A HISTORY OF MOBILITY IN NEW MEXICO

A History of Mobility in New Mexico uses the often-enigmatic chipped stone assemblages of the Taos Plateau to chart patterns of historical mobility in northern New Mexico.

Drawing on evidence of spatial patterning and geochemical analyses of stone tools across archaeological landscapes, the book examines the distinctive mobile modalities of different human communities, documenting evolving logics of mobility—residential, logistical, pastoral, and settler colonial. In particular, it focuses on the diversity of ways that Indigenous peoples have used and moved across the Plateau landscape from deep time into the present. The analysis of Indigenous movement patterns is grounded in critical Indigenous philosophy, which applies core principles within Indigenous thought to the archaeological record in order to challenge conventional understandings of occupation, use, and abandonment.

Providing an Indigenizing approach to archaeological research and new evidence for the long-term use of specific landscape features, *A History of Mobility in New Mexico* presents an innovative approach to human-environment interaction for readers and scholars of North American history.

Lindsay M. Montgomery is an assistant professor in the School of Anthropology at the University of Arizona, USA. She is co-author of *Objects of Survivance* (2019), and has published in the *Journal of Social Archeology*, *International Journal of Heritage Studies*, *American Indian Quarterly*, and *Advances in Archaeological Practice*. Her research focuses on the ethnohistory of Indigenous people in the North American West, with particular emphasis on documenting interethnic interaction, settler colonialism, and cultural resiliency.

A HISTORY OF MOBILITY IN NEW MEXICO

Mobile Landscapes and Persistent Places

Lindsay M. Montgomery

Routledge
Taylor & Francis Group
LONDON AND NEW YORK

First published 2021
by Routledge
2 Park Square, Milton Park, Abingdon, Oxon OX14 4RN

and by Routledge
52 Vanderbilt Avenue, New York, NY 10017

Routledge is an imprint of the Taylor & Francis Group, an informa business

British Library Cataloguing-in-Publication Data
A catalogue record for this book is available from the British Library

Library of Congress Cataloging-in-Publication Data
A catalog record has been requested for this book

ISBN: 978-0-367-34801-4 (hbk)
ISBN: 978-0-367-34800-7 (pbk)
ISBN: 978-0-429-32815-2 (ebk)

Typeset in Bembo
by MPS Limited, Dehradun

For my grandfather David Montgomery (1927–2011), who taught me the art of storytelling and the power of history.

CONTENTS

LIST OF FIGURES

ACKNOWLEDGMENTS

Many people and organizations have supported this work over the past decade. I would first and foremost like to acknowledge all the support and love that my family and partner have provided over the years. As my great-grandfather Julius Wilcher always said, family comes first. I am also deeply indebted to the Radcliffe Institute for affording me the time, funding, and incredible intellectual community necessary to write this book. Over the course of writing this book, I have had the opportunity to work closely with several fantasitic undergraduate and graduate research assistants, including Jessica Gebhard, Nam Hyun Kim, Mairead Poulin, and Danielle Soza who were instrumental in helping to process the data presented in this book. The fieldwork which forms the core of this monograph was graciously supported by the National-Geographic Waitt Foundation, the National Science Foundation, Stanford University, the University of Arizona, and Barnard College. In addition to this institutional support, I would like to acknowledge the central role that Merrill Dicks and the Bureau of Land Management Taos Office have played in providing research permits and related research reports as well as the amazing team of archivist, librarians, and archaeologists at the Laboratory of Anthropology in Santa Fe, without whom much of this work would not have been possible. Finally, I would like to recognize the incredible intellectual support provided by my advisors and mentors over the years, including Lynn Meskell, Michael Wilcox, Barbara Voss, and Chip Colwell. I would like to espeically thank Severin Fowles, to whom I am eternally grateful for the many opportunities he has provided for me to conduct research in the northern Rio Grande under his guidance. Finally, a special thanks to Sarah C. Murray, who contributed the amazing artwork for the frontcover of this book.

IN SEARCH OF SONGS

For many Indigenous Peoples in the North American Southwest, the land is part of an intricate web connected together by songs and song series. Each verse lyrically traces the physical experience of traveling between, and residing within, certain places, creating a shared cognitive map. For the O'odham in southern Arizona, songs follow the same narrative structure as orally transmitted narratives, having a beginning, middle, and end. Each of these segments contains information about a particular quality of action or a specific geographic place.[1] Similarly, among Tewa-speaking communities like *Ohkay Owingeh* (San Juan Pueblo) in New Mexico, songs are associated with features of the natural environment, including the cardinal directions, mountains, clouds, lightning, rain, birds, insects, plants, and animals. While the imagery evoked by song lyrics can often be vivid and highly specific, in other instances such details are only hinted at, allowing the listener to draw from their own well of mental images to fill in the gaps.[2] The power of song lyrics lies not in their specificity but rather in their ability to transport the singer and listener through time and space to a particular place on the land and its local environment. As Northern Ute elder, Clifford Duncan, has commented, "each place in the landscape has its own song … and when you sing these songs, they bring back the feeling of that place."[3] To sing, then, is in some ways to breathe a place into being. It is to connect the human, the natural, and the spiritual worlds together with a single note.

This book is my song.

Each word, an echo on the wind taking me (and you) to New Mexico.

Each chapter, a story about a place on the northern Rio Grande landscape and the peoples who traveled through and lived there.

1

PLACE ON THE MOVE

The Taos Plateau in an expansive landscape etched with trails, rivers, roads, and arroyos. The smooth spaces of its open grasslands disrupted by the cavernous Rio Grande Gorge and volcanic cones—Cerro San Antonio, Cerro de la Olla, and Cerro del Yuta—towering thousands of feet in the air. Caused by cataclysmic eruptions some 20 million years ago, these mountains contain a rich archive of materials left behind by human occupants between roughly 5500 BCE and the 19th century.[4] As discussed by Sarah Schlanger, the sustained use of particular places is often a result of their unique ecological characteristics—for example, access to seasonal springs—or proximity to easily exploitable resources, such as workable stone. These land forms may also have particular topographic elements, like ridge tops or caves, which make them desirable locations as shelters, hunting locales, defensive outposts, or ceremonial sites. Places may become persistent because they were previously occupied.[5] Over time, these locations become known and used by successive generations through orally shared knowledge. A growing body of evidence suggests that Indigenous people return to ancestral places both physically and spiritually through stories, songs, and prayers, evidence that contradicts archaeological models of use and abandonment.[6] Rather than a cycle of intensive occupation followed by dispersion and migration human engagements with the landscape are better understood as a series of visitations, which vary in duration and frequency over time in response to changing ecological, economic, and social conditions.

The accumulative nature of most culturally modified places and landscapes pushes back against conventionalized archaeological chronologies, which organize human social processes into bounded temporal phases. As Rachel Crellin has argued, this *block-time* approach creates the impression that human history is a compilation of "periods of stasis punctuated by moments of radical transformation."[7] The arrival of Europeans to the North American Southwest in the late

16th century has often been viewed by historians and archaeologists as the most "radical" of such transformative; propelling Indigenous people out of the dark primitivism of previous millennia and into civilization. Such block-time thinking has produced a tripartite chronological system (pre-historic, proto-historic, and historical periods) that places undue influence on the development of writing in recording history while glossing over the accumulative nature of such histories. As a growing number of scholars have pointed out, archaeologists need to attend to the dynamic ways that Indigenous people continuously adapted to changes in their locale and social environments over time.[8] Rather than searching for material markers of disruption, this book seeks out small-scale evidence for change and continuity in human engagements with the landscape.

The persistent places of the Taos Plateau are connected together through trails etched across its vast expanses—migration routes, pilgrimage pathways, trading throughfares, roads of conquest, and asphalt highways. Over the past 10,000 years, these trails have been used, expanded upon, and covered up by the inhabitants of the region, creating a rich, multi-vocal landscape. A focus on place-based movement in the northern Rio Grande sheds light on an often-overlooked facet of the region's archaeological record—the enigmatic record of residentially mobile communities. In the New Mexico, great quantities of ink have been spilt documenting how "sedentary" Indigenous people, and their immediate ancestors, constructed sophisticated agricultural landscapes using elaborate canal systems and extensive terrace networks.[9] The study of pre-Hispanic farming systems in the region has been a hallmark of Southwest archaeology, dating to the landmark research of Adolph F. Bandelier and Frank Hamilton Cushing in late 19th century.[10] More recently, archaeologists in the northern Rio Grande region have focused their efforts on studying the relationship between Indigenous settlements, their surrounding landscapes, and associated beliefs about land, water, plants, and animals. Drawing on Indigenous ontologies and epistemologies, these studies have examined the subjective and objective creation of place within the region.[11] This culturally grounded approach has done much to enhance our understanding of the occupational patterns and social systems of ancestral Tiwa and Tewa-speaking people. The scholarly focus on doing village-centered archaeology has meant that the short-term occupations which characterize a significant proportion of the archaeological landscape in northern New Mexico have gone comparatively understudied. By examining those places and the pathways created by highly mobile Indigenous communities, this book shifts scholarly attention away from the settlements and fields of the Rio Grande Valley and towards the ephemeral material signatures of human-environment interactions along New Mexico's borderlands.

In an effort to move away from the environmentally driven functionalist models often employed by archaeologists to interpret human mobility patterns, I draw upon an Indigenous worldview which posits an intimate connection between the spiritual and natural worlds. The approach taken up in this book builds on and moves beyond Lewis Binford's original definition of "place" as a discreet and bounded locus of human behavior. Instead of simply adapting to the physical and natural environment of the Taos Plateau, Indigenous individuals and communities actively shaped these places through perception, cognition, and behavior.[12] The archaeological record of such places reflects the material accumulation of distinct social meanings which are often quite different and occasionally antithetical to one another.[13] In tracing out the deep histories of particular places on the Taos Plateau, this book aims to tease apart such instances of difference while highlighting the often-overlooked connections across peoples engaged in varying types of mobility.

▼▽▼

This is a book about place and how these places were used over time. It is also about the role of particular places within larger networks of mobility. These mobility systems were informed by a variety of factors, including changes in environmental and ecological conditions, the reintroduction of horses into North America, and the advent of steam-powered locomotion. These social and ecological developments form the back drop upon which I interpret patterns in the material record of the Taos Plateau. To varying degrees, each of the place-based chapters within this book discuss the ways in which changing environmental dynamics informed the socioeconomic practices of the regions inhabitants, the impact of horses on movement systems and inter-ethnic interaction, and the effects of industrial capitalism on regional demography and settlement patterns. What follows is a broad overview of these topics with the aim of providing a set of historical touchstones that the reader can reference as you make your way through the subsequent discussions of persistent places on the Plateau.

The climate and ecology

The Taos Plateau is part of the larger Rio Grande Rift Zone, extending from Chihuahua, Mexico, into Colorado.[14] Despite only receiving 6–12 inches of rain per year, the area has a diverse ecology comprised of intermountain basins filled with sagebrush and semi-desert shrub, wetland and riparian areas, as well as piñon-juniper forests.[15] While a largely high desert environment, ample water is provided by perennial lakes, known as playas, and intermittent mountain streams, which serve as tributaries to the Rio Grande.[16]

Over time, inhabitants of the northern Rio Grande region experienced several significant shifts in environmental and ecological conditions, which directly influenced subsistence choices, stone tool technologies, and residential patterns. The earliest human occupants in the Southwest experienced a cold, wet climate referred to as the Younger Dryas period, lasting between roughly 10,900 and 9700 BCE.[17] By 8000 BCE, this cold period had ended and had been replaced by a warm, dry environment. Stable carbon isotope data collected from central New Mexico by

Stephan Hall and William Penner indicate that between 8,000 and 4,000 BCE there was a gradual increase in mean annual temperature, from 10°C to 12°C, and a corresponding decrease in annual precipitation, from 400 to 320 mm.[18 19] These climatic shifts were brought on by a decline in the number of annual El Niño events leading to a progressive decrease in spring flow and wet meadow formation as well as reducing sagebrush and grass pollen on the valley floor.[20] This dryer warmer climate spurred the expansion of spruce-fir forests, ponderosa pine, and oak along the lower mountain slopes of Taos Plateau.[19] For the next several thousand years, dry conditions and higher temperatures prevailed, with lake levels declining significantly over this time. Accompanying this increasing aridity was a marked transition in the types of tools and hunting strategies employed by Indigenous people. Rather than producing fluted spears for use in communal big game hunts, Indigenous communities developed a residential mobility pattern focused on exploiting smaller game within particular resource niches. Although tool styles and land-use patterns continue to evolve after 8000 BCE, this seasonally based mobility pattern characterizes much of the regional archaeological record for the next 7,000 years. During this expansive time frame, Indigenous people living in the northern Southwest engaged in a sophisticated long-distance mobility round, centered on the exploitation of particular wild game and plant resources between the San Luis and northern Rio Grande Valleys.[21]

Around 2500 BCE, paleoenvironmental data drawn from pluvial lakes, sand sheets, streams, rivers, and springs indicate a shift to cooler and wetter weather as the strength and frequency of El Niños increased. The increased frequency in El Niño events and associated shifts in rainfall intensity during this period are inferred from measurements of sand content from well-dated core samples taken from El Junco Crater Lake on the Galápagos Islands.[22] As springs rejuvenated, sagebrush steppes and piñon-pine woodlands also expanded across the Colorado Plateau and adjacent areas.[23] Indigenous people responded to these changing conditions by increasingly concentrating their seasonal hunting and gathering activities on upland wooded environments and by developing new projectile point technologies with thinner, shorter blades and serrated edges.[24] The Taos Plateau became an important fall-time resource node for groups moving between upland and lowland areas within this more localized land-use pattern.[25]

A comparatively high moisture climate continued for the next several thousand years, facilitating early experimentation with maize domestication.[26] During this time, maize was primarily used to fill in subsistence gaps during seasonal shortfalls and Indigenous people in the northern Rio Grande continued to engage in various degrees of residential mobility, focused on exploiting high-ranking game and pine nut harvesting. This subsistence pattern continued well after Indigenous communities to the south had settled into agriculturally centered villages. The archaeological record of the Taos Plateau, which contains large numbers of dispersed lithic scatters and specialized point types, reflects the evolution and persistence of this northern hunting-gathering tradition.[27]

This northern hunting-gathering tradition continued to dominate the material record of the region into the 10th century in part due to the sustained availability of protein sources like antelope, elk, deer, and big horn sheep and the particularities of the local environment—the high elevation along with small deviations in average temperature create a short growing season for maize.[28] While many of the Indigenous people living in the Taos Valley eventually shifted to a village-centered subsistence system, hunting and gathering remained an important part of the socioeconomic systems of the region's inhabitants. For example, the *Ĭăłap°ăĭbâ* (Taos Pueblo) have oral histories that document the merger of northern hunting-focused groups occupying the Trinidad and Cimarron districts with southern Peoples from the Espanola valley influenced by a Chacoan tradition.[29] These accounts record the persistence of these two social groups and their economic orientations—the "Summer people" associated with agriculture and superior ceremonial and military skills and the "Winter people" who were primarily hunters—into the 21st century.

The cooler-wetter climate and pattern of worldwide alpine glaciation of the previous era continued into the 14th century. While Indigenous groups, like the Ĭăłap°ăĭbâ, came to rely less and less on residential mobility and foraging during this time, others were actively moving into new territories in order to continue this subsistence system. Numic-speaking groups occupying the intermountain areas to the north and west of Taos and Athabaskan-speaking groups largely living to the north and east developed important trading relationships with the emergent agricultural communities living in the northern Rio Grande. Within this evolving subsistence landscape, the Taos Plateau remained a sort of "nomadic land"; an unsettled space inhabited but not occupied by highly mobile Indigenous peoples.

Tree-ring data indicates that during the initial exploratory endeavors of Spanish colonizers in the northern Rio Grande, the San Luis Valley experienced a major drought interval between 1570 and 1600. This severe drought was followed by a century of higher precipitation levels which enabled a large degree of vegetation growth.[30] The newly revived landscape of the late 17th and 18th centuries made possible the development of a distinctive agro-pastoral subsistence system among Hispano settlers. This system centered on small-scale farming endeavors and sheep herding. Sheep herding introduced a new mobility circuit onto the Taos Plateau, as herders moved their sheep between high- and low-elevation pastures. These herds also became new targets of lightning-fast raids by now mounted Numic and Athabaskan-speaking nomads.

Beginning in the late 19th century, the geomorphology of the northern Southwest has undergone a series of radical shifts as deep arroyos formed and the once-rich desert grasslands of the region were depleted by overgrazing. Coppice dunes formed from wind-swept sands and mesquite shrubs have replaced the once-sweeping rangelands of the region.[31] As will be discussed in greater detail below, many of these environmental changes were set in motion by a dramatic increase in ranching and mining activities accompanying the expansion of US imperial interests west of the Mississippi and Anglo-American settlement across New Mexico.

The horse

Relatives of modern horses were widespread across North America during the last major ice age 18,000 years ago. By 9000 BCE, changing environmental conditions had caused most of the megafauna on the continent, including the ancestors of domesticated horses, to become extinct. The first horses to re-enter the northern Southwest accompanied Oñate's wagon train on his 700-mile entrada from Mexico City in the late 16th century. This hardy breed of Spanish Barbs was one of several *Ganado mayor*—larger domesticated animals such as horses, mules, and cattle—introduced into the northern Rio Grande by Spanish colonizers.[32] Semi-formal prohibitions under colonial law initially limited the possession and use of horses by Indigenous peoples. Despite these regulations, over the course of the 17th century equestrianism was gradually integrated into the lifeways of Indigenous communities living along the Rio Grande.

The Pueblo Revolt of 1680 was a watershed moment for Indigenous equestrianism. Aided by *Ndee* (Apache) allies, "Puebloan" communities from across the region united to drive New Mexico's then-Governor Antonio de Otermin out of Santa Fe. As the violence of the revolt escalated, over 2,000 Hispano inhabitants fled south into Texas, leaving the vast majority of their valuable horse herds behind. Over the course of the next 12 years, a growing number of Indigenous Peoples, particularly the *Nuutsiyu* (Ute), *Diné* (Navajo), *Ndee*, and *Numunu* (Comanche), began raiding the former colony for horses. By the time, the Spanish colonial government re-imposed formal, if not total, imperial control over the region in 1692, these Indigenous communities had enfolded horses into their socioeconomic systems.

The long growing season and ample supply of grass across the southern Plains provided pasturage for Indigenous horse herds, facilitating the emergence of a sophisticated horse culture among Indigenous communities in the region.[33] New Mexico eastern Plains were also home to a then-bountiful supply of bison, made more accessible by travel on horseback. Before horses, bison hunting expeditions were largely a communal enterprise undertaken by large groups of men and entailed many days of planning. On horseback, an individual hunter could take down a buffalo virtually single handedly. As the efficiency of bison hunting increased, many Indigenous Peoples re-oriented their subsistence practices around year-round big game hunting and trade on horseback.[34]

Horses had both spatial and social impacts on Indigenous people throughout the region. At a very basic level, horses dramatically extended the area that Indigenous communities could travel, expanding the territorial radius of hunting, gathering, raiding, and trading activities. For example, as one of the earliest Indigenous Peoples to gain access to horses in the 1600s, *Ndee* groups rapidly stretched their hunting-gathering economy into Texas, Oklahoma, and northern

FIGURE 1.1 George Catlin, *Comanche Feats of Horsemanship*, 1834–1835, Oil on Canvas, Smithsonian American Art Museum, Gift of Mrs. Joseph Harrison, Jr. 1985.66.487.

Mexico.[35] Territorial expansion was accompanied by increasingly violent raiding for horses and mules. Spanish archival documents indicate that between 1778 and 1795 alone, *Ndee* raiders took over 23,000 Spanish-owned horses, mules, and cattle from New Mexico and its bordering outposts.

As *Ndee* groups expanded their territorial reach to the south, in the north, the *Numunu*, and their *Nuutsiyu* allies, began a parallel territorial and economic expansion, out of the Great Basin and into the southern Plains. (Figure 1.1).
By the mid-eighteenth century multiethnic trading parties were traveling to western *Numunu* camps in the upper Arkansas basin to purchase horses and mules, distributing these animals to markets in New Mexico, the Mississippi Valley, and across the Plains. It was certainly not without irony that *Numunu* intermediaries sold the horses they had acquired through raiding in New Mexico back to Hispano traders living in the territory. By the late 1700s, nomadic raiding had so depleted the horse and mule population of New Mexico that Governor Pedro Fermín de Mendinueta was annually requesting some 1,500 horses to be sent to the colony from Mexico.[34–36] By the 1730s, Indigenous groups living in Montana, Saskatchewan, and Alberta, had regular access to horses largely through *Numunu* trade networks. As historian Pekka Hämäläinen has aptly demonstrated, the *Numunu* came to control a

vast political and economic empire that stretched from the Arkansas River Valley, north to Alberta and south to the Balcones escarpment in Texas, largely through stealing, breeding, and selling horses.[37]

Although *Ĭăłap°ăĭbâ* (Taos), *P'į̨wwweltha* (Picuris), and *Cicuye* (Pecos) Pueblos had been important inter-ethnic trading hubs prior to the 18th century, equestrianism both expanded the scale of this exchange and diversified the participants in these networks. Trade fairs were lively scenes during which colonial oversight was often ineffective and Christian morality had little sway. Fray Pedro Serrano described one such fair at Taos in 1761,

> When the Indian trading embassy comes to these governors and their alcalde, here all prudence forsakes them, or rather I shall say that they do not guess how completely they lose their bearings, because the fleet is in. The fleet being in this case, some two hundred or at least fifty, tents of barbarous heathen Indians, Comanches as well as other nations, of whom the multitude is so great that it is impossible to enumerate them … Here in short, is gathered everything possible for trade and barter with these barbarians in exchange for deer and buffalo hides, and what is saddest, in exchange for Indian slaves, men and women, small and large, a great multitude of both sexes. …[38]

This letter reveals the general disdain that colonial administrators appear to have had towards equestrian groups, like the *Numunu*, who were viewed as "barbarians" despite the important role these Indigenous interlocutors played in supplying much need commodities to the isolated colony.

Serrano's account also speaks to the important role that raiding for captives played within the evolving equestrian exchange networks of the region. *Indios bárbaros*—the term used to refer to all non-Christian and usually nomadic Indigenous Peoples—could be captured legally under the just war doctrine enacted through the *vale* system established in 1610 by Governor Pedro de Peralta. Under the *vale* system, individual citizens were allowed to capture or sell unbaptized Indigenous peoples at Spanish and Indigenous-led trade fairs.[39] These legal restrictions incentivized slave raiding across *Ndee*, *Diné*, *Nuutsiyu*, and *Numunu* groups, with *Ndee* settlements like *La Jicarilla* and *El Cuartelejo* particularly hard hit by slave raiders.[40] The majority of Indigenous captives were sold to Hispano landholders as domestic and agricultural laborers. Typically referred to as *genizaros*, these individuals often became important cultural intermediaries between Hispano and equestrian traders. In this sense, horses also played an intimate role in the emergence of new ethnic identities and familial structures in New Mexico.

In addition to altering territorial boundaries, economic strategies, and ethnic identities, horses influenced and were influenced by Indigenous social practices. Surrounding Indigenous equestrianism is a whole set of innovative rituals and ceremonies, including the application of certain herbal medicines to promote vitality and the use of decorated masks, bridles, and paint to ensure the power, swiftness, and success of horses in hunting, combat, races, and raids.

Oral narratives documenting the incorporation of horses into tribal histories developed alongside many of these material traditions. For example, among the *Diné*, the following story emerged to explain how and why they first received horses:

> The deities of the Navajo kept horses in great numbers long before people had them and both sun and moon rode them across the heavens. But when the twin war gods asked sun for weapons to fight the monsters devouring all living beings, they preferred to accept lightning instead. Horses and other livestock thus came first into the possession of Europeans. Only later did turquoise boy, the elder twin succeed, after much searching, in obtaining the stone and shell fetishes needed to create the Navajo's first horses, which were then sung into life by his mother, Changing Woman.[41]

As the *Diné* origin story indicates, horses were enfolded into an already well-established set of stories and narrative conventions about the creation of the world and associated culture heroes.

Horses also came to play an important role in heightening the already individualistic nature of residentially mobile Indigenous societies. Within this self-aggrandizing system, the capture of horses took on symbolic meaning; it was both a means of asserting control over territory, signaling one's bravery, and achieving social distinction. In this sense, horse capture was "not only the means of war; it was also the end[s]."[42] During this time, a heraldic art tradition was developed to record the heroic deeds of equestrian warriors which were inscribed onto war shirts, buffalo hides, tipi liners, rock walls, and ledgers. While this "cultural interest in self-aggrandizement" certainly fueled violence between Indigenous and non-Indigenous communities in northern New Mexico, it also encouraged an ethos of generosity.[43] By acquiring property through combat and then giving it away to less wealthy members of society, men demonstrated their prowess and munificence thereby gaining status in society.

The growing horse herds of Indigenous Peoples also restructured seasonal mobility circuits and residential patterns. While the location of bison herds had primarily determined the placement of aggregated encampments in the pre-horse era, in the post-horse age adequate pasturage and water supply became key drivers of camp selection. The carrying capacity of the Southwest and southern Plains grasslands was not as elastic as the equine population, making large aggregations of families and their horse herds impractical and unsustainable. As a result, Indigenous equestrian groups increasingly came to live in dispersed small-scale settlements for most of the year.[44] Accompanying these shifts were new patterns of seasonal transhumance in which families would move their herds from low-lying grass lands into highland mountain ranges during hotter dryer months of the year. In 1776, one Spanish observer remarked on this seasonal pattern among the *Numunu*, reporting that they had moved some 1,000 horses into the Sangre de Cristo foothills during the summer months, returning to the Plains in the winter.[45]

Though much more could be said about the transformative role of horses on mobile communities, what I hope has become clear is the profound impact equines had on Indigenous mobility patterns and accompanying socioeconomic systems and material practices. Enabling Indigenous actors to travel farther and faster, horses dismantled prior physical constraints on political and economic networks. In light of such changes, there is perhaps a good argument to be made that the only good thing that European colonization has ever done for Indigenous people is to bring horses back to North America. In addition to altering where mobile groups could travel and whom they could raid or trade with, horses transformed the rationales driving movement. A new set of factors, including the availability of pasturage, access to trade goods (including human capital in the form of slaves), and opportunities for achieving status through counting coup came to determine where and why mobile groups were moving.

The locomotive

The late 19th century, issued in another series of profound changes in the region's landscape and human movement patterns across it. Up until this date, New Mexico had largely been perceived by colonial conquerors as an economic and political backwater, a small-scale outpost at the edge of the Spanish empire. This all changed in December of 1878, when the first locomotive on the Atchison, Topeka, and Santa Fe Railway (AT&SF) crossed into New Mexico from Colorado. The new line of the AT&SF railroad followed the original path of the Santa Fe Trail—an important Indigenous and Hispano trading thoroughfare which gained prominence during the 18th century—across the Raton Mountains, connecting the coal mines of Trinidad, Colorado to Las Vegas, New Mexico. The line marked an extraordinary feat of engineering, passing through Raton, at a gauge of 186 feet per mile and an elevation of 7,720 feet above sea level, the steepest gauge ever attained by a standard railroad in the world at the time.[46]

Journalists from across the United States flocked to New Mexico to report on the sheer magnitude of this mechanical marvel. One such account, written by Mrs. Susan T. Perry for the *New York Evangelist* in 1880 is worth quoting at length:

> It is doubtful if any other portion of the United States there is so beautiful and so interesting a stretch of country as that through which the Atchison, Topeka and Santa Fé railroad passes southward through Colorado and New Mexico. The wonderful mechanical skill of man is shown in the construction of this railroad. From the Colorado line to the point where the road enters the Rio Grande valley the road has been built through a mountainous country, where the obstacle to be overcome were greater, and engineering skill demanded has been of a higher order, than in the construction of such lines as the Baltimore and Ohio, and the Pennsylvania … Standing on the

> platform of the car the traveler realizes that he is passing through a wonderful line of travel. Imagination runs rampant as he rides through the narrow passageway in the canon and sees the rocks hanging over him seemingly just ready to fall from their insecure positions in the side of the mountain. What if one of the coaches should be detached from the train and make a rapid descent! What if the engineer should forget himself for even one moment! Eyes are eagerly strained toward the locomotive to see if the engineer looks equal to the emergency. We hint at our fears but are assured that only the best and more experienced engineers are allowed the responsibility of "this run."[47]

Perry's vivid description of her first voyage on the AT&SF line, also known as the Santa Fe railroad, oozes excitement, conveying the thrilling sense of adventure that swirled around locomotive travel at the turn of the century. Her reporting also points to a deeper truth behind the railroad's purpose. In moving commodities over a vast perceptibly untamed wilderness at an unprecedented rate, locomotive travel announced Western man's mastery over nature.

By March 1881, the AT&SF line stretched the entire length of New Mexico, connecting the small towns dotting the territory's northern periphery from Albuquerque to Deming where the line connected with the Southern Pacific Railway (Figure 1.2). The Deming station was the lynch pin in a newly established east-west transcontinental system, the second of such networks in all of North

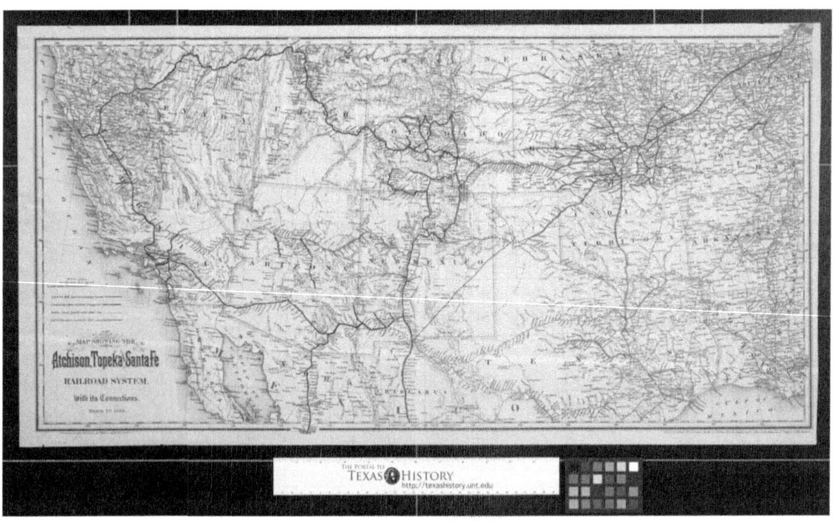

FIGURE 1.2 G.W. & C.B. Colton & Co. Map of the Atchison, Topeka, and Santa Fe Railroad System with Its Connections. March 1, 1888. New York. University of North Texas Libraries, The Portal to Texas History, texashistory.unt.edu; crediting University of Texas at Arlington Library.

America. Within a decade of its arrival into the isolated mountain town of Raton, the steam engine had drawn Spain's former frontier colony into the capitalist era.

The railroad, and American colonization more broadly, fundamentally transformed the way people moved across the open stretches of the desert West. Earlier generations of Indigenous and Hispano occupants had a relatively minimal impact on the landscape, shaping their settlement patterns and trail networks around the local topography. The railroad altered this land-use system, blasting through igneous rock and crossing cavernous canyon lands to create direct lines of travel between an ever-growing number of cities. Connecting more people to more places, more rapidly, the railroad collapsed the time-space continuum, speeding up the rate at which people could move across distances at an unprecedented level.

In addition to enhancing the efficiency of commerce, the railroad intensified economic interactions across the region. Both before and during the Spanish colonial period, the inhabitants of New Mexico practiced a form of subsistence economics rooted in a relatively diversified use of the environment. Barter was the principal mode of exchange due to consistent currency shortages throughout New Spain. This barter system centered upon the exchange of bison products, captives, horses from the Plains for sheep, textiles, agricultural goods, cotton, and piñon nuts. Archival records documenting the annual mule trains from New Mexico to Sonora, Vizcaya, and Coahuila indicate that the annual earnings from this export trade were roughly 14,000 pesos.[48] Although the Santa Fe Trail significantly expanded New Mexico's trade economy, in 1823, only about $12,000 worth of merchandise was transported by a mere 30 traders along this route. The AT&SF railroad blew these figures out of the water, earning about the same amount of money in freight over the course of 3 weeks.[49] Seventy years later, the Santa Fe line could move twice that much business from Santa Fe to Chicago in 2 days![50]

Much like the Spanish empire, American colonialism ushered in a new system of animal transhumance, this time focused on cattle rather than horses and sheep. The preference for sheep over cattle among settlers during the 17th and 18th centuries was largely due to the fact that bison herds on the eastern Plains already provided a reliable source of high-protein meat. Sheep were also easier to protect from equestrian raiders—a major thorn in the side of most herders. In 1827, there were an estimated 250,000 sheep within the colony compared to 5,000 head of cattle and a meager 850 horses.[51] At the end of the Civil War in 1865, beef demand in the eastern United States steadily increased, fueling a burgeoning ranching industry in the West. Estimates suggest that the number of cattle in the territory had skyrocketed from 347,000 in 1880 to over 1.5 million by 1890.[52]

The railroad played a seminal role in the cattle industry's growth, shipping cattle, with fewer risks of injury or death, across vast distances. The rapid growth in Western cattle populations in response to the demand for beef in the major metropolises of the East accelerated the processes of overgrazing initiated by sheep and horses, denuding New Mexico's lush landscape of natural grasses—the magnitude of which Anglo-American ranchers were likely unaware of at the time.

The railroad also altered settlement patterns across New Mexico. Until the late 19th century, New Mexico was a sparsely populated landscape. In 1750, there was an estimated 12,000 "Pueblo" Peoples and some 4,000 Hispanos occupying about 1% of the land base. Although the Hispano population in New Mexico gradually increased over the preceding century, the total number of settlers in the region remained small, with 5,603 residents reported as living in the capital city of Santa Fe while Albuquerque—the largest city in the state—had a modest population of 6,238.[53] These statistics are particularly striking when compared to other cities in the American West during this same period. Despite being founded over 100 years after Santa Fe, Denver had around 35,000 people living within its city limits and San Francisco boasted a population of over 233,000.[54] With the help of the railroad, New Mexico's demography gradually began to change. Euro-American settlers followed fast on the heels of the AT&SF section hands laying rail ties. These settlers established a whole string of small towns across the northern Rio Grande—Lamy, Rincon, Holbrook, Springer, Dillon—lighting up the desert like Christmas lights. Thirty years after the Santa Fe line reached Albuquerque, the city's population had nearly doubled in size and the territory's total population had finally cracked the 300,000 threshold.[55]

As the AT&SF line expanded its reach across the United States, once quiet towns in New Mexico became bustling tourist hubs. Railroad cars teeming with disaffected East Coasters hoping to regain physical and mental health while observing Indigenous Peoples in their "natural" environment came streaming into New Mexico.[56] At the head of this new army of frontier enthusiasts was a man named Frederick Henry Harvey. Harvey was born on June 27, 1835, in London. Arriving in New York City at the fresh age of 15, Harvey bought a small space in the old Topeka depot of the Santa Fe railroad in 1875, establishing a restaurant and boarding house affectionately called the Harvey House.[57] The Harvey–Santa Fe partnership was one of the most lucrative business enterprises in the American Southwest.

In 1899, Harvey formally expanded his operations to include a curio business. Part restaurant, part hotel, part curio shop, Harvey Houses provided tourists with room and board, guided tours of scenic locations, and trinkets to commemorate their exotic adventures.[58] Each Harvey House along the Santa Fe line mimicked the local adobe architecture and offered passengers an opportunity to buy "Indian wares" and postcards inked with romantic images of the frontier. Each day, Indigenous women came to these stations to sell pots, baskets, beadwork, silver-and-turquoise jewelry, and weavings. Other families began performing social dances or live demonstrations of their artistry for eager travelers. Soon there was a Harvey House at every major stop along the AT&SF line in the Southwest, including Albuquerque, Santa Fe, and Flagstaff. By 1901, when Harvey died, the Santa Fe system owned and operated 15 hotels, 47 restaurants, and 30 dining cars.[59]

By creating a market for hand-made "traditional" crafts, the tourism industry ushered in by Harvey and the railroad incentivized a move away from intertribal trade in domestic products. Instead, Indigenous artisans began to produce goods that appealed to the aesthetic sensibilities and interests of Euro-American travelers. Over the course of the 20th century, New Mexico's once isolated markets were integrated into America's cash economy. Accompanying this new influx of capital was a growing number of manufactured goods and technologies, including electricity and the automobile. In response to these changing socioeconomic dynamics, more and more Indigenous people took up full-time positions as artisans and day laborers to earn the money needed to operate within a wage economy.[60] As with climatic shifts and the introduction of horses, human communities adapted to the railroad by adjusting their mobility networks, creating new settlement systems, and engaging in innovative economic and social practices.

▼▽▼

Mobility patterns and settlement systems were intimately shaped by a variety of factors over the past 10,000 years, including the climate, the introduction of new domesticates, and the development of novel modes of transportation. The ways in which human communities responded to these changes has left behind material remnants that archaeologists may use to document localized and large-scale changes in human land-use practices. This book takes up the challenge of narrating this history of mobility in New Mexico.

Section 1 is divided into three chapters and serves as the theoretical and methodological scaffolding for the analyses presented in the second part of the book. Chapter 2 elaborates upon the unique ways that Indigenous people and, more specifically, residentially mobile Indigenous Peoples, construct history. The land based ontologies of these Indigenous communities offer an alternative framework to the chronologically oriented paradigms which have been used to reconstruct much of Indigenous history. The material records of particular places and archaeological residues of movement between these places provides a powerful corrective to Western histories that have erased Indigenous Peoples from the landscape. Chapter 3 expands on the Indigenizing approach presented in the previous chapter by developing a alternative vocabulary and grammar for talking about Indigenous history. The stylistic and rhetorical interventions presented in this chapter challenge engrained modes of thinking and writing about Indigenous people, conventions which often have the unintended effect of disconnecting living Indigenous communities from their ancestors and cultural heritage. The last chapter in this section, Chapter 4, provides a brief overview of the interpretive challenges which accompany the study of mobile landscapes and how these analytical hurdles are addressed throughout the manuscript.

Section 2 traces out the particular ways in which Indigenous and non-Indigenous groups used, marked, and altered the Taos Plateau over time. The archaeological record discussed in these chapters is comprised of isolated diagnostic projectile points, chipped stonescatters, and rock features, including stone rings, rock piles, cairns, and linear alignments. While Chapter 5 focuses on the archaeological record at three playa sites located on the west side of the Rio Grande

Gorge near Cerro San Antonio, Chapters 6 and 7 document the findings of non-collection-based landscape surveys conducted on the slopes of Cerro de la Olla and Cerro del Yuta, respectively. Through the stylistic analysis of bifacial tools, assessments of feature morphology, geospatial statistics, and geochemical sourcing, these chapters provide an in-depth look into land-use patterns at each locale.

Finally, Chapter 8 takes a step back from these detailed discussions of place in order to examine how human mobility systems shaped and were shaped by different landscape features, including playas, mountains, and the Rio Grande Gorge itself. These findings offer broader insights into how the northern Rio Grande was used over time by Indigenous and non-Indigenous groups.

Notes

1 Darling, 2009: 68.
2 Garcia Sr. et al., 2013: 493.
3 Patterson and Duncan, 2013: 160.
4 Lipman and Mehnert, 1979: 289; Schlanger, 1992: 92; Shackley, 2011: 1002.
5 Schlanger, 1992: 97.
6 Over the past 30 years a robust body of scholarship has developed around Indigenous cultural landscapes. For some notable examples see Basso, 1996; Nelson, 2000; Tomka and Stevenson, 1993; Zedeno, 1997.
7 Crellin, 2020: 135.
8 For other critiques of the "prehistory-history" divide in archaeology, see Lightfoot, 1995; Panich, 2013; Silliman, 2009.
9 There are numerous examples of archaeological studies of cultural landscapes in the northern Rio Grande region including Anschuetz et al., 2001; Duwe and Anschuetz, 2013; Fish, 1984; ; Herhahn and Hill, 1998; Snead, 2008.
10 Anschuetz et al., 2017.
11 Fowles, 2010: 461. For examples of other works that draw on Pueblo worldviews to interpret the archaeological record see, Anschuetz, 2001; Fowles, 2009, Ortman, 2009; Snead, 2002; Swentzell, 1993.
12 David and Thompson, 2008: 38; Whittlesey, 2008: 74.
13 Schein, 1997: 660.
14 Julyan, 2006: 23.
15 Wescott et al., 2016: 9.
16 Wescott et al., 2016: 9.
17 Hall, 2017: 20.
18 Hall, 2017: Figure 2.7; Hall and Penner, 2013.
19 Jodry, 1999.
20 Dicks et al., 2016: I-19; Hall, 2017: 20.
21 Vierra, 2013: 147.
22 Conroy et al., 2008, 2009; Hall, 2017: Figure 2.1
23 Hall, 2017: 24; 26.
24 Vierra, 2013: 149.
25 Vierra, 2003.
26 Vierra et al., 2018: 246.
27 Vierra, 2013: 150.
28 Fowles, 2004: 151.
29 Boyer, 2008: 24; Fowles, 2005: 43, 2004; McNutt, 1959; Trager, 1967.
30 Dicks et al., 2016: I-20.
31 Hall, 2017: 28.

32 Dunmire, 2013: 18.
33 Hämäläinen, 2003: 836.
34 Levine, 1991: 160.
35 Mitchell, 2015: 139.
36 Dunmire, 2013: 56.
37 Dunmire, 2013: 19; Hämäläinen, 1998: 121; Montgomery, 2019.
38 Hackett, 1937: 486–487.
39 Eiselt, 2012: 112.
40 John, 1996: 243.
41 Mitchell, 2015: 102.
42 Roe, 1955: 227.
43 Brownstone, 2015: 9.
44 Betty, 2005.
45 Mitchell, 2015: 123.
46 N.A., 1881: 2.
47 Perry, 1880: 1.
48 MacCameron, 1998: 24–25; Mancal, 2011: 741.
49 Frost, 2015: 16.
50 Marshall, 1945: 131.
51 MacCameron, 1998: 45.
52 Conron, 1984.
53 Frost, 2015: 16.
54 N.A., 1860–2000; N.A., 1880–2017.
55 Census, 1910: 158; Melzer, 2012: 1.
56 Tisdale, 1996: 434.
57 Marshall, 1945: 97.
58 Tisdale, 1996: 436.
59 Marshall, 1945: 100.
60 Tisdale, 1996: 435.

Bibliography

Anschuetz, Kurt F. 2001. Soaking It All in: Northern New Mexican Pueblo Lessons of Water Management and Landscape Ecology. In *Native Peoples of the Southwest: Negotiating Land, Water, and Ethnicities*, edited by L. Winston, pp. 49–78. Greenwood Publishing Group, Westport.

Anschuetz, Kurt F., Eileen L. Camilla, and Christopher D. Banet. 2017. Agricltural Landscapes. In *The Oxford Handbook of Southwest Archaeology*, edited by B.J. Mills and S. Fowles. Oxford University Press. DOI: 10.1093/oxfordhb/9780199978427.013.12.

Anschuetz, Kurt F., Richard H. Wilshusen, and Cherie L. Scheick. 2001. Archaeology of Landscapes: Perspectives and Directions. *Journal of Archaeological Research* 9(2):157–211.

Basso, Keith. 1996. Wisdom Sits in Places: Notes on a Western Apache Landscape. In *Sense of Place*, edited by S. Field and K. Basso, pp. 53–90. School of American Research Press, Santa Fe.

Betty, Gerald. 2005. *Comanche Society: Before the Reservation.* Texas A&M University College Station.

Boyer, Jefferey L. 2008. North People and South People: Ethnohistorical and Archaeological Evidence for the Origins and Organization of Taos Pueblo. In *Chasing Chaco and the Southwest: Papers in Honor of Frances Joan Mathien*, edited by R.N. Wiseman, T.C. O'Laughlin, C.T. Snow, and C. Travis, pp. 19–35. Archaeological Society of New Mexico, Albuquerque.

Brownstone, Arni. 2015. *War Paintings of the Tsuu T'ina Nation.* University of New Mexico Press, Albuquerque.

Census, U.S. Bureau. 1910. *Thirteenth Census of the United States. Population. Vol. 3. Nebraksa-Wyoming, Alsaka, Hawaii, and Porto Rico.* United States Department of Commerce, Government Printing Press, Washington, DC.

Conron, John P. 1984. Santa Fe and the Santa Fe Railroad. *La Cronic de Nuevo Mexico*, vol. 2. Historical Society of New Mexico, Albuquerque.

Conroy, Jessica L., Jonathan T. Overpeck, Julia E. Cole, Timothy M. Shanahan, and Miriam Steinitz-Kannan. 2008. Holocene Changes in Eastern Tropical Pacific Climate Inferred from a Galápagos Lake Sediment Record. *Quaternary Science Reviews* 27: 116–118.

Conroy, Jessica L., Alejandra Restrepo, Jonathan T. Overpeck, Mirian Steinitz-Kannan, Julia E. Cole, Mark B. Bush, and Paul A. Colinvaux. 2009. Unprecedented Recent Warming of Surface Temperatures in the Eastern Tropical Pacific Ocean. *Nature Geoscience* 2: 46–50.

Crellin, Rachel J. 2020. Discussing Posthuman Approaches to Power: Marxism, Politics, and Affect. In *Archaeological Theory in Dialogue: Situating Relationality, Ontology, Posthumanism, and Indigenous Paradigms*, edited by R.J. Crellin, C.N. Cipolla, L.M. Montgomery, O.J.T. Harris, and S.V. Moore. Routledge Press, London.

Darling, J. Andrew. 2009. O'odham Trails and the Archaeology of Space. In *Landscapes of Movement: Trails, Paths, and Roads in Anthropological Perspective*, edited by J.E. Snead, C.L. Erickson, and J.A. Darling, pp. 61–83. University of Pennsylvania Museum of Archaeology and Anthropology, Philadelphia.

David, Bruno, and Julian Thomas. 2008. Landscape Archaeology: Introduction. In *Handbook of Landscape Archaeology*, edited by B. David and J. Thomas, pp. 27–43. LeftCoast Press, Walnut Creek.

Dicks, Merrill, Arron C. Anderson, Jessica Mrstik, Peter Rogers, and Todd Scarbourgh. 2016. *Rio Grande Del Norte National Monument Class III Cultural Resources Survey of the Cerro Montoso Project Area, Taos County, New Mexico.* Taos: Bureau of Land Management, Toas.

Dunmire, William W. 2013. *New Mexico's Spanish Livestock Heritage Four Centuries of Animals, Land, and People.* University of New Mexico, Albuquerque.

Duwe, Samuel, and Kurt F. Anschuetz. 2013. Ecological Uncertainty and Organizational Flexibility on the Prehispanic Tewa Landscape: Notes from the Northern Frontier. In *From Mountain Top to Valley Bottom: Understanding Past Land Use in the Northern Rio Grande Valley, New Mexico*, edited by B.J. Vierra, pp. 95–112. University of Utah Press, Salt Lake City.

Eiselt, B. Sunday. 2012. *Becoming White Clay: A History and Archaeology of Jicarilla Apache Enclavement.* University of Utah Press, Salt Lake City.

Fish, Suzanne K., and Paul R. Fish (editors) 1984. *Prehistoric Agricultural Strategies in the Southwest*, p. 33. Arizona State University Press, Tempe.

Fowles, Severin. 2004. The Making of Made People: The Prehistoric Evolution of Hierocracy Among the Northern Tiwa of New Mexico. Unpublished PhD dissertation, Anthropology Department, University of Michigan, Ann Arbor.

Fowles, Severin. 2005. Historical Contingency and the Prehistoric Foundations of Eastern Pueblo Moiety Organization. *Journal of Anthropological Research* 61(1): 25–52.

Fowles, Severin. 2009. The Enshrined Pueblo: Villagescape and Cosmos in the Northern Rio Grande. *American Antiquity* 74(3): 448–466.

Fowles, Severin. 2010. The Southwest School of Landscape Archaeology. *Annual Review of Anthropology* 39: 453–468.

Frost, Richard H. 2015. *The Railroad and the Pueblo Indians: The Impact of the Atchison, Topeka, and Santa Fe on the Pueblos of the Rio Grande, 1880–1930.* University of Utah Press, Salt Lake City.

Garcia Sr., Peter, Reycita Garcia, Patricia Ortiz, Beverly Garcia, Gordon Garcia, Giseld Saufkie, Gregg Shutiva, and Linda J. Goodman. 2013. Four Springtime Tewa Songs. In *Inside Dazzling Mountains: Southwest Native Verbal Arts*, edited by D.L. Kozak, pp. 487–524. University of Nebraska Press, Lincoln.

Hackett, Charles W. (editor). 1937. *Historical Documents Relating to New Mexico, Nueva Vizcaya, and Approaches Thereto, to 1773,* p. 3. Carnegie Institution, Washington, DC.

Hall, Stephen A. 2017. Paleoenvironments of the American Southwest. In *The Archaic Southwest: Foragers in an Arid Land*, edited by B.J. Viera, pp. 16–30. The University of Utah Press, Salt Lake City.

Hall, Stephan A., and William L. Penner. 2013. Stable Carbon Isotopes, C3-C4, Vegetation, and 12,8000 Years of Climate Change in Central New Mexico, USA. *Palaeogeography, Palaeoclimatology, and Palaecology* 369: 272–281.

Hämäläinen, Pekka. 1998. The Western Comanche Trade Center: Rethinking the Plains Indian Trade System. *The Western Historical Quarterly* 29(4): 485–513.

Hämäläinen, Pekka. 2003. The Rise and Fall of Plains Indian Horse Cultures. *The Journal of American History* 90: 833–862.

Herhahn, Cynthia L., and J. Brett Hill. 1998. Modeling Agricultural Production Strategies in the Northern Rio Grande Valley, New Mexico. *Human Ecology* 26: 469–487.

Jodry, Margaret A. 1999. Paleoindian Stage Paleoecological Records. In *Colorado Prehistory: A Context for the Rio Grande Basin*, edited by M.A. Martorano, T. Hoefer III, M.A. Jodry, V. Spero, and M.L. Taylor, pp. 12–26. Colorado Council of Professional Archaeologists, Denver.

John, Elizabeth A.H. 1996. *Storms Brewed in Other Men's Worlds: The Confrontation of Indians, Spanish, and French in the Southwest, 1540-1795.* University of Oklahoma Press, Norman.

Julyan, Robert Hixson. 2006. *The Mountains of New Mexico.* University of New Mexico Press, Albuquerque.

Levine, Francis. 1991. Economic Perspectives on the Comanchero Trade. In *Farmers, Hunters, and Colonists: Interaction between the Southwest and the Southern Plains*, edited by K.A. Spielmann, pp. 155–170. University of Arizona Press, Tucson.

Lightfoot, Kent G. 1995. Culture Contact Studies: Redefining the Relationship between Prehistoric and Historical Archaeology. *American Antiquity* 60(2): 199–217.

Lipman, Peter W., and Mehnert, Harald H. 1979. The Taos Plateau Volcanic Field, northern Rio Grande Rift, New Mexico. In *Rio Grande Rift: Tectonics and Magnetism*, edited by R.E. Riecker, pp. 289–311. American Geophysical Union, Washington, DC.

MacCameron, Robert. 1998. Environmental Change in Colonial New Mexico. In *A Sense of the American West: An Anthology of Environmental History*, edited by J.E. Sherow, pp. 41–64. University of New Mexico Press, Albuquerque.

Mancall, Peter C. 2011. Santa Fe Trail. In *Encyclopedia of Native American History.* Facts On File, New York.

Marshall, James. 1945. *Santa Fe: The Railroad that Built and Empire.* Random House, New York.

Melzer, Richard. 2012. New Mexico on the Eve of Statehood, 1910–1912. *Historical Review* 1.

Mitchell, Peter. 2015. *Horse Nations: The World Impact of Horses on Indigenous Societies Post-1492*. Oxford University Press, Oxford.
McNutt, Charles H. 1959. *Excavation and Interpretation of Early Puebloan occupations at Tesuque Bypass Site in the Upper Rio Grande Valley*, Department of Anthropology, University of Michigan, Ann Arbor.
Montgomery, Lindsay M. 2019. Nomadic Economics: The Logic and Logistics of Comanche Imperialism in New Mexico. *Journal of Social Archaeology*. DOI. org/10. 1177/1469605319859667.
NA. 1880–2017. Denver, Colorado Population History.
NA. 1881. The Atchison, Topeka, and Santa Fe Railroad over the Raton Mountains (Jan 3, 1880). *Scientific American (1845–1908)* 42(1): 2.
Nelson, Margaret C. 2000. Abandonment: Conceptualization, Representation, and Social Change. In *Social Theory in Archaeology*, edited by M.B. Schiffer, pp. 52–62. University of Utah Press, Salt Lake City.
Ortman, Scott. 2009. Action, Place, and Space in the Castle Rock Community. In *The Social Construction of Communities: Agency, Structure, and Identity in the Prehispanic Southwest*, edited by M.D. Varien and J.M. Potter, pp. 125–154. Altamira, New York.
Panich, Lee M. 2013. Archaeologies of Persistence: Reconsidering the Legacies of Colonialism in Native North America. *American Antiquity* 78(1): 105–122.
Patterson, Carol, and Clifford Duncan. 2013. Concepts of Spirit in Prehistoric Art According to Clifford Duncan, Ute Spiritual Elder. In *Rock Art and Sacred Landscapes*, edited by D.L. Gillette, M. Greer, M.H. Hayward, and W.B. Murray, pp. 139–162. Springer, London.
Perry, Susan T. 1880. Observations in New Mexico. *New York Evangelist (1830–1902)*.
Roe, Frank Gilbert. 1955. *The Indian and the Horse*. University of Nebraska Press, Norman.
Schlanger, Sarah H. 1992. Recognizing Persistent Places in Anasazi Settlement Systems. In *Space, Time, and Archaeological Landscapes*, edited by J. Rossignol and L. Wandsnider, pp. 91–112. Plenum Press, New York & London.
Schein, Richard H. 1997. The Place of Landscape: A Conceptual Framework for Interpreting an American Scene. *Annals of the Association of American Geographers* 87(4): 660–680.
Shackley, M. Steven. 2011. Sources of Archaeological Dacite in Northern New Mexico. *Journal of Archaeological Science* 38: 1001–1007.
Silliman, Stephen W. 2009. Change and Continuity, Practice and Memory: Native American Persistence in Colonial New England. *American Antiquity* 74(2): 211–230.
Snead, James E. 2002. An Imperishable Record: History, Theory, and the Cultural Landscape of the Northern Rio Grande. In *Traditions, Transitions, and Technologies: Themes in Southwestern Archaeology in the Year 2000*, edited by S.H. Schlanger, pp. 16–32. University of Colorado Press, Niwot.
Snead, James E. 2008. *Ancestral Landscapes of the Pueblo World*. University of Arizona Press, Tucson.
Swentzell, Rina. 1993. Mountain Form, Village Form: Unity in the Pueblo World. In *Ancient Land, Ancestral Places: Paul Logsdon in the Pueblo Southwest*, edited by S.H. Lekson and R. Swentzell, pp. 139–147. Museum of New Mexico Press, Santa Fe.
Tisdale, Shelby J. 1996. Railroads, Tourism, and Native Americans in the Greater Southwest. *Journal of the Southwest* 38(4): 433–462.
Tomka, Steve A., and Marc G. Stevenson. 1993. Understanding Abandonment Processes: Summary and Remaining Concerns. In *Abandonments of Settlements and Regions: Ethnoarchaeological and Archaeological Approaches*, edited by C.M. Cameron and S.A. Tomka, pp. 191–196. Cambridge University Press.

Trager, George L. 1967. The Tanoan Settlement of the Rio Grande Area: A Possible Chronology. In *Studies in Southwestern Ethnolinguistics: Meaning and History in the Lanugages of the American Southwest*, edited by D.H. Hymes, W.E. Bittle and H. Hoijer, pp. 335–350. The Hauge, Mouton.
Vierra, Bradley J. 2003. Late Archaic Settlement Systems in the Northern Rio Grande. Paper Presented at the Annual Meetings of the Society for American Arachaeology. Seattle, Washington.
Vierra, Bradley J. 2013. Archaic Foraging Technology and Land Use in the Northern Rio Grande, New Mexico. In *From Mountaintop to Valley Bottom: Papers in Honor of Paul Williams*, edited by B.J. Vierra, p. 145–160. University of Utah Press, Salt Lake City.
Vierra, Bradley J., Richard I. Ford, and Stephen S. Post. 2018. Archaic Foragers of the Northern Rio Grande. In *The Archaic Southweset: Foragers in an Arid Land*, edited by B.J. Vierra, pp. 235–253. Univeristy of Utah Press, Salt Lake City.
Wescott, Konnie L., Jennifer M. Abplanalp, Jeff Brown, Brian Cantwell, Merrill Dicks, Brian Fredericks, Angie Krall, Katherine E. Rollins, Robert Sullivan, Arnie Valdez, Bruce Verhaaren, Joseph Vieira, Lee Walston, and Emily A. Zvolanek. 2016. San Luis Valley-Taos Plateau Landscape-Level Cultural Heritage Values and Risk Assessment Final Report. Report Prepared for the Bureau of Land Management by Argonne National Laboratory, Argonne, Illinois.
Whittlesey, Stephanie M. 2008. Mountains, Mounds, and Meaning: Metaphor in the Hohokam Cultural Landscape. In *The Archaeology of Meaningful Places*, edited by B.J. Bowser and M.N. Zedeno, pp. 73–89. University of Utah Press, Salt Lake City.
Zedeno, M. Nieves 1997. Landscapes, Land Use, and the History of Territory Formation: An Example from the Puebloan Southwest. *Journal of Archaeological Method and Theory* 4: 67–103.

PART I

Indigenizing the archaeology of mobility

IN SEARCH OF INDIGENOUS FUTURISM

Indigenous people live in an upside-down world, the kind of disutopian society that most Americans only see on television or read about in books. Kathryn Tijerina, an enrolled member of the Comanche Nation, has called this alternative reality, "post-apocalyptic." Describing her love for science-fiction novels on a sunny afternoon at the Mercado San Augustin in Tucson, Tijerina told me: "It was like an epiphany to me. That's why I like apocalyptic science fiction so much, because we [Native Americans] went through our own apocalypse. It makes sense to me to look at how people survive."[1] Rather than a fantastical literary premise, the provocative notion that one's entire way of life could be violently turned on its head is history for Indigenous people like Tijerina.

Following the initial waves of cultural and physical genocide which reverberated throughout Native North America upon the arrival of Europeans, Indigenous people have been politcally disenranchised, economically undermined, systematically silenced, and publicly forgotten. The disappearance of living Indigenous people from North America was heralded by Supreme Court Justice Joseph Story, who, in 1828, declared that Native Americans "seem destined to a slow but sure extinction. Everywhere, at the approach of the white man, they fade away."[2] Story's comments are echoed in William Cullen Bryant's poem *An Indian at the Burial Place of His Fathers,* which regales readers with a harrowing account of Indigenous extinction at the hands of Euro-American colonizers:

> They waste us—ay—like April snow
> In the warm noon, we shrink away
> And fast they follow, as we go
> Towards the setting day,—
> Till they shall fill the land, and we
> Are driven into the western sea.

> But I behold a fearful sign,
> To which the white men's eyes are blind;
> Their race may vanish hence, like mine,
> And leave no trace behind,
> Save ruins o'er the region spread,
> And the white stones above the dead[3]

As the haunting prose of Bryant's poem reveals, to be Indigenous in North America today is in many ways to be invisible; a shadow; a ghost.

The surreal nature of Indigenous life in the 21st century has been turned on its head by Native artists and filmmakers in ways that draw out the tragedy and horror of colonization while highlighting the resiliency of Indigenous people. In September 2019, Mi'kmaq filmmaker Jeff Barnaby released the movie *Blood Quantum*, which depicts the effects of a zombie pandemic on a fictional version of the Mi'kmaq Reserve, a First Nations group in northeastern Canada, who are immune to the virus. The movie is a sardonic twist on the deadly effects of infectious disease on Indigenous peoples during the initial waves of European settlement in the Americas. As hinted at in the title, the film provides a gory commentary on the reservation—a colonial institution quite literally intended to quarantine Indigenous people—and on the politics of tribal membership as measured by degree of "Indian blood." Cannupa Hanska Luger (Mandan, Hidatsa, Arikara, Lakota, Austrian, and Norwegian) has also drawn on science fiction motifs in his installation entitled *Future Ancestral Technologies: nágshibi,* which imagines a post-apocalyptic world where Indigenous people are the only survivors. Debuted in 2018 at the University of South Dakota, the multi-media art pieces and performances in Luger's exhibition posit a dynamic Indigenous future in which tipis are solar-powered, regalia is considered everyday wear, and ceremony is central to daily life.

While settler zombies and solar-powered tipis may seem a far cry from the lithic landscapes of the Taos Plateau, upon further reflection they appear vitally important. Visual and material expressions of Indigenous survivance are central to archaeological praxis in North America because they place in stark relief the ways in which colonialism has unsettled and shaped the present and future of Indigenous descendants. Archaeology, until relatively recently, has been complicit in this disruption. It has done so in a plethora of ways, including the plundering of Indigenous-made objects and bodies, the construction of anthropological cultures disconnected from contemporary communities, and the publication of scientific narratives which have historically excluded Indigenous voices, opinions, and stories. The following chapter seek to disrupt these alienating practices by developing an alternative set of interpretive frameworks which emulate Barnaby and Luger's message of Indigenous resiliency and persistence.

2

INDIGENOUS HISTORY

Indigenous people today continue to experience the alienating effects of anthropological discourses of Native disappearance. A 2018 poll by the Reclaiming Native Truth project found that some 40% of Americans do not believe that Native Americans exist today.[4] Not only do "authentic" Native American's continue to be portrayed as extinct within popular discourse, but, museums, universities, and archives, maintain a monopoly on truth vis a vie Indigenous histories. These settler colonial institutions, control access to Indigenous material culture while occupying, often without acknowledgement, the traditional territories of Indigenous Peoples. This chapter traces the various ways in which settler colonial interests and anthropological discourses have intersected to disenfranchise and disempower Indigenous people. It goes on to present an alternative approach to Native North American historiography which draws from core tenets within Indigenous philosophy. This "Indigenous" framework takes the ongoing connection between Indigenous Peoples and the land as the starting place from which to develop ethical and culturally grounded narratives that support Indigenous assertions of sovereignty over their cultural heritage and history.

▼▽▼

Anthropological narratives have unmoored Indigenous Peoples from history and modernity. In *Custer Died for Your Sins*, Vine Deloria Jr. captures this a-historicity, arguing that

> To be an Indian in modern American society is in a very real sense to be unreal and ahistorical. Experts paint us as they would like us to be. Often, we paint ourselves as we wish we were or as we might have been. The more we try to be ourselves the more we defend what we have never been.[5]

Deloria's comments suggest that Indigenous people living in the 21st century are simulations of a more "authentic" Native American that no longer exists. Rather than soverign Peoples, Indigenous people are nostalgic figures, pop culture icons, and the inspiration for a deluge of dreamcatchers and flute player curios that fill the shelves of every gas station and roadside shop west of the Mississippi.[6]

To fill the void left by the "disappearance" of "real" Indigenous people, a plethora of stereotypes have emerged; the most iconic duo perhaps being the blood-thirsty Plains warrior of Buffalo Bills Wild West show and the Powhatan princess, who graced the carton of Land O Lakes butter for a century. In portraying modern Native Americans as simulations of a mythological authentic ancestor, the popular media has effectively placed Indigenous people outside of modernity, rendering them silent in American politics today and irrelevant for America's future as a nation. Deloria's comments also suggest that American intellectuals have played a critical role in perpetuating such faulty narratives. Within the field of archaeology, the most long-lasting and pernicious of these disenfranchising ideas has been the concept of social "complexity."

During the 19th century, American anthropologists developed evolutionary frameworks to explain the relationship between complexity and civilization. In *Ancient Society*, published in 1877, Lewis Henry Morgan draws on observations of non-Western communities to develop a theory of unilineal social evolution, in which societies passed through successive stages of savagery, barbarism, and civilization. According to Morgan, the Indigenous Peoples of North America "exemplified the condition of mankind in three successive ethnical periods … especially those of the lower and of the middle status of barbarism, more elaborately and completely than any other portion of mankind."[7]

Morgan's approach required a clever reconfiguration of the relationship between culture and chronology. Indigenous people practicing a residentially mobile hunting- and gathering-based lifestyle were conceived as the sociological predecessors of Indigenous people engaged in farming and living in aggregated villages, even though these two groups often lived side by side in the same region. While Morgan's original theory used a variety of criteria including subsistence, governance, language, family structure, "religion," architecture, and property to rank societies, the matter of lifestyle (i.e., sedentary agriculturalist versus mobile hunter-gatherer) became the most salient factor for colonial policymakers looking to rationalize their efforts to claim Indigenous lands on behalf of white civilization.

Federal policy during the 19th century drew on Morgan's ideas as well as earlier legal documents that equated civilization with mastery over nature through cultivation and the exploitation of natural resources.[8] The explicit link between agriculture, sedentism, and land rights was codified by *The Law of Nations* written by Emer de Vateel:

> We have already observed (§81), in establishing the obligation to cultivate the earth, that those nations cannot exclusively appropriate to themselves

> more land than they have occasion for, or more than they are able to settle and cultivate. Their unsettled habitation in those immense regions cannot be accounted a true and legal possession; and the people of Europe, too closely pent up at home, finding land of which the savages stood in no particular need, and of which they made no actual and constant use, were lawfully entitled to take possession of it, and settle it with colonies.[9]

de Vateel clearly states that legal possession of land is based on proof of permeant occupation and cultivation.

The principles laid out in *The Law of Nations* directly informed the Homestead Act passed in 1862, which granted all adult (Anglo-European) citizens who had not borne arms against the US government the right to claim 160 acres of surveyed territory under the stipulation that they "improve" the plot by building a dwelling and cultivating the land.[10] These plots were typically located within the traditional territories of Indigenous people deemed incapable of satisfactorily demonstrating a long-term investment in the land. The notion that Indigenous people were incapable of improving the land was expressed by Thomas Jefferson in a series of notes on the States of Virginia:

> I know of no such thing existing as an Indian monument: for I would not honor with that name arrow points, stone hatchets, stone pipes, and half-shapen images. Of labour on the large scale, I think there is no remain as respectable as would be a common ditch for the draining of lands …"[11]

Jefferson's comments explicitly exclude the vast majority of the archaeological record associated with Indigenous people in the United States from serving as proof of occupation under American law.

American politicians like Jefferson strategically marshalled the ideas of de Vateel, Morgan, and other intellectuals of the age to rationalize the removal, dispossession, and assimilation of Indigenous Peoples across the United States.[12] As Alexis de Tocqueville so aptly noted, "the dispossession of the Indians often takes place today in regular and, so to speak, entirely legal manner".[13] As part of a broader effort to clear Indigenous people from the land and assimilate them into American society, Jefferson argued explicitly for the need to "speed up" the social evolution of Indigenous people by transforming mobile foragers into settled agriculturalists. According to Jefferson, the promotion of agriculture and household manufacture, "will enable them [Indians] to live on much small[er] portions of land, and indeed will render their vast forests useless but for the range of cattle … while they are learning to do better on less land, our increasing numbers will be calling for more land."[14]

Echoing Jefferson's sentiments, Massachusetts Congressman Edward Everett declared in 1820 that "it is not necessary to exterminate a savage tribe—place the germ of civilization in their soil—and such is its living principle, such the *vis conservatrix* of the arts of civilized life, that it will strike root, shoot up, and spread."[15] Both Jefferson and Everett use a moralizing discourse in which assimilation was evoked as a responsible alternative to total war. Education, in Western-style agriculture, then, offered the best means of opening up Indigenous lands for colonization.

While the idea that Indigenous people simply needed to abandon their "wandering" ways seemed an efficient approach to pacifying the hunter-gatheres of the Great Basin and equestrian nomads of the Plains, this same logic placed the federal government in a double bind *vis-a-vis* Tribal Nations already engaged in intensive forms of agriculture. For instance, many Indigenous Peoples in the Southeast had tried to use the Euro-American legal system to claim proprietary ownership over their traditional territories by demonstrating permanent occupation. These efforts undermined settler ambitions to possess the fertile farm lands occupied by Cherokee, Creek, Choctaw, Chickasaw, and Seminole communities.[16]

To remedy this problem, colonial administrators pivoted, eschewing evolutionary arguments for the rheotric of de Tocqueville regarding the inherent disposition of all Indigenous people. In *Democracy in America*, de Tocqueville argued that the preference for a "wandering" life among Indigenous peoples would prevent them from "settling" down and adapting to Western democracy.[17] According to this racialized logic, nomadism was anti-democratic and therefore stood in direct opposition to the American "civi-territorial complex." However, this did not mean that the "nomadic" disposition of Indigenous people could not be changed.

In a letter from Secretary of War John H. Eaton to the Cherokee Delegation in 1829, Eaton proposed the following solution for opening up Cherokee lands in Georgia for White settlement: "while with the aid of schools a hope may be indulged, that ere long industry and refinement, will take the place of those wandering habits now so peculiar to the Indian character, the tendency of which is to impede them in their march to civilization."[18] Eaton's policy was premised on the belief that Indigenous people could in fact change their essential *esprit de corps* through Western-style education. President Andrew Jackson made a similar argument to Congress in December of that same year, stating that the "arts of civilization" could be taught to Indigenous people as a way of "reclaiming them from a wondering life."[19]

This larger history of Indigenous displacement from the land reveals the role of Euro-American perceptions and scholarly writings about Indigenous "nomadism" in the formation of settler colonial policies. As Deloria noted, intellectuals are not only complicit in settler colonialism they are an essential cog in the imperial machine. In the end, it was almost irrelevant whether any particular Indigenous People fit the anthropological definition of a "hunting-gathering" or "agricultural" society. From a colonial optic, the fact that these Tribal Nations were not seen as using the land to its maximal extent—as defined by a capitalist logic of efficency—made them "wanderers," a designation sufficient to justify their removal and eventual replacement by settlers who could use that land properly. While this destructive period of federal land appropriation ended during the mid-20th century, the underlying discourses and conceptual categories which underpinned these policies continue to percolate within anthropological archaeology.

Despite a discipline-wide reckoning with this colonial history during the 1980s and 1990s, archaeologist, remain deeply committed to notions of social "complexity". For early anthropologists like Morgan, agriculture was a key facet of any "civilized" society and a prerequisite for "social complexity."

> From these causes, but more particularly from the increased abundance of *subsistence through field agriculture* [emphasis added], nations began to develop, numbering many thousands under one government, where before they would be reckoned by a few thousands. The localization of tribes in fixed areas and in fortified cities, with the increase of the numbers of the people, intensified the struggle for the possession of the most desirable territories. It tended to advance the art of war, and to increase the rewards of individual prowess. These changes of condition and of the plan of life indicate the approach of civilization, which was to overthrow gentile and establish political society.[20]

In essence, Morgan was arguing that cultivation was an imaginary socioeconomic hurdle, which human societies were either moving towards or elaborating upon. While no longer cloaked in raciliazed assumptions of Indigenous inferiority and European civility, archaeological writings tody often echo the assumptions of Morgan and other scholars about how societies evolve (incrementally and linearly) as well as what they are evolving toward (hierarchy).

As Michelle Leliévre has argued in reference to the Mi'kmaq—a mobile Indigenous People living in Nova Scotia, Canada, "the presumptive relationship between subsistence and social evolution" proposed by teleological models of social evolution developed by Morgan and Engels have "had deep and lasting effects on the development of anthropology and especially the subdiscipline of archaeology."[21] One need only flip to the table of contents of commonly assigned introductory archaeology textbooks to see the engrained nature of Morgan's linear progression from hunter-gatherer to agriculturalist to "state-level" society.[22] These sources draw on and perpetuate definitions of social complexity linked to the presence of stratification, material accumulation, large concentrated populations, formal "religion," writing, and permanent settlements. For example, in *Patterns in Prehistory*—a popular archaeology textbook now in its 5th edition—sociocultural complexity is defined by

> ranking particular societies on a single scale but on the basis of several primary variables … [including] (1) the degree of *differential access* to wealth, power, and prestige; (2) the extent to which differential access to wealth, power, and

> prestige are *inherited*, as opposed to earned; (3) the degree to which individuals in a community are *specialized* in their *occupations* … and (4) the degree to which political power is *centralized* in a government [origional emphasis].[23]

The authors of this textbook also put forward the argument that "the largest and most complex civilizations throughout history have been based on the cultivation of only a few genera—in fact, just six plant genera—wheat, barley, millet, rice, maize, and potatoes."[24] This definition of complexity reflects a Western capitalist bias towards material accumulation and a model of land use that presumes sedentary agriculture is the inevitable and best means of engaging with the environment.

This type of evolutionary thinking is echoed in many popular academic texts like Jared Diamond's now-famous *Guns, Germs, and Steel*. The narrative arc of this book is framed as an extended response to a question posed to Diamond by Yali, a Papua New Guinea man who asked, "Why is it that you white people developed so much cargo and brought it to New Guinea, but we black people had little cargo of our own?"[25] In addressing Yali's question, Diamond points to the superiority of certain European technologies, particularly guns and steel weaponry, as proximate factors contributing to the West's dominance in the modern world. Drawing on anthropological definitions of social complexity discussed previously, much of Diamond's argumentation relies on the assumption that the development of agriculture, and agricultural surplus, is a precursor to things like cities, stratification, state religion, writing, and other such innovations; criteria which bare a striking resemblance to Morgan's list. Specifically, he argues that, "the availability of domestic plants and animals ultimately explains why empires, literacy, and steel weapons developed earliest in Eurasia and later, or not at all, on other continents."[26] Although Diamond's work has often been critiqued by anthropologists for painting too simple a picture of large-scale social processes, what is particularly notable about this example is the way in which textbooks and popular literature draw on shared assumptions about the significance of agriculture in social "development" without considering the origins of these criteria and who they serve.

A land-based model of Indigenous History

To date, Indigenous history has been "written from the sedentary [and I would add Western] point of view."[27] This fixation on village-based agriculture is perhaps most salient within the archaeological literature of the American Southwest, which has largely focused either on explaining the transition of Indigenous people from "Archaic" hunter-gatherers into sedentary agriculturalists or on the evolution of "sedentary" agricultural societies prior to the mid-19th century.[28] As Bradley Vierra and Maxine McBrinn point out, "Despite its [the Archaic period] length, it is probably the least studied period in the

Southwest (and in the rest of North America)."[29] With some notable exceptions, much of the history of non-agricultural Indigenous Peoples in the region has either been glossed over or explained in relationship to plant and animal domestication. This focus on cultivation flattens the heterogeneity of Indigenous socioeconomic practices and engagements with the land.

Rather than documenting domestication and population aggregation, I use the material record of the Taos Plateau to discuss human connections to particular places and their movements between these places. This requires a "deep" approach to history, tracing patterns in how different human societies used and conceptualized places over time. Shifting our scholarly gaze away from village sites and towards the broader landscape is particularly important for understanding the histories of residentially mobile Indigenous communities who have been glossed over by Southwest archaeologists and targeted by genocidal policies of erasure.In addition to focusing on landscape, the alternative approach advocated for in this book draws on Indigenous oral histories, personal narratives, ontologies, and epistemologies as important sources of knowledge for interpreting the archaeological record. Indigenous oral traditions and thier material culture comprise an *Indigenous archive.*[30] Rooted in the experiences of Native communities and individuals, the Indigenous archive contains evidence, sometimes suppressed or overlooked, that casts "doubt upon the validity of assumptions and myths, especially ones held by those in power" and directly contributes to the creation of collective narratives about the past.[31]

Indigenous people have a unique way of approaching history, which is distinct from those traditionally drawn on by archaeologists. Western forms of history have typically produced chronological narratives of important events based on linear understanding to time. Rather than linear time marked by calendrical dates, many Indigenous communities think about time as cyclical. As Vine Deloria Jr. argued in *God is Red*, "[T]he western preoccupation with history and a chronological description of reality was not a dominant factor in any tribal conception of either time or history."[32] For example, the Hopituh-Shi-nu-mu (Hopi) conceptualize their history as a cycle of worlds that exist(ed) in the past, present, and future. Each of these four worlds align with catastrophic environmental events, places on the landscape, and oral narratives which explain the community's origins, migrations, social practices, and cultural values.[33] Similarly, Tsitsistas (Cheyenne) oral traditions reflect a spatially anchored cyclical approach to time. Cheyenne narratives document the community's migration through five different worlds defined by particular geographical locations and important animals, like rabbits, dogs, and bison, that they came to depend on.[34]

In addition to drawing on cyclical notions of time, most Indigenous peoples hold a place-based understanding of history in which particular landscape features act as reservoirs of collective memories and narratives.[35] These places and associated narratives constitute a community's *cosmogeography*. Drawing on oral histories among the Jicarilla Apache, Sunday B. Eiselt has defined a cosmogeography as a system of territorial organization in which space is structured around astronomical and geographic markers that orient individuals within the supernatural and physical world. Cosmogeographies are embodied and therefore highly malleable, changing over time in response to the acquisition of new territories or the incorporation of new people into the group.[36]

Indigenous approaches to place differ in fundamental ways from those of the Western colonial state. For European nation-states, the land is an inanimate space to be organized into bounded controllable geographical units. These units are codified within maps drawn using the orthagonal precision of the Cartesian coordinate system. Colonial acts of map making were intimately tied to territorial conquest and "gave no recognition to preexisting Aboriginal boundaries or spatial conventions, let alone any form of pre-existing Aboriginal land title."[37] Through the creation of Cartesian maps, the Spanish, Mexican, and American colonial projects imposed bounded grids and associated notions of private and collective property onto the cyclical place-based approach to the land held by Indigenous peoples.

Archaeological mapping projects have typically perpetuated the settler colonial habit of reordering and dividing up Indigenous landscapes into gridded spatial units. The creation of archaeological site maps divides out the land into culturally modified and "natural" areas. Traditional methods of spatializing the archaeological record excludes large swaths of the landscape used, but not materially marked by, Indigenous peoples from historical narratives. Although seemingly benign, this piecemeal approach to mapping is profoundly political. As T.J. Ferguson and Chip Colwell have argued, "projections of time and space onto the territory of Native people is not innocuous" and has very real repercussions for Indigenous Peoples seeking to make legal claims to traditional territories and natural resources.[38] The high-stakes of archaeological praxis in North America ought to compel us to incorporate Indigenous understandings of place-based history into our interpretations of the past.

▼▽▼

The cosmogeographies of Indigenous people are comprised of origin stories, migration narratives, place names, and place lore. These cosmogeographies link particular natural resources to a larger body of narratives about communal origins and events. As Keith Basso has argued, important places are created and maintained through collective acts of remembering that create a direct connection between the present and past.[39] These places may be singular, for example the red clay source near Questa, New Mexico, used by Jicarilla Apache runners during ceremonial relay races. Or they may be more prevalent, for example the multitude of micaceous clay shrines inhabited by *Hactcins*—personifications of objects and natural forces.[40] Oral histories provide detailed accounts of how the clay *Hactcin* taught *Ndee* women how to make micaceous pottery, creating an historical framework for contemporary practices among Jicarilla community members.

In addition to recording places linked with specific natural resources and ceremonial activities, place-based histories document the relationships between different Indigenous communities. Take, for example, Apache Springs, which is located near Taos. Fed by Taos Blue Lake, Apache Springs flows south into the Rio Pueblo, which eventually ends in a large buffalo pasture historically used by the Jicarilla as a campsite. According to stories shared by Gilbert Velarde (Jicarilla Apache) during a meeting with Taos, Picuris, and other Jicarilla tribal members in August of 2017, the spring is a place where Jicarilla traders and families would stop during their annual journey to Taos for the San Geronimo feast day in September.[41] Although archaeologically unmarked, this pasture embodies the long-standing economic and social relationship between the *Ĭăłap°ăĭbâ* and the Jicarilla.

The oral tradition preserves memories linked to communal origins and social practices. While the link between origin stories and collective identity may be obvious, personal narratives and teachings linked to place also engender a shared sense of history. The telling and re-telling of personal narratives creates a sense of cultural belonging grounded in the land. As these stories circulate among direct descendants of the narrative's protagonist they become part of the community's collective memory.

For Indigenous peoples engaging in highly mobile bison-hunting lifestyles, personal narratives typically reference events and places linked to hunting journeys, raiding parties, and military excursions. *Arrows Fall on the Hunt* is one such narrative and was told to anthropologist Pliny Goddard in 1911 by a Jicarilla man named Casa Maria.[42] The story begins with a group of Jicarilla men camped along the Canadian River in preparation for a bison hunt. According to Casa Maria, the hunting party traveled east towards the Plains in search of bison, stopping at three different locations to camp along the way. Their first stop along their journey was called *DzîLts'îdgaiye* (mountains stand), which likely references Laughlin Peak, a prominent landmark visible while traveling east from Cimarron along the Canadian River. The party then proceeded east, stopping at *LiyeLdeseLye* (saddle-washed-away) and *Balisoye*. After 2 days of preparations at Balisoye, the hunting party moved one last time to a place called *Gadjaeyi* and camped below in an arroyo. Over the course of 3 days, the party conducted a successful hunt, killing many bison and leaving the ground littered with arrows. After the third day of hunting, the party decided to head back to Cimarron lest they encounter any enemies. By verbally documenting the relationship between points across an expansive landscape, Casa Maria's story creates a sort of memory web, connecting personal experiences to a broader set of shared places and narratives.[43]

The way in which place-based personal narratives connect community members over time is demonstrated in a story shared with me by Fred and LaDonna Harris (Comanche). This narrative focuses on the raiding exploits of LaDonna's great grandfather, a man named Hoawah. As told to Fred and LaDonna by her grandfather Tabitha, the story takes place prior to a battle between a *Numunu-Kai-i-guu* (Kiowa) encampment and the US military at Adobe Walls in north Texas:

> Some old adobe ruins that had been built, and sometimes used, although mostly abandoned, by buffalo hunters. They were just kind of an irritant for the Plains Indians who depended on the buffalo. There was allot of ferment going on ... There was a lot of bring back the buffalo, or let's get the old days back, or whatever ... So, there was these young guys looking for something to do, and they said well hell let's get together and go out there and kill those people who are in Adobe walls, those buffalo hunters. So, a huge group of them, it's very unusual, because war parties are generally pretty small, but this was a big group of several tribes. Well Tabitha's father, Hoawah, was in that group. He told me, what his father told him. He said that they rode out there and camped out at Adobe walls. The adobe ruins are down in kind of a prairie and then there is a kind of stream, and then to the east, way up high is a kind of bluff. And the ruins, or the buildings, and the top of that bluff is about a mile. They came in there in the evening, late afternoon, and camped, made camp on top of that bluff. And Hoawah and some of the other young guys, wanted to steal some horses before the battle ... he and some of the other young guys went down there at night to where those buffalo hunters were sleeping. And he found a white horse that had a halter on and a long rope. And he wanted to get as long a rope as possible, and he had a knife. So, he kept feeling down this rope and all of a sudden, he gets to a guy's hand who was sleeping and holding the rope. I think he cut the rope anyway and got out of there with the horse ...[44]

Rather than recounting the battle, Hoawah's story focuses on his personal aggrandizing acts prior to combat. This account contrasts with the American version of events, which recounts the specific details of the battle that transpired on November 25, 1864. The American version of events is materially commemorated by an official marker placed next to the battle site by the Texas State Historical Survey Committee in 1964 (Figure 2.1).

In addition to its textual rather than oral form, the American version of the Adobe Walls battle precisely documents aspects of the encounter absent from Hoawah's story. These details include: (1) the actual date of the battle; (2) the number of *Numunu*, *Kai-i-gwu*, and American soldiers present; (3) the total number of casualties as well as the victor of the encounter; and (4) the precise location of the Adobe Wall ruins laid out on a cardinal grid. The emphasis placed on quantifying aspects of the battle as well as the various references to chronological time within the historical marker are key features of a Western approach to history, the goal of which is to produce an objective review of particular events. In contrast, the Harris' retelling of this event does not focus on the actual details of the encounter at all but rather on a single act of bravery undertaken by Hoawah as a young warrior before the action of the battle even takes place. This focus on personal aggrandizing deeds reflects *Numunu* cultural practices in

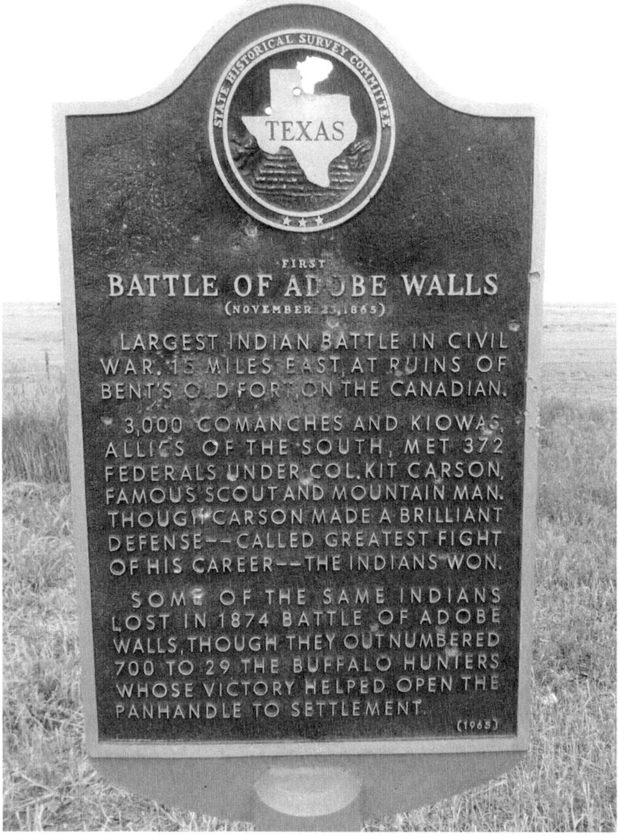

FIGURE 2.1 Battle of Adobe Walls Historical Marker 1690, Bent's Old Fort, Texas. Public domain photograph taken on November 3, 2005.

which social status and prestige was acquired through counting coup and subsequent oral recitations of the brave deed. Hoawah's narrative is also notable in its use of natural features on the landscape, like streams and bluffs, as spatial anchors for the action which unfolds rather than the use of cardinal directions or mile markers. As discussed previously, referencing physical features of the natural environment is a common narrative technique within a place-based approach to history.

There is a growing body of evidence to suggest that residential mobility was viewed as a spiritual as well as a functional practice by Indigenous Peoples. During the late 19th century anthropologist John Wesley Powell made the following observation about the *Nuutsiyu*:

> It is curious to notice with what tenacity an Indian clings to a trail; a path which has been followed by his forefathers is sacred to him, and though in

> the constant and rapid erosion of the gulches and sides of the hills and mountains these trails have become very difficult yet he never abandons them when they can by any possibility be followed, even though a shorter and better road is very perceptible.[45]

Powell's comments suggest that movement along the trail was considered "sacred" by *Nuutsiyu* people based on their ontological belief in a recipricoal connection between the physical and spiritual worlds.

The spiritually charged nature of Indigenous engagements with, and conceptualizations of, the land is materially marked by the vast trail systems created by the *Ndee*, *Nuutsiyu*, and *Numunu* across the southern Plains and Great Basin regions. For example, the northern branch of the Santa Fe Trail follows a well-known protohistoric *Nuutsiyu* road from New Mexico across the Continental Divide into California. The *Numunu* made similarly extensive trail networks (Figure 2.2).[46] In 1841, American settler John Arrowsmith described several such trails.

One of these routes was a north-south trail known as "Comanche Road" that ran south through Sabinal River canyon. A similarly extensive east-west trail extended from the upper Brazos River drainage deep into east Texas.[47]

For the resdientally mobile communities who made these trails , traveling, was not simply a functional means of moving from one resource patch to another but was a way of connecting to one's ancestral past through the land. Echoing Powell's statements, linguist James Goss summarized *Nuutsiyu* beliefs regarding the relationship between mobility and sacred geography, stating, "movement was a basic value. That is, you could say they had a sacred mandate, passed on to them by tradition from deity that they were supposed to do this."

In addition to the sacred role of mobility within Indigenous worldviews, Numic-speaking groups, like the *Nuutsiyu* and *Numunu*, approach place-making in highly individualist ways. Elaborating upon this idea, Clifford Duncan (Northern Ute) stated, "as far as sacred sites, I don't think there were places, like, for everyone to use and call sacred. I think those were narrowed down to the family or single unit."[48] Duncan's comment suggests that for the *Nuutsiyu*, landscape features became significant spaces through repeated use by individuals or family units. This approach to place-making reflects the social structure of highly mobile Indigenous people who historically spent much of the year living in bilateral kin groups.

The autonomous worldview of residentially mobile communities suggests that places attached to hunting areas or travel routes, acrue significance over time largely through repeated use. For the *Nuutsiyu*, *coochumpah* (River of Buffaloes), marks an historically used location for bison hunting. This place-name refers to a river that issues from Coochatope Pass and joins the Sahwatch River running eastward from the Continental Divide in Colorado.[49] Among the *Numunu*, Tucumcari in northeastern New Mexico, is also considered a significant place. The word Tucumcari derives from the term *tucumcane*, which translates as "House after Dark." As the name would suggest, *tucumcane* is a well-known

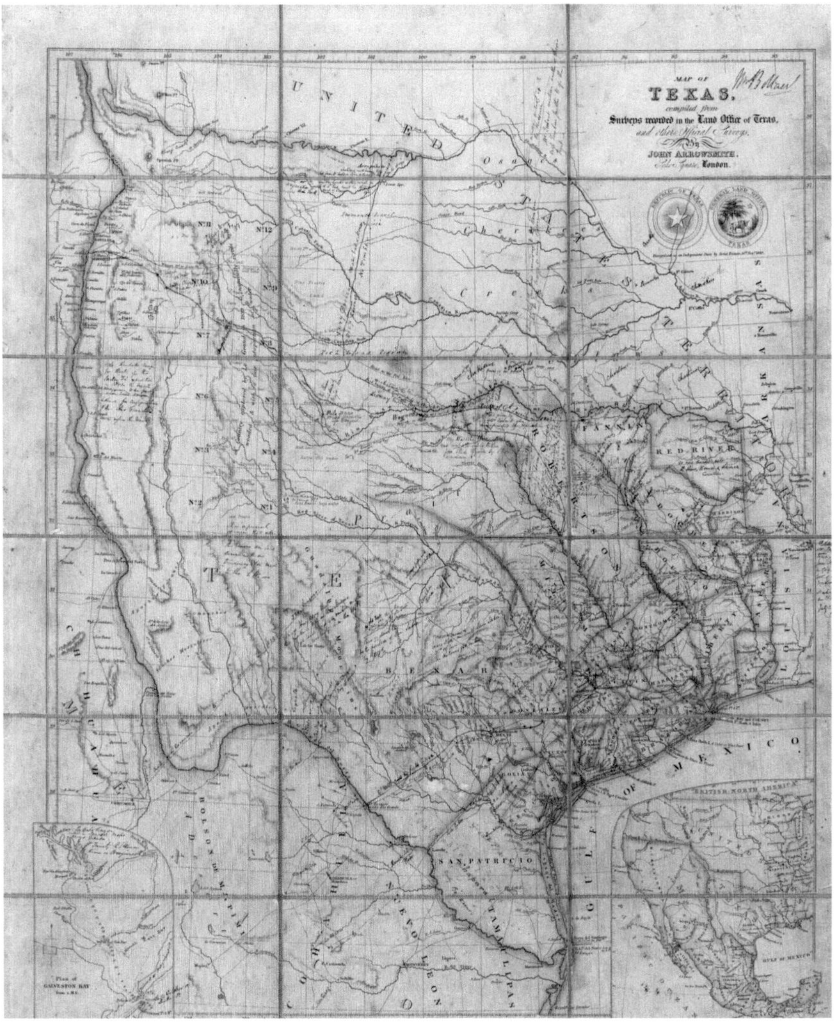

FIGURE 2.2 Map of Texas by John Arrowsmith and William Bollaert.[50]

camping place frequently used by *Numunu* activity groups traveling south from the Arkansas River valley. While the scale at which these more personal engagements with place circulate is smaller than for widely shared origin or migration stories, these place-names and narratives are nonetheless informed by a collective cultural framework which that makes them intelligible and relevant to other community members.

Kathryn Tijerina has also commented on the unique ways in which residential mobility structured the relationship between sacredness and the landscape for Numic-speaking peoples:

> I hear a lot from other Indians about the sacred connection to place. It is somewhat hard when you are nomadic. So, I think a lot of that is invested in the tipis. The tipis were their place, and that is why sometimes you would paint tipis with your medicine or just adorn them in ways that you liked … because you sort of, you took your place with you wherever you went.[51]

Tijerina's comments indicate that for at least some Comanche tribal members, ephemeral structures like tipis were equivalent to more permanent landscape features like the mountains, springs, hunting grounds, and raw material sources. As a fixed feature of everyday life, tipis grounded an individual's identity while the topography and ecology surrounding that mobile home changed. If we extend this framework to its logical extent, any place where a *Numunu* person sets up a tipi may have become an important place within the cosmogeography of the family or aggregated community who camped there.

There are several lessons archaeologists can learn from a careful consideration of the unique ways Indigenous peoples approach movement and the landscape. First, embracing an land-based approach to history draws our attention to *where* an event occurred, not *when* it occurred. The traditional obsession with chronology within North American archaeology has led to the expenditure of tremendous amounts of energy on perfecting the accuracy of chronometric dating methods and a plethora of typologies matching artifacts to calendrical dates. Instead of timelines and typologies, Indigenous people produce sacred cosmogeographies—cognitive maps comprised of physical points on the landscape (mountains, rivers, valleys, resource nodes, etc.) and orally transmitted narratives about the people, events, and resources associated with these places.[52] Duncan and Tijerina's comments suggest that the cosmogeographies of residentially mobile Indigenous peoples in particular exist at multiple scales, including the personal, familial, and communal. The collective cognitive maps produced by these various individuals and groups contain lines of flight connecting together temporary yet significant stopping places within a continuous cycle of movement.[53] Embracing this sort of land-centered historiography will require archaeologists to record the material and narrative evidence surrounding collectively shared place-names, points of individual or familial significance, and the pathways that connect these individual and communal spaces.

Second, for residentially mobile groups the journey between places is paramount and serves several important purposes. Through journeying, each new generation acquires an internal map of the landscape and resources within it. Traveling is also connected to identity formation and the creation of a collective memory. It is while traveling on the trail that certain stories, personal narratives, and songs are shared, which connect the present to the past and provide cultural instruction. Of course, traveling is also functional; it is a means of accessing the natural resources and goods that sustain(ed) everyday life. The importance of journeying to mobile Indigenous peoples draws attention to the broader use of space rather than habitation sites cordoned off from the natural landscape based on artifact density. Documenting trail systems along with geochemical sourcing studies offer two conventional archaeological methods for reconstructing the larger networks of movement in which Indigenous people were engaged. When placed in dialogue with oral histories and personal narratives, these material traces can significantly enhance archaeological histories of Indigenous peoples.

A mobile place-based framework demands a different approach to answering archaeological questions that integrates but also goes beyond ethnographically informed analyses to include the world views oflndigenous people. For example, the *Nuutsiyu* historically followed an ecologically informed mobility circuit that mapped onto culturally significant landscape features. Among the Muache Ute, family groups would camp to the north of Blanca Peak in the San Luis Valley during the spring and summer months, moving into lower-elevation grassland during the fall and winter.[54] This seasonal cycle was informed by the location of specific ecological resources, a series of astrologically based ceremonies and dances, colors linked to cardinal directions, and ancestral mythical characters found in origin stories. This cosmogeography creates a culturally grounded framework with which to interpret material evidence of seasonality, social practices, and economic activities associated with *Nuutsiyu* encampments within this mobility circuit.[55]

Finally, a land-based approach to history also requires a new method for defining the traditional territories of residentially mobile communities. Definitions of "occupation" or "settlement" typically used by archaeologists reflects a sedentary (and settler colonial) perspective that uses architecture, agriculture, and artifact accumulation as signifiers of use. These criteria exclude from the historical record many Indigenous places and spaces, which may lack substantial or for that matter any form of material culture. For Indigenous people, particularly those who historically practiced residential mobility, territorial use was asserted through the making of trails, the creation of perishable structures, or the use of natural resources. In order to capture this continuous cycle of use-abandonment-reuse, a more dynamic and flexible characterization of "occupation" is needed. A place-based approach to the archaeological record that focuses on evidence of long-term, albeit ephemeral, uses of particular places offers one productive alternative to traditional site focused forms of analysis.

▼▽▼

Settler colonialism intentionally attacks the foundational connection between Indigenous people and the land by physically removing them from or appropriating pieces of their traditional territories. Historian Peter Decker renders the devastating effects of such erasure clear, "The Americans forcibly broke the Ute connection to their land. Doing so caused great havoc, since the land provided them not only with their sustenance, but also served as the basis for their culture (religion, ceremonies, and to some extent, their language). Their land was their being."[56] Archaeologists have been complicit in these alienating processes, all too often ignoring the intersectionality of both settler colonialism and disciplinary practices and their impacts on contemporary Tribal Nations. In order to *Indigenize*—the process of naturalizing and legitimizing Indigenous forms of knowledge and beliefs—North American archaeology, we must actively seek to document and dismantle those methods and narratives that have contributed to the silencing of Indigenous peoples.

The archaeological record can serve as a counter-archive with which to *re-territorialize* the North American landscape and, in this particular case, the northern Rio Grande. Reterritorialization entails the physical and discursive reclamation of the land as an Inidgenous space. Archaeologists can serve as allies in this process by identifying and documenting the often-scant material remains left by Indigenous people. In addition to carefully attending to a broader swath of the material record in certain places rather than sites, reterritorialization entails incorporating Indigenous oral histories, personal narratives, and worldviews into our interpretive frameworks. Integrating Indigenous worldviews and narratives into the writing of archaeological histories is more likely to reveal processes of persistence rather than disappearance.[57] Ultimately, this integrative approach to archaeology can help to reconnect descendant communities to places across the North American landscape, thereby denying the completeness of settler colonialism.

Notes

1 Kathryn Tijerina, 2016, personal communication.
2 Dippie, 1982: 1.
3 Bryant, 2009: 58.
4 Inbody, 2018.
5 Deloria Jr., 1988 [1969]: 2.
6 Moos, 2005: 156.
7 Morgan, 1877: 16.
8 Connolly, 1995.
9 Vattel, 2008 [1758]: 209.
10 Act of May 20, 1862 (Homestead Act).
11 Jefferson, 1977: 138.
12 McQueen and Hendrix, 2017: 664.
13 Tocqueville, 2010: 527.
14 Jefferson, 2010: 447.
15 Everett, 1973: 13.
16 McQueen and Hendrix, 2017: 670.
17 McQueen and Hendrix, 2017: 664.
18 Prucha, 2000: 46.
19 Jackson, 2000: 47.
20 Morgan, 1877: 540.
21 Leliévre, 2017: 68.
22 Collins, 2016; Fagan, 2007; Spielvogel, 2008; Wenke and Olszewski, 2006.
23 Wenke and Olzewski, 2007: 280.

24 Wenke and Olzewski, 2007: 230.
25 Diamond, 1997: 14.
26 Diamond, 1997: 97.
27 Deleuze and Guattari, 1987: 23.
28 McBrinn and Vierra, 2016: 58. For examples of a focus on agricultural development in the American Southwest see Cordell, 1997; Damp et al., 2002; Ezzo and Deaver, 1998; Mabry, 2005; Merrill et al., 2009; Roth, 2016; Wills, 1988a,b.
29 McBrinn and Vierra, 2016: 232.
30 Montgomery and Fowles, 2020: 199.
31 Delgard, 2001: 9.
32 Deloria, 2003 [1973]: 112.
33 Killsback, 2013: 96.
34 Killsback, 2013: 103.
35 The concept of place-based history was perhaps most famously discussed by Vine Deloria Jr., 2003 [1973] and Keith Basso, 1996. Since then, many archaeologists have drawn on this notion of place-based history to talk about Indigenous cultural landscapes. For a few examples of this approach in Southwest archaeology, see Ferguson and Colwell, 2006; Laluk, 2017; Snead, 2002.
36 Eiselt, 2012: 144.
37 Byrne, 2003: 172.
38 Ferguson and Colwell-Chanthaphonh, 2008: 39.
39 Basso, 1996.
40 Eiselt, 2012: 159.
41 Gilbert Velarde, 2017, personal communication.
42 Goddard, 1911: 254–255.
43 Lynch, 2011: 361.
44 Fred Harris, 2017, personal communication; LaDonna Harris, 2017, personal communication.
45 Fowler and Fowler, 1971: 39.
46 Campbell and Field, 1968.
47 Burns, 2004.
48 Hafen and Hafen, 1957.
49 Gelo and Wickham, 2017.
50 Arrowsmith and Bollaert, 1841.
51 Kathryn Tijerina, 2016, personal communication.
52 Ferguson and Colwell-Chanthaphonh, 2008: 29.
53 Deleuze and Guattari, 1986: 43.
54 Goss, 2000.
55 Montgomery, 2020.
56 Dees, 2004.
57 Although few archaeologists to date have conceptualized their work as "indigenizing" or "reterritorializing," a growing list of scholars are documenting the subtle ways that Ndee, Nuutsiyu, and Numunu communities have used and marked the landscape in New Mexico. For some examples see the work of Brugge, 2012; Eiselt, 2009, 2012, 2013; Seymour, 2015, 2017; Towner, 2016.

Bibliography

Act of May 20, 1862. (Homestead Act) Public Law 37-64, 05/20/1862. Record Group 11. General Records of the United States Government. National Archives, Washington, DC.

Arrowsmith, John, and William Bollaert. 1841. Map of Texas. Retrieved from the Library of Congress, Washington, DC. https://www.loc.gov/item/2002627151.

Basso, Keith. 1996. Wisdom Sits in Places: Notes on a Western Apache Landscape. In *Sense of Place*, edited by S. Field and K. Basso, pp. 53–90. School of American Research Press, Santa Fe.

Bennett, Tony. 2013. *The Birth of the Museum: History, Theory, Politics*. Routledge, London.

Berlo, Janet Catherine. 1992. Introduction: The Formative Years of Native American Art History. In *The Early Years of Native American Art History: The Politics of Scholarship and Collecting*, edited by J.C. Berlo, pp. 1–21.University of Washington Press, Seattle.

Brugge, David. 2012. Emergence of the Navajo People. In *From the Land of Ever Winter to the American Southwest: Athapaskan Migrations and Ethnogenesis*, edited by D.J. Seymour, pp. 124–149. University of Utah Press, Salt Lake City.

Bryant, William Cullen. 2009. *Poetical Works Poems of William Cullen Bryant. The Project Gutenberg*. D. Appleton & Co., New York.

Burns, Sam. 2004. *The Ute Relationships to the Lands of West Central Colorado: An Ethnographic Overview Prepared for the U.S. Forest Service by the Office of Community Services*. Fort Lewis College, CO.

Byrne, Dennis R. 2003. Nervous Landscapes: Race and Space in Australia. *Journal of Social Archaeology* 3(2): 160–193.

Campbell, T.N., and William T. Field. 1968. Identifican of Comanche Raiding Trails in Trans-Pecos Texas. *West Texas Historical and Scientific Society Publications* 44: 128–144.

Clifford, James. 1987. Of Other Peoples: Beyond the 'Salvage' Paradigm. In Discussions in Contemporary Culture, edited by H. Foster, pp. 121–130. Bay Press, Seattle.

Collins, Roman. 2016. *History: The Civilizations that Defined World History*. CreateSpace Independent Publishing Platform, Scotts Valley.

Conn, Steven. 2004. *History's Shadow: Native Americans and Historical Consciousness in the Nineteenth Century*. University of Chicago, Chicago.

Connolly, William E. 1995. *The Ethos of Pluralization*. University of Minnesota Press, Minneapolis.

Dees, Lisel. 2004. Part II: Ute Ethnographic Research: Grand Mesa, Uncompahgre, and Gunnison National Forests. In *The Ute relationships to the lands of West Central Colorado: An Ethnographic Overview Prepared for the U.S. Forest Service by the Office of Community Services*, edited by S. Burns. Fort Lewis College, Durango.

Deleuze, Gilles, and Felix Guattari. 1986. *Nomadology: The War Machine*. Columbia University, New York.

Deleuze, Gilles, and Felix Guattar. 1987. *A Thousand Plateaus: Capitlaism and Schizophrenia*. University of Minnesota Press, Minneapolis.

Diamond, Jared. 1997. *Guns, Germs, and Steel*. W.W. Norton & Company, New York.

Delgard, Richard, and Jean Stefancic. 2001. *Critical Race Theory: An Introduction*. New York University Press, New York.

Deloria Jr., Vine. 1988 [1969]. *Custer Died for Your Sins: An Indian Manifesto*. University of Oklahoma Press, Norman.

Deloria Jr., Vine. 2003 [1973]. *God Is Red: a Native View of Religion*. Fulcrum Publishing, Golden.

de Tocqueville, Alexis. 2010. *Democracy in America*. Edited by E.N. Trans. J.T. Schleifer. Liberty Fund, Indianaopolis.

de Vattel, Emrich 2008 [1758]. *The Law of Nations: Or, Principles of the Law of Nature, Applied to the Conduct and Affairs of Nations and Soverigns, with Three Early Essays on the Origin and Nature of Natural Law and on Luxury*, edited by B. Kapossy and R. Whatmore. Book 1, Chapter XVIII. Liberty Fund, Indianopolis.

Dippie, Brian W. 1982. *The Vanishing American: White Attitudes and U.S. Indian Policy*. University Press of Kansas, Lawerence.

Dorchester, Danielle. 1893. Report of the Superintendent of Indian Schools, Department of the Interior UW-Madison Libraries Digial Collections, Washington, DC.

Dubin, Steven C. 1999. *Displays of Power: Memory and Amnesia in the American Museum*. New York University Press, New York.

Eiselt, B. Sunday. 2009. The Jicarilla Apaches and the Archaeology of the Taos Region. In *Between the Mountains-Beyond the Mountain: Papers in Honor of Paul R Williams*, edited by E. Brown, K. Armstrong, D.M. Brugge, and C. Condie, pp. 57–69. Papers of the Archaeological Society of New Mexico vol. 35, Albuquerque.

Eiselt, B. Sunday. 2012. *Becoming White Clay: A History and Archaeology of Jicarilla Apache Enclavement*. University of Utah Press, Salt Lake City.

Eiselt, B. Sunday. 2013. Upland-Lowland Corridors and Historic Jicarilla Apache Settlement in the Northern Rio Grande. In *From Mountain Top to Valley Bottom: Understanding Past Land Use in the Northern Rio Grande Valley, New Mexico*, edited by B.J. Vierra, pp. 131–141. University of Utah Press, Salt Lake City.

Everett, Edward. 1973. On the State of the Indians (January 1823). *The North American Review* 238(4): 10–14.

Fagan, Brian M. 2007. *People of the Earth: An Introduction to World Prehistory*. Pearson Education Inc., New Jersey.

Ferguson, T.J., and Chip Colwell-Chanthaphonh. 2006. *History Is in the Land: Multivocal Tribal Traditions in Arizona's San Pedro Valley*. University of Arizona Press, Tucson.

Ferguson, T.J., and Chip Colwell-Chanthaphonh. 2008. *Collaboration in Archaeological Practice: Engaging Descendant Communities*. AltaMira Press, Lanham.

Fowler, Don D., and Catherine S. Fowler (editors). 1971. *Anthropology of the Numa: John Wesley Powell's Manuscripts on the Numic Peoples of Western North America, 1868-1880*. Smithsonian Institution Press, Washington, DC.

Gelo, Daniel J., and Christopher J. Wickham. 2017. *Comanche and Germans on the Texas Frontier: The Ethnology of Heinrich Berghaus*. Texas A & M University Press, College Station.

Goddard, Pliny Earle. 1911. *Jicarilla Apache Texts*. Anthropological Papers of the American Museum of Natural History, New York.

Goss, James A. 2000. Traditional Cosmology, Ecology, and Language of the Ute Indians. In *Ute Indian Arts and Culture: From Prehistory to the New Millennium*, edited by W. Wroth, pp. 27–52. Taylor Museum of the Colorado Springs Fine Arts Center, Colorado Springs.

Gruber, Jacob W. 1970. Ethnographic Salvage and the Shaping of Anthropology. *American Anthropologist* 72(6): 1289–1299.

Hafen, LeRoy R., and Ann W. Hafen (editors). 1957. *Central Route to the Pacific by Gwinn Harris Heap with Related Material on Railroad Explorations and Indian Affairs by Edward F. Beale, Thomas H. Benton, Kit Carson, and Col. E.A. Hitchcock, and in Other Documents, 1853–54*. Arthur H. Clark Co., Glendale.

Inbody, Kristen. 2018. Survey: People Think Native Americans Don't Exist/Aren't Discriminated Against. *Great Falls Tribune*, August 7, 2018. https://www.greatfallstribune.com/story/news/2018/08/09/survey-native-american-discrimination/952349002/.

Jefferson, Thomas. 1977. Notes on the State of Virginia (1787). In *The Portable Thomas Jefferson*, edited by M.D. Peterson. Penguin Books, Harmondsworth.

Jefferson, Thomas. 2010. *The Works of Thomas Jefferson: 1799–1803*, edited by Paul L. Ford. Cosimo Inc., New York.

Killsback, Leo. 2013. Indigenous Perceptions of Time: Decolonizing Theory, World

History, and the Fates of Human Societies. *American Indian Culture and Research Journal* 37(4): 84–113.

Laluk, Nicholas C. 2017. The Indivisibility of Land and Mind: Indigenous Knowledge and Collaborative Archaeology within Apache Contexts. *Journal of Social Archaeology* 17(1): 92–112.

Leliévre, Michelle. 2017. *Unsettling Mobility: Mediating Mi'kmaw Soverignty in Post-contact Nova Scotia*. University of Arizona Press, Tucson.

Lynch, Elizabeth M. 2011. Navigating Regional Landscapes with Jicarilla Personal Narratives. In *Landscape in Language: Transdisciplinary Perspectives*, edited by D.M. Mark, A.G. Turk, N. Burenhult, and D. Stea, pp. 353–368. John Benjamin's Publishing Co., Amsterdam.

McBrinn, Maxine E., and Bradley J. Vierra. 2017. The Southwest Archaic. In *The Oxford Handbook of Southwest Archaeology*, edited by B. Mills and S. Fowles. Oxford University Press. DOI: 10.1093/oxfordhb/9780199978427.013.12.

McQueen, Alison, and Burke A. Hendrix. 2017. Tocqueville in Jacksonian Context: American Expansionism and Discourses of American Indian Nomadism in Democracy in America. *American Political Science Association* 15(3): 663–677.

Montgomery, Lindsay M. 2020. When the Mountain People Came to Taos: Ute Archaeology in the Northern Rio Grande. In *Spirit Lands of the Eagle and Bear: Numic Archaeology and Ethnohistory in the American Rocky Mountains and Borderlands*, edited by R. Brunswig and D. Hill, pp. 257–281. University Press of Colorado, Boulder.

Montgomery, Lindsay M., and Severin Fowles. 2020. An Indigenous Archive: Documenting Comanche History through Rock Art. *American Indian Quarterly* 44(2): 196–220.

Morgan, Lewis Henry. 1877. *Ancient Society*. Charles H Kerr & Co Chicago.

Moos, Dan. 2005. *Outside America*. Dartmouth College, Hanover.

Price, Sally. 2001. *Primitive Art in Civilized Places*. University of Chicago Press, Chicago.

Prucha, Francis Paul. 2000. *Documents of the United States Indian Policy*. University of Nebraska Press, Lincoln.

Seymour, Deni J. 2015. Mobile Group Visitation at the Eastern Frontier Pueblos: An Archaeological Example from Tabira. *Plains Anthropologist* 60(233): 4–39.

Seymour, Deni J. (editor). 2017. *Fierce and Indomitable: The Protohistoric Non-Pueblo World in the American Southwest*. University of Utah Press, Salt Lake City.

Snead, James E. 2002. An Imperishable Record: History, Theory, and the Cultural Landscape of the Northern Rio Grande. In *Traditions, Transitions, and Technologies: Themes in Southwestern Archaeology in the Year 2000*, edited by S.H. Schlanger, pp. 16–32. University of Colorado Press, Niwot.

Spielvogel, Jackson J. 2008. *Ancient Civilizations: Discovering Our Past*. McGraw-Hill Education, New York.

Stocking, George W., Jr. (editor). 1985. *Objects and Others: Essays on Museums and Material Culture*. University of Wisconsin Press, Madison.

Towner, Ron H. 2016. Early Navajo Land Use in Northwestern New Mexico: Big Bead Mesa in Regional Perspective. *Journal of Field Archaeolgoy* 41(1): 118–129.

Wenke, Robert J., and Deborah I. Olszewski. 2007. *Patterns in Prehistory: Humankind's First Three Million Years*. Oxford University Press.

IN SEARCH OF THE RIGHT WORDS

In *Map to the Next World*, poet laureate Joy Harjo (Muskogee (Creek)) writes: "In the last days of the fourth world I wished to make a map for those who would climb through the hole in the sky … In the legend are instructions on the language of the land, how it was we forgot to acknowledge the gift, as if we were not in it or of it."[1] The concept of a fourth world reflects an Indigenous approach to history, in which people move through different worlds over time rather than proceeding from point A to point B along a linear timeline. The tone of Harjo's poem is future oriented. Hinting at the eminent emergence of a fifth world, the narrator reflects on their past actions revealing that the people of the fourth world have made a critical mistake in forgetting the "language of the land". The gift of the land which the fourth worlders have failed to acknowledge references Indigenous beliefs in the animacy of the physical world, which exists in a en-tangled web of relations with humans, non-humans, and spiritual beings. Although Harjo does not explain how or why the people of the current era forgot about these land-centered teachings, her statement bears a striking resemblance to the processes of alienation and dispossession brought on by settler colonialism.

North American archaeology exists in a similarly prescient moment to the one described in *Map to the Next World*. The discipline sits at the cusp of a new "fifth world." We might think of these previous "worlds" in terms of major theoretical paradigms within the field. World 1, the culture history approach, World 2, the processual approach, World 3, the post-processual approach, and World 4, the collaborative turn. The passage of the Native American Graves and Repatriation Act some 30 years ago marks the emergence of this fourth archaeological world; a legal precedent which informed the development of Indigenous archaeology as a subdiscipline, and the increasing assertion of sovereignty over cultural heritage by Tribal Historic Preservation Offices and Indigenous-led organizations. These developments radically altered archaeological praxis with descendant communities and have pushed forward a ethically based and publicly oriented form of archaeology.

But what of this emergent fifth world?

We have already seen glimmers of what this world might be in the increasing attention afforded to collaborative methodologies within the discipline. As Harjo's poem suggests, the "map," which will structure this disciplinary fifth world ought to be rooted in Indigenous worldviews, which center reciprocity (i.e. social justice), relationships (i.e. collaboration), and connections with the land (i.e. place-based reasoning). The question that we must answer as we enter into this new world is: How are my words, narratives, and maps connecting or disconnecting Indigenous peoples to the land and their relations? What follows is an attempt, although admittedly imperfect, to answer this question.

3

A NOTE ON INDIGENOUS STYLE

Taking into consideration the damaging ways in which the English language has been used to construct laws, policies, and narratives that disenfranchise Indigenous peoples can often induce a sort of literary paralysis. This "writer's block" can take the form of a nagging apprehension that not enough Indigenous people have been consulted or contributed to the work. At other times, it may be a feeling of panic in the realization of a misunderstanding or misrepresentation. While it is difficult for Western-trained archaeologists, like myself, to fully decolonize how we think and write, we can allocate more of our intellectual efforts toward critically examining the vocabularies, concepts, and assumptions that inform our writings.

To be clear, the Indigenous peoples discussed throughout this monograph are not my direct ancestors and I do not claim to write "for" them. However, I do hope to help Indigenize archaeological discourse in North America by altering commonly used concepts and terminology in the discipline to more accurately reflect the goals and perspectives of Indigenous people. Some of these changes will likely seem minor while others may feel clumsy or unnecessary. These terms may appear awkward for the reader precisely because they overturn engrained conventions that govern how we, as archaeologists, write about Indigenous peoples and their material culture. The title of this chapter, along with the proposed terminologies discussed, were informed by *Elements of Indigenous Style,* written by Opsakwayak Cree editor Gregory Younging. *Elements of Indigenous Style* is a comprehensive stylistic guide for scholars from a range of disciplines who write about First Nations, Métis, and Inuit peoples in Canada. As Younging points out, the aim of "Indigenous style" is to develop a new body of terms and frameworks drawn from collaborative conversations with Indigenous people and which recognize and respect the cultural integrity of these communities.[2] Although far from comprehensive, the following style guide adapts Younging's ideas to the United States, and particularly the Southwest, context. This literary map is organized into three sections: principles for writing with and about Indigenous peoples, principles for writing about time, and principles for writing about culture. Within each of these sections, I explain why I find particular concepts problematic from an Indigenizing perspective and provide a set of alternative terms which I will then use throughout the remainder of this book.

Principles for writing with and about Indigenous Peoples

Historically anthropologists and archaeologists have used terminology that homogenizes (e.g., native), denigrates (e.g., squaw), or disempowers (e.g., unrecognized) Indigenous people. While the following list is by no means an exhaustive compilation of all such troubling terms, it does represent those words which I find most problematic or have encountered most frequently in archaeological writings. Replacing these terms contributes to broader efforts within academia to acknowledge and respect the sovereignty and cultural integrity of Indigenous people.

Indian: Today, the term "Indian" occupies a controversial space within Native North America. For some Indigenous people, typically from the generations born before 1970, the term "Indian" is part of their common vernacular and is seen as an appropriate word when used by cultural insiders. Other Indigenous people strongly reject the legitimacy of this misnomer, arguing that it should be avoided unless referring specifically to legal constructs, like "Indian Country" or policies, like the Indian Removal Act (1830).

The term "Indian" homogenizes vastly different communities in an attempt to capture in a single racialized category hundreds of regionally, culturally, and ethnically distinct Indigenous peoples. This simplistic classificatory scheme has been used by various different settler colonial states to identify a special class of people to be subdued, disenfranchised, and assimilated. As a result of these colonial processes, the "Indian" has come to signify a set of derogatory beliefs about the intellectual and cultural inferiority of Indigenous people. Beyond the ethical dilemma associated with using terms steeped in racist ideologies, the very origins of the word are problematic. As is now well known, the Spanish word *Indios*, from which the English term "Indian" derives, was first used by Christopher Columbus to refer to the people he encountered after landing upon the island of Guanahani (San Salvador).[3] Of course, the people Columbus and his crew encountered were not in fact "Indians" (from the Indian subcontinent) at all but rather members of the Taíno People, who had inhabited the islands of the Caribbean for over a thousand years prior to that fateful voyage in 1492. Columbus's geographic misnomer has traditionally been corrected through the use of terms like "American Indian" or "Native American" instead.

As a stand-alone term, "Indian" is less frequently used in scholarly writings than it once was during the 19th and early 20th centuries, none the less, it remains a persistent feature of archaeological parlance in North America. The continued used of this word is found in Stephen H. Lekson's recent book, *A Study of*

Southwestern Archaeology, published in 2018. Throughout the book, Lekson interchangeably uses the terms "Indian" and "Native American" to refer to Indigenous peoples in the Southwest. For example, in Chapter 5 he writes that, "Indians have been conspicuous by their absence in most of this book, but in this chapter, Indians are everywhere. This segregation is not out any disrespect for Indian tribes; rather, the organization of this book reflect my firm belief that archaeology is not, inherently, a Native American enterprise."[4] Lekson's use of the term "Indian" here is worrying because of the way in which he summarily excludes a category of people central to North American archaeology from participating in the discipline as traditionally conceived. Similar terminology can also be found in popular textbooks like *Southwest Archaeology in the 20th Century*, in which Katherine A. Spielmann writes that, "southwestern archaeologists are once again working directly with Indian peoples in structuring their research questions and research designs."[5] My aim in using these examples is not to unfairly point fingers at the interesting work of well-established Southwest scholars like Lekson and Spielmann, but rather to draw the reader's attention to the slippery ways in which this problematic term continues to circulate within archaeological discourse without acknowledging its controversial origins or racialized use in settler colonial policies.

While some may argue that these examples are simply exceptions being used to prove a rule, I would point the reader towards a more prolific, yet hidden, use of the term "Indian" in the form of the "Paleo-Indian." A JSTOR search for publications using the word "Paleo-Indian" between 2000 and 2020 yields around 3,579 scholarly articles and book chapters. When broken down to its constituent parts, this term becomes confusing: "Paleo" meaning ancient and "Indian" a word used to incorrectly refer to the Indigenous People Columbus encountered in the Caribbean and subsequently applied to all Indigenous groups in the Americas. If there were ever "Paleo-Indians," they certainly did not live in North America. Instead, this term is perhaps better suited for the original inhabitant of the Indian subcontinent.

The term "Paleo-Indian" is a convenient shorthand used by North American archaeologists to classify the earliest material culture of Indigenous peoples. The use of such a generic term largely reflects the limitations of archaeological modeling which maps material remains onto temporal-cultural-ethnic categories. The uniformity of stone tools dating to the "Paleo-Indian Period"—roughly 13,000 (perhaps earlier) to 8000 BCE creates a false sense of cultural heterogeneity and has obscured the connections between contemporary Indigenous people and their ancestors. One solution to this dilemma, suggested by Indigenous archaeologist Roger Echo-Hawk, is to use the origin stories and migration narratives of specific Indigenous people as models for reconstructing cultural categories and technological traditions in the deep past.[6]

In light of such critiques, I will avoid the term "Indian" as well as its hyphenated form "Paleo-Indian," as general descriptors of identity. Drawing on the precedent set by the *UN Declaration on the Rights of Indigenous People*, I will instead use the term **Indigenous people or person** when referring to individuals directly descended from the First Peoples of North America.[7] Capitalizing the term "Indigenous" here is an important grammatical gesture that acknowledges the sovereignty of these communities as independent Nations prior to, and under, colonization.

Band/Tribe: Anthropologists, archaeologists, and historians alike have used the terms "band" and "tribe" to describe the sociopolitical systems of small non-state societies. Indigenous people living in family-based units and practicing a hunting and gathering subsistence pattern are typically considered "band-level societies," while "tribal" societies include Indigenous people living in larger aggregated communities divided into well-defined subsidiary albeit egalitarian groups. These terms are part of an influential schema of sociocultural integration, which included bands, tribes, chiefdoms, and states developed by Elman Service in the *Origins of the State and Civilization*.[8] Although writing nearly a century after Lewis Henry Morgan, Service's understanding of political organization created a similar set of hierarchical distinctions between small-scale (typically Indigenous) egalitarian social systems and large-scale stratified states (represented by European nations or other modern states). As the title to Service's volume indicates, "civilization" was equated with political complexity and understood to be something that human societies were inevitably and incrementally moving towards.

Service's sociopolitical framework was directly informed by the historical models laid out by Fredrich Engle in *The Origin of the Family, Private Property, and the State.* Engle's theory documented the evolution of primitive societies from production-for-use to production-of-commodities economies—a transition linked to technological advancement, the accumulation of wealth, and the formation of social classes.[9] The concept of "bands" and "tribes" unproblematically applies a theoretical concept rooted in 20th-century social norms and critiques of Western capitalism to Indigenous people in the past. In addition to the poor fit between Indigenous social systems and Marxist historical materialism, this explanatory framework fails to recognize how Indigenous communities conceptualize their sociopolitical structures or the territorial nature of Indigenous identity.[10]

When the appropriate cultural information is publicly available, I will adopt the **particular terminologies** used by Indigenous People to describe their social-political-territorial systems. For example, the *Numunu* refer to the group of people who historically lived in the Texas-Panhandle area as *Kutsutuhka* (Buffalo Eater), the *Nuutsiyu* refer to the peoples who occupied the region around the Sangre de Cristo and San Juan mountain ranges as *Kapota*, and the Jicarilla Apache divide their society into two social-territorial groups—those people historically living to the east of New Mexico, called *gołgaihèń* (Plains people) and those living to west, referred to as *saidindèh* (Sand people).[11]

Much like the term "band," the words "tribe" or "tribal" ignore the specific ways that Indigenous people conceptualize their socio-political worlds. This term is based on a Western understanding of power premised upon individual leadership.

This may be true in some cases but is certainly not a generalizable principle defining Indigenous leadership structures and associated systems of control. When applied to Indigenous communities in the United States, the term "tribe" imposes a timeless and false sense of coherency on to Indigenous social structures which were in reality fluid, often decentralized, or distributed power through groups rather than individuals. Furthermore, this concept collapses important cultural differences between Indigenous Peoples and flattens the complexity of their political systems. Rather than accurately representing the nature of Indigenous society in the past (or present for that matter), this model of governance was imposed upon Indigenous communities by colonial administrators accustomed to negotiating with male sovereigns. These assumptions were codified in the 1823, 1831, and 1832 rulings of US Supreme Court Chief Justice John Marshall. Known as the "Marshall Triology", these court decisions legally recognized the nationhood and inherent sovereignty of Native American "tribes". While it is hard to say whether Elman Service was aware of this particular history of the word "tribe", in the United States this term possess a legal status which has significant consequences for how we construct Indigenous social groups in the past. Instead of trying to fit the diverse social structures of Indigenous people into a classificatory scheme based on Western assumptions and conventions, I will instead us the phrase **Indigenous People(s)** or **Tribal Nation(s)** to refer to distinct Indigenous entities regardless of their federal or state status. These terms explicitly recognize the fact that Indigenous societies meet the four criteria of a sovereign nation under international customary law: (1) permanent populations, (2) definite occupied territory, (3) a government, and (4) the ability to enter into relations with other nations.[12]

Culture Area(s): Anthropologists and archaeologists have had a longstanding interest in spatializing culture; an interest captured in the culture area concept. This idea emerged during the 19th century as a means of organizing the growing ethnographic collections of World museums based on their geographical origins rather than by artifact type.[13] This method of arranging objects was first implemented by Adolf Bastian at the Ethnological Museum in Berlin but was most fully realized as a classificatory scheme within the halls of the American Museum of Natural History (AMNH) under the direction of Franz Boas.[14] As originally conceived, the culture area concept was applied explicitly to the material culture of "primitive" (i.e., non-Western) groups. The proper subjects of this organizational logic was summarized by Boas in a letter to Morris K. Jessup, the president of the AMNH: "The character of the exhibits should be such as to show how the most primitive tribes depend entirely upon the products of their home, and how with the progress of civilization wider and wider areas are made to contribute to the needs of man."[15] The link between subsistence and material culture was at the center of Boas's culture area framework, which was informed by an evolutionary logic that placed Indigenous people outside of "civilization."

Clark Wissler was among the earliest champions of the culture area concept as an analytical approach rather than an organizational scheme.[16] Wissler's model created lists of culture traits, "(a) in terms of geography; (b) according to the constituent tribal groups; and (c) in the coincident relations of the traits, irrespective of tribal units."[17] These three categories were used to aggregate Indigenous people into spatially anchored groups based on similarities in material culture, such as stone tools, textiles, ceramics, and architecture as well as social practices linked to food and ceremonies.[18] Wissler's model used a core-periphery framework of cultural diffusion which held up some Tribal Nations as "ideal" or "central" exemplars of a given culture type based on their environmental-geographical location. It was hypothesized that these regionally defined cultures diffused across various "zones" with traits becoming less "pure" as they moved towards the borders of a given culture area.[19] This approach created a false division between more and less culturally "authentic" Tribal Nations based on their geographic location during the 19th and early 20th century. Subsequent work by well-known North American anthropologists like Alfred L. Kroeber challenged such uncritical applications of the "ethnographic present," instead using the culture area approach to exam the development of cultural complexes over time.[20]

While anthropological interest in constructing and analyzing culture areas has significantly waned since the mid-20th century, the central precept—the areal expression of culture—continues to inform archaeological practice today. The enduring nature of culture areas can be seen in most major natural history museums in the United States today, which continue to organize their collections into broad geographical areas including the Southwest, Plains, Northwest Coast, Great Basin, etc., (Figure 3.1).

Outside of museum halls, scholars are also compelled, in part by law and in part by disciplinary convention, create maps outlining the boundaries of archaeological cultures and the traditional territories of Indigenous People. This approach is perhaps best captured in the most definitive publication written on Indigenous Peoples, *The Handbook for the North American Indian*, each volume of which is dedicated to a regional culture area (vol. 6: Artic, vol. 7: Subarctic, vol. 8: Northwest Coast, vol. 9 & 10: California, vol. 11: Southwest, etc.).[21]

Such culture areas are in many ways an essential aspect of archaeological research, which relies on our ability to draw comparisons across material types and to recreate the rich social worlds of Indigenous people in the past using fragmentary data. While grouping material culture is an essential feature of archaeological research, we must also acknowledge the very political nature of such practices. Whether one likes to admit it or not, archaeological narratives and concepts shape policies governing who controls the culture heritage of Indigenous communities and inform legal cases over land claims and natural resources. The political nature of archaeological praxis requires a more careful consideration of how archaeological cultures and culture areas may facilitate or hinder Indigenous assertions of territorial and representational sovereignty in the present.

FIGURE 3.1 Northwest Coast Hall. American Museum of Natural History, New York. Photograph by George Holden.

In depicting bounded stagnate territories, such engrained classificatory exercises flatten the dynamic nature of Indigenous social systems and histories of movement and migration. Furthermore, in many cases American colonial policies of relocation and allotment have created a disconnect between archaeological and anthropological culture areas and the geopolitical boundaries of modern Tribal Nations. As Michael Wilcox points out in the case of the Hohokam–Pima–O'odham, archaeological cultures like the "Hohokam" distance contemporary Tribal Nations from their ancestral cultural heritage while placing the burden of demonstrating a cultural connection on often underfunded and understaffed Indigenous governments.[22]

While abandoning the culture areas used by archaeologists is not entirely possible, I will use quotation marks when referencing archaeological cultures like "Hohokam" or "Dismal River" to demarcate their subjectivity. I will also try to connect these archaeological culture areas as much as possible to historic and contemporary Indigenous Peoples. Along these same lines, I will avoid using ethnic identifiers like Ute, Apache, Navajo, Comanche, and Shoshone when referring to the archaeological record of New Mexico. These names are often mispronunciations of Indigenous words, names used by outsider groups, or made up by Western settlers based on observation. Using these terms perpetuates the power of academics to name, quantify, and control Indigenous People and their histories. When a clear cultural connection can be made between the archaeological record and contemporary Tribal Nations, I will use the terms and associated territorial boundaries that these Indigenous People claim for themselves:

Numunu **(Comanche)**
Nuutsiyu **(Ute)**
Ndee **(Apache)**
Newe **(Shoshone)**
Diné **(Navajo)**
Kai-i-gwu **(Kiowa)**
Inuna-ina **(Arapaho)**
Tsitsistas **(Cheyenne)**
Nuwuvi **(Southern Paiute)**
Numu **(Northern Paiute)**
Ĭăłap°ăĭbâ **(Taos Pueblo)**

Due to the often-fragmentary nature of the archaeological record and fluidity of Indigenous land-use practices, evidence for a direct connection between the archaeological record and contemporary communities is often unclear. In these instances, I will use hyphenated terms such as **Ancestral *Numunu-Ndee*** to recognize the ambiguity of their overlapping territories prior to and preceding European colonization. In other instances I will refer to Indigenous people by language group, using the terms **Numic, Athabaskan, Tiwa, and Tewa-speaking** to describe the material culture of Indigenous Peoples speaking these languages.

Principles for writing about time

Much like the culture area concept, the creation of bounded temporal categories linked to shifts in material practices is a fundamental aspect of archaeological research. Without a linear sense of time, the majority of archaeological and historical arguments about culture change and social processes become analytically unmoored. While completely abandoning chronological sequences may not be realistic within the discipline of archaeology, this does not mean that we should continue on blindly with business as usual. Instead, I argue for a critical examination of conventional approaches to time, specifically the notion of "prehistory" and the "Archiac", which limit and undermine the representational sovereignty of Indigenous Peoples.

Prehistory: North American archaeologists have often drawn a clear disciplinary distinction between those scholars who study Indigenous people in the deep past (i.e., Prehistory) and those that study Indigenous People who appear in the archival records of colonial officials (i.e., History). This divide has resulted in different theoretical and methodological practices. While functional and environmentally driven explanatory frameworks are often used to interpret the economic and social practices of small-scale societies prior to the 15th century, a more social approach has often been applied alongside documentary evidence to understand inter-ethnic interaction and social change in the centuries preceding European colonization. These analytical differences reflect legitimate limitations in the types of evidence available; there are simply no "written" documents about or ethnographies of Indigenous life in 5000 BCE. However, these methodological differences also reflect a lingering hesitancy among most archaeologists trained in scientific rationalism to regard the oral traditions of Indigenous Peoples as valid data sources.

The prehistory-history divide enshrines a very particular definition of "History" as directly associated with the use of writing and the formation of permanent documentary archives. The implication being that Indigenous Peoples have history, but they do not have History. This formulation of "history," rather than its broader definition as the study of past social processes, creates a subjective hierarchy, in which written sources produced by Western colonizers are given a proprietary status regarding the Truth. The prehistory-history divide creates a radical disjuncture between Indigenous Peoples today and ancestral Indigenous communities. This artificial separation ignores how Indigenous people conceptualize their relationship to the past and hinders the ability of Tribal Nations to access and control their cultural heritage.

These critiques are, of course, not new. Kent Lightfoot, Stephen Silliman, and Matthew Liebmann, among others have argued for over a decade now that the bifurcation of Native North American archaeology into "history" and "prehistory" problematically positions the arrival of Europeans as the definitive historical moment in over 10,000 years of Indigenous life on the continent.[23] In an effort to produce more engaging long-term histories, many North American archaeologists have embraced a diachronic approach which situates Indigenous-settler colonial interactions within a longer history of Native accommodation, transculturation, adaptation, and resiliency.[24] Despite these efforts, "prehistory" remains a persistent analytical construct that continues to inform archaeological thinking about Indigenous Peoples and their pasts. A review of the Society for American Archaeology's (SAA) conference programs from 2009 to 2019 reveals that the word "prehistory" appears on average 23 times in every conference proceeding (Figure 3.2).

In fact, this terminology actually appears more frequently in SAA programs dating to the past 5 years than in those prior to 2013. While these numbers offer only a rough metric of "prehistory" popularity within archaeological parlance, they do indicate that this concept is still a core part of how experts in the discipline think about the past.

The continued use of the term "prehistory" belies its naturalization as a temporal construct and the reticence of archaeologists to seriously develop an alternative set of analytical categories. The slow decline of "prehistory" also reflects the general anti-disinterest among of archaeologists in relinquishing their gatekeeping status over Indigenous pasts. In an effort to further dismantle the prehistory-history divide, I will use specific chronological terminology, including **time ranges** (e.g., 5500–3200 BCE), **centuries** (e.g., 17th century), and **dates** when appropriate. Furthermore, all chronological references throughout this book will be designated using **Before**

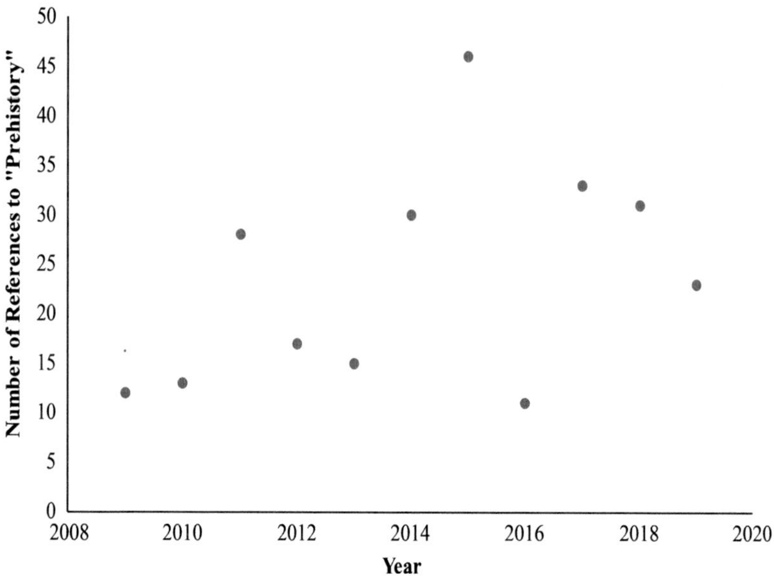

FIGURE 3.2 References to Prehistory in the SAA Conference Program, 2009–2019.

Common Era (BCE) or **Common Era** (CE) to eschew the imposition of Christian calendrical time onto Indigenous spaces and events.

Archaic: In North American archaeology, the term "Archaic" is used as a sociological category and a time period. Much like the term "Paleo-Indian", the word "Archaic" is applied to a range of Indigenous Peoples living across the continent who practiced a foraging-based subsistence system involving high levels of seasonally driven residential mobility. In the American Southwest and Great Basin regions, Jesse Jennings was one of the first archaeologists to use the term "Archaic" as a cultural construct. Jennings's fieldwork at Danger Cave in Western Utah in the 1950s became the type-site for what came to be known as the archaic "Desert culture." The "Desert culture" referred to the socio-economic system of residential mobility used by Indigenous people in the semiarid environment of the Great Basin from roughly 9000 BCE to 500 CE. The material assemblages associated with the "Desert culture" included evidence of hunting medium to small game ground stone implements for processing plant-based resources, stone tool technologies, including spears, atlatls, and projectile point technologies.[25]

As a temporal classification, the "Archaic" is an equally broad category, referring to the period "during which people were no longer big-game specialists but were not yet farmers."[26] In northern New Mexico, Alfred Kidder was one of the first scholars to work explicitly on the material record of the "Archaic period," laying the groundwork for what later became the "Basketmaker tradition"—defined by the use of the atlatl and coiled basketry.[27]

The pioneering work of Cynthia Irwin-Williams during the 1960s in northwestern New Mexico was a seminal moment in the development of "Archaic" archaeology in the region. Synthesizing the past several decades of work on this period in the northern Southwest, Irwin-Williams's research led to the formation of a formal cultural-historical sequence with which to classify different technological phases over the course of this extensive period of broad-spectrum hunting and gathering. Irwin-Williams's fieldwork at Arroyo Cuervo produced yet another archaeological culture, the "Oshara Tradition." Using stylistic changes in projectile point morphology over time, Irwin-Williams identified five subsidiary cultural phases within the "Oshara Tradition": Jay (5500–4800 BCE), Bajada (4800–3200 BCE), San Jose (3200–1800 BCE), Armijo (1800–800 BCE), and En Medio (800 BCE–400 CE).[28]

The cultural-technological phases created by Irwin-Williams have directly informed the three broad chronological categories used by Southwest archaeologists today: Early (5500–3200 BCE), Middle (3200–1800 BCE), and Late (1800 BCE–400 CE).[29] While such periodization provides a helpful framework for classifying stone tools and talking about large swaths of time, from an historical perspective, these categories lack the chronological clarity needed to make fine grained arguments about shifts in the socioeconomic practices of Indigenous people over time. In addition to such seemingly insurmountable analytical shortcomings, from a political perspective, the "Archaic" as a general phase in Native North American history, disconnects Indigenous Peoples in the deep past from those Indigenous People identified in settler colonial documents as well as contemporary Tribal Nations. While this may seem like a simple matter of semantics, by consigning Indigenous people in the deep past to distinct temporal-cultural categories, archaeologists unintentionally reinforce settler colonial narratives that seek to separate Indigenous Peoples from the land in order to erase any prior or competing claims to sovereignty.

Critics of doing away with the "Archaic" will likely point out that without such helpful short hands as the "Desert Culture" or the "Middle Archaic," archaeological texts would become laden down with long-winded descriptions of socioeconomic practices and their material correlates. I agree. The temporal breath of the Early, Middle, and Late "Archaic" periods is in many ways unsolvable. The material focus of archaeological research is fundamentally limited when it comes to the objects preserved in the archaeological record from the deep past—a record characterized primarily by stone tool technologies which are morphologically and stylistically consistent for long periods of time.

While I acknowledge these barriers, I would also draw the reader's attention to the classificatory possibilities that may arise when we de-center traditional archaeological models of chronological time and instead draw on Indigenous ones. As discussed in Chapter 2, many Indigenous groups understand time in terms of cyclical worlds rather than as linear temporal phases. If one was to draw on such culturally grounded approaches to deep time, then we might think about the material record as corresponding to a series of worlds spatially anchored within

North America, and that are associated with particular material and cultural practices that map onto oral histories. While a promising potential avenue, such a complex revisioning of the Taos Plateau material record would require a more targeted form of collaboration with Indigenous Peoples in the area and is therefore beyond the current scope of this book. For the purposes of this manuscript, I will instead make a much more modest shift, and use **specific dates** or **date ranges** to situate the archaeological record in time (e.g., 1800 BCE or 1st century CE). When drawing from or referring to other scholars' work on this subject, I will use the terms **"Early," "Middle,"** and **"Late Archaic"** in quotation marks.

Principles for writing about culture

As a discipline that straddles the humanities and social sciences, American archaeology is torn between the urge to create detailed culturally specific case studies and a desire to produce generalizable claims about social and historical processes. This latter facet of the discipline has informed the formation of a specialized vocabulary to discuss the material culture of Indigenous Peoples. Perhaps not surprisingly given the disciplines origins in Western thought, archaeological jargon has typically failed to capture the worldviews of, or terminologies used by, Indigenous people themselves. While many of the concepts and terms archaeologists use, such as "folklore," "mythology/myths," and "religion," may seem benign, these words often have an alienating effect. These terms are alienating because they reinforce an epistemological hierarchy in which Indigenous frameworks are considered irrelevant or inferior to Western ones.

Folklore: Although the term "folklore" has increasingly fallen out of use within anthropology, this concept continues to circulate in heritage management circles as a means of describing the oral traditions of predominantly non-Western groups.[30] For example, the word "folklore" can be found in the title of international heritage agencies such as the "World Intellectual Property Organization Intergovernmental Committee on Intellectual Property and Genetic Resources, Traditional Knowledge, and Folklore" and in the "United Nations Educational, Scientific and Cultural Organization's Recommendations on the Safeguarding of Traditional Culture and Folklore." While these subcommittees to the United Nations help to protect the intangible heritage of Indigenous Peoples, they do so by using Western cultural categories, frameworks, and values. Specifically, the term "folklore" is problematic because it is based on a perceived distinction between "popular or traditional" practices such as storytelling, dance, and music among non-Western groups and "high culture", things like literature, philosophy, and art which are seen as being of exceptional universal value and which have historically been the domain of Western societies.[31]

Rather than placing folklore in a separate heritage category based on Western definitions of "culture," we might instead incorporate Indigenous perspectives into the institutional frameworks meant to protect and preserve their patrimony. From an Indigenizing perspective, folklore is a form of traditional knowledge that contains historical, philosophical, and cultural information. With this framework in mind, I will use the term **oral tradition** or **traditional knowledge** to refer to intangible elements of Indigenous cultural heritage.

Mythology/Myths: The terms "myth" and "mythology" have been traditionally used by anthropologists and archaeologists to describe stories associated with the supernatural and natural worlds of Indigenous Peoples. As Ian Barbour suggests, Indigenous myths are distinguished from the stories which circulate within religions like Christianity, Judaism, and Islam because the latter are "tied primarily to historical events rather than to phenomena in nature."[32] Underlying Barbour's distinction between Indigenous myths and Abrahamic narratives are two problematic assumptions: (1) the belief that Indigenous people are governed by the environment and (2) the belief that Indigenous stories are fictional accounts rather than historically grounded facts. As Gregory Younging has argued, this particular understanding of mythology is offensive to Indigenous People because it implies that oral traditions and stories are not based in reality.[33]

The partitioning of mythology from history in archaeological thought is informed by the primacy of scientific rationalism within academia. The perceived divide between myth and science that emerged during the Enlightenment era in Europe obscures the ways in which Western narratives also take on mythological forms. In *Evolution, Creationism, and Other Modern Myths*, Vine Deloria Jr. skillfully draws attention to the ways in which "our entrenched belief in scientific folklore and its myth of rigorous rationalism, generally discounts the fact that mystical insights has played a critically important role in the creation of new scientific theories."[34] Leveling the playing field, so to speak, between Indigenous and Western knowledge systems, involves incorporating Indigenous "myths" into archaeological histories.

For many Indigenous communities, history is conveyed through two types of stories: stories about the distant past and historical accounts. Stories about the distant past take place during what anthropologists have referred to as the "mythical age" and explain how and why the world and its creatures came to be. Accompanying these ancient narratives are more recently developed stories, including prophecies, cautionary narratives, and metaphorical accounts intended to shape collective behavior in the present.[35] In an effort to acknowledge this alternative historical framework, I will use the terms **origin stories** and **deep time narratives** to refer to stories about the distant past and will use the term **personal narrative** or **oral history** to refer to stories from the more recent past.

Religion: The Franciscan and Dominican missionaries were among the first Europeans to draw a distinction between the ceremonial practices of Indigenous Peoples, which they considered "rituals," and the "religious" practices of the

Catholic church. While Indigenous practices were seen as evil, cult-like, and barbaric by European colonizers, Christian practices were deemed righteous, civilized, and factually grounded. Anthropologists have, of course, distanced themselves from the moralizing overtones of these early missionary distinctions, instead framing religion as either an explanatory framework for natural events and phenomena (as proposed by E.B. Tylor) or as symbolic statements about the social order (as argued by Emil Durkheim).[36] Subsequent anthropological engagements with religion have acknowledged the often-blurry boundary the exists between philosophy and religious doctrine. Such theoretical musings complicate the once strict division between formally codified "world religions" like Christianity, Islam, Judaism, Buddhism, and Hinduism and the orally transmitted practices and beliefs of Indigenous peoples. The notion that Indigenous ceremonial practices were in fact "religions" has since been codified in heritage-based laws, such as the 1978 American Indian Religious Freedom Act.

While the terminological shift from ritual to religion legitimizes Indigenous belief systems and offers legal protection for associated ceremonial and spiritual practices, the concept of religion brings its own ontological baggage to the table. As Severin Fowles has argued, the term "religion" embodies a perceived division between the sacred and profane that may not accurately represent the fact that for many Indigenous people pretty much everything could be considered "sacred."[37] As Vine Deloria Jr. argued in *God Is Red*, "Tribal religions in the old days did no create an external ethical system. Cultural considerations involving total tribal life enabled people to merge all societal functions in a unity from which all forms of behavior derived."[38] Building on the arguments of Deloria and Fowles, I will use the word **doings**, rather than religion, to refer to Indigenous cultural practices "characterized by a heightened awareness of interconnectedness and the relations between things."[39]

▼▽▼

The grammatical and conceptual changes proposed in this chapter are admittedly imperfect alternatives to existing concepts. At a very practical level, synthesizing fragmentary material evidence requires generalization and distillation; processes which inevitably result in sometimes broad categories (e.g., the Archaic) and imprecise definitions (e.g., myth or religion). Indeed, the terminological changes proposed in this chapter are also broad and imprecise in some ways. For example, although the term "Indigenous Peoples" acknowledges the sovereignty of Tribal Nations, it also homogenizes the distinct identities and histories of these groups and glosses over salient differences in their political and legal statuses. In a similar vein, although using locally derived identity markers (e.g., Numunu) helps to Indigenize archaeological practice, these terms also flatten intra-group differences in identity. Critics may also rightly point out that applying these ethnic markers to the deep past creates a false sense of cultural and ethnic coherency over time when in reality Indigenous identities and social configurations were as dynamic and fluid in the deep past as they are in the present.

Rather than a perfect solution to the limitations of archaeological analyses, the proposed vocabulary changes are intended to draw the reader's attention to the political nature of taken for granted terminologies and categories. Although we may choose to go on using ideas like "prehistory" and creating archaeological culture areas, we should also acknowledge how such choices may undermine the representational sovereignty of Indigenous People. Until relatively recently, Indigenous worldviews have been the subject of anthropological study rather than the basis of archaeological theory. The proposed vocabulary changes implemented in this book are part of a growing effort by Indigenous archaeologists to more fully incorporate Indigenous epistemologies and ontologies into discipline.

In the end, adopting an "Indigenous style" requires having conversations with Indigenous communities. These conversations, along with the specific context of settler colonialism one is writing from within, will inevitably produce differences in preferred terminologies. While many other changes could be proposed to the literary style of North American archaeologists, this chapter offers a preliminary map for how one might write about Indigenous Peoples and histories in an Indigenizing way.

Notes

1 Harjo, 2002.
2 Younging, 2018: 99.
3 Younging, 2018: 56.
4 Lekson, 2018: 145.
5 Spielman, 2005: 202.
6 Echo-Hawk, 2000.
7 Younging, 2018: 65.
8 Service, 1975.
9 Service, 1975: 34; Engels, 1891.
10 Younging, 2018: 53.
11 Kavanagh, 2008 :13, 348; Opler, 1940: 127; Opler, 1971: 311.
12 Younging, 2018: 68.
13 Newman, 1971: 9.
14 Newman, 1971: 10.
15 Boas, 1898.
16 Wissler, 1917.
17 Wissler, 1927: 886.
18 Newman, 1971: 10.
19 Newman, 1971: 10.
20 Kroeber, 1931, 1939; Newman, 1971: 12.
21 Sturtevant, 1978.
22 Wilcox, 2010.
23 Hart et al., 2012; Lightfoot, 1995; Liebmann, 2012; Mitchell and Scheiber, 2010; Silliman, 2010, 2012.
24 For examples of studies that have embraced the creation of long-term Indigenous histories over the past 20 years, see Cipolla, 2013; Martinez et al., 2013; Panich, 2013; Schneider and Panich, 2019; Seymour, 2017.
25 Jennings, 1956, 1964; Vierra, 1990: 57.
26 Vierra and McBrinn, 2017: 232.

27 Vierra, 1990: 58.
28 Irwin-Williams, 1968, 1973.
29 Irwin-Williams, 1973.
30 Younging, 2018: 55.
31 UNESCO, 1989.
32 Barbour, 1974: 23.
33 Younging, 2018: 55.
34 Deloria, 2002: 58.
35 Meland, 2002: 138.
36 Barfield, 2000: 402.
37 Fowles, 2012: 102.
38 Deloria, 2003 [1973]: 250.
39 Fowles, 2012: 103.

Bibliography

Barbour, Ian. 1974. *Myths, Models, and Paradigms.* San Francisco: Harper and Row, San Franciso.

Barfield, Thomas J. (editor). 2000. *The Dictionary of Anthropology.* Blackwell Publishers, Oxford.

Boas, Franz. 1989. Letter from Franz Boas to Morris K. Jessup (May 28, 1898). American Museum of Natural History, Department of Anthropology, New York.

Cipolla, Craig N. 2013. *Becoming Brothertown: Native American Ethnogenesis and Endurance in the Modern World.* University of Arizona Press, Tucson.

Deloria, Vine Jr. 2002. *Evolution, Creationsim, and Other Modern Myths: A Critical Inquiry.* Fulcrum Publishing, Golden.

Deloria, Vine Jr. 2003 [1973]. *God Is Red: A Native View of Religion.* Fulcrum Publishing, Golden.

Echo-Hawk, Roger C. 2000. Ancient History in the New World: Integrating Oral Traditions and the Archaeological Record in Deep Time. *American Antiquity* 65(2): 267–290.

Engles, Friedrich. 1891. *The Origin of the Family, Private Property, and the State.* Reprint ed. 1972. Edited with an introduction by E.B. Leacock. International Publishers, New York.

Fowles, Severin M. 2012. *An Archaeology of Doings: Secularism and the Study of Pueblo Religion.* School for Advanced Research, Santa Fe.

Harjo, Joy. 2002. A Map to the New World. In *How We Became Human New and Selected Poems: 1975-2001.* W.W. Norton & Company, New York.

Hart, Michael Anthony. 2010. Indigenous Worldviews, Knowledge, and Research: The Development of an Indigenous Research Paradigm. *Journal of Indigenous Voices in Social Work* 1(1): 1–16.

Irwin-Williams, Cynthia. 1968. Archaic Culture History in the Southwestern United States. In *Early Man in Western North America,* edited by C. Irwin-Williams. Eastern New Mexico University, Portales.

Irwin-Williams, Cynthia. 1973. The Oshara Tradition: Origins of Anasazi Culture. *Eastern New Mexico University Contributions in Anthropology* 5(1): 1–19.

Jennings, Jesse D. 1956. The American Southwest: A Problem in Cultural Isolation. In *Seminars in Archaeology: 1955,* edited by R. Wauchope, pp. 59–127. Cambridge University Press, Cambridge.

Jennings, Jesse D. 1964. The Desert West. In *Prehistoric Man in the New World*, edited by J. Jennings and E. Norbeck, pp. 149–174. University of Chicago Press, Chicago.

Kavanagh, Thomas W. (editor). 2008. *Comanche Ethnography: Field Notes of E. Adamson Hoebel, Waldo R. Wedel, Gustav G. Carlson, and Rober H. Lowie*. University of Nebraska Press, Lincoln.

Kroeber, Alfred L. 1931. The Culture-Area and Age-Area Concepts of Clark Wissler. In *Methods in Social Science- A Case Book*, edited by S.A. Rice, pp. 248–265. University of Chicago Press, Chicago.

Kroeber, Alfred L. 1939. *Cultural and Natural History of Native North America*. University of California Press, Berkeley.

Lekson, Stephen H. 2018. *A Study of Southwest Archaeology*. University of Utah Press, Salt Lake City.

Liebmann, Mathew. 2012. The Rest is History: Devaluing the Recent Past in the Archaeology of the Pueblo Southwest. In *Decolonizing Indigenous Histories: Exploring prehistoric/Colonial Transitions in Archaeology*, edited by S.M. Hart, M. Oland, and L. Frink, pp. 19–44. University of Arizona Press, Tucson.

Lightfoot, Kent G. 1995. Culture Contact Studies: Redefining the Relationship between Prehistoric and Historical Archaeology. *American Antiquity* 60(2): 199–217.

Martinez, Desire Renee, Wendy G. Teeter, and Karimah O. Kennedy Richardson. 2013. Human Occupation and Landscape Alterations on Catalina Island, California. In *Small Islands, Big Implications*, edited by J. Perry and C. Jazwa. University of Utah Press, Salt Lake City.

Meland, Carter Thomas. 2002. The Trickster Is History: Tribal Tricksters and American Cultural History in Contemporary Native Writing. Unpublished PhD thesis, Department of History, University of Minnesota, Minneapolis.

Mitchell, Mark D. and Larua L. Scheiber. 2010. Crossing Divides: Archaeology as Long-Term History. In *Across a Great Divide: Continuity and Change in Native North American Societies, 1400-1900*, edited by L.L. Scheiber and M.D. Mitchell, pp. 1–22. University of Arizona, Tucson.

Newman, James L. 1971. The Cutlure Area Concept in Anthropology. *Journal of Geography* 70(1): 8–15.

Opler, Marvin K. 1940. The Southern Ute of Colorado. In *Acculturation in Seven American Indian Tribes*, edited by R. Linton, pp. 119–203. D. Appleton Century Co., New York.

Opler, Morris E. 1971. Jicarilla Apache Territory, Economy, and Society in 1850. *Southwestern Journal of Anthropology* 27(4): 309–329.

Panich, Lee M. 2013. Archaeologies of Persistence: Reconsidering the Legacies of Colonialism in Native North America. *American Antiquity* 78(1): 105–122.

Schneider, Tsim, and Lee Panich. 2019. Landscapes of Refuge and Resiliency: Native Californian Persistence at Tomales Bay California, 1770s-1870s. *Ethnohistory* 66(1): 21–47.

Service, Elman. 1975. *Origins of the State and Civilization: The Process of Cultural Evolution*. W.W. Norton, New York.

Seymour, Deni J. (editor). 2017. *Fierce and Indomitable: The Protohistoric Non-Pueblo World in the American Southwest*. University of Utah Press, Salt Lake City.

Silliman, Stephen. 2010. Crossing, Bridging, and Transgressing Divides in the Study of Native North America. In *Across a Great Divide: Continuity and Change in Native North American Societies, 1400-1900*, edited by L.L. Scheiber and M.D. Mitchell, pp. 258–276. University of Arizona Press, Tucson.

Silliman, Stephen. 2012. Between the Long Duree and the Short Puree: Postcolonial Archaeologies of Indigenous History in Colonial North America. In *Decolonizing*

Indigenous Histories: Exploring Prehistoric/Colonial Transitions in Archaeology, edited by M. Oland, S.M. Hart and L. Frink, pp. 113–131. University of Arizona Press, Tucson.

Spielmann, Katherine. 2005. Ethnographic Analogy and Ancestral Pueblo Archaeology. In *Southwest Archaeology in the Twentieth Century*, edited by L.S. Cordell and D.D. Fowler, pp. 194–203. University of Utah Press, Salt Lake City.

Sturtevant, William C. (editor). 1978. *Handbook of North American Indians*. Smithsonian Institution, Washington DC.

United Nations Educational, Scientific, and Cultural Organization. 1989. Recommendation on the Safeguarding of Traditional Culture and Folklore. Retrieved from the UNESCO website: http://portal.unesco.org/en/ev.php-URL_ID=13141&URL_DO=DO_TOPIC&URL_SECTION=201.html.

Vierra, Bradley J. 1990. Archaic Hunter-Gatherer Archaeology in Northwestern New Mexico. In *Perspectives on Southwest Prehistory*, edited by P. Minnis and C.L. Redman, pp. 57–67. Westview Press, Boulder.

Vierra, Bradley J., and Maxine McBrinn. 2017. The Southwest Archaic. In *The Oxford Handbook of Southwest Archaeology*, edited by B.J. Mills and S. Fowles. Oxford University Press. DOI: 10.1093/oxfordhb/9780199978427.013.12.

Wilcox, Michael V. 2010. Marketing Conquest and the Vanishing Indian: An Indigenous Response to Jared Diamond's Guns, Germs, and Steel and Collapse. *Journal of Social Archaeology* 10(1): 92–117.

Wissler, Clark. 1917. *The American Indian: An Introduction to the Anthropology of the New World*. Douglas C. McMurtrie, New York.

Wissler, Clark. 1927. The Culture-Area Concept in Social Anthropology. *American Journal of Sociology* 32(6): 881–891.

Younging, Gregory. 2018. *Elements of Indigenous Style*. Brush Education Inc, Toronto.

IN SEARCH OF NOMADS

In the summer of 2013, I ventured onto the Taos Plateau in search of nomads. By nomads, I mean Indigenous people practicing significant levels of residential mobility and engaged in either sheep or horse pastoralism. Within New Mexico, this category typically describes Indigenous Peoples like the *Diné*, *Ndee*, *Numunu*, and *Nuutsiyu*, although many other Indigenous equestrians traveled through the region as part of their seasonal rounds, trading expeditions, or raiding exploits.

As my rented Chevy suburban emerged out of the Rio Grande gorge, heading towards the Colorado boarder with field crew and gear in tow, I remember feeling a sense of awe at the sheer magnitude of the landscape, its open prairies punctuated by volcanic cones. As I drove north along Highway 285 in search of a possible tipi site tentatively identified by Bureau of Land Management (BLM) archaeologist Merrill Dicks, I was struck (strangely enough) by the resonances between the landscape outside my window and the writings of Giles Deleuze and Felix Guattari: "The nomads are there, on the land, wherever there forms a smooth space that gnaws, and tends to grow, in all directions. The nomads inhabit these places; they remain in them, and they themselves make them grow."[1] Although Deleuze and Guattari almost certainly never visited northern New Mexico before writing *Nomadology*, their idea that "nomads" engage with time and space in distinctive ways offers insights into where one might look for material evidence of nomadism. Rather than surveying river valleys where village sites are often constructed, nomadic encampments are more often found in smooth open spaces—the playas, mountain foothills, and grassy basins of the northern Rio Grande landscape.

Over the course of the field season, it became clear that the archaeological history of this landscape was much richer and more varied than I had anticipated. The gnawing expanses of the Taos Plateau were in reality thickly layered cultural palimpsests, offering up evidence for the changing mobility practices of a variety of human groups over the *longue durée*. It is this complex material history that I hope to disentangle in order to understand how Indigenous and non-Indigenous people used particular places on the landscape and how each successive occupation in these places "made them grow," investing them with new functions and meanings over time.

4

THE MESSY WORK OF MOBILE ARCHAEOLOGY

The study of residentially mobile hunting-gathering populations has been a consistent facet of anthropological research since the discipline's inception in late 19th century. Archaeological studies of residential mobility have typically focused either on pre-agricultural foragers (i.e., "Archaic" and "Paleo-Indian" periods) or on equestrian nomads. Despite the vast temporal divide that separates foragers in the deep past from the bison hunting Peoples of the late-16th century onward, the actual "stuff" left behind by these residentially mobile groups is remarkably consistent across time and space. The archaeological record of these Indigenous groups is dominated by lithics, including chipped stone tools, stone piles, alignments, and circles, as well as rock art.

The material residues of mobility present various interpretive hurdles for archaeologists. For example, such sites often consist of small numbers of artifacts and undiagnostic chipped stone debris which pose challenges for temporally dating occupations or distinguishing distinct occupational events. Furthermore, surface artifacts are subject to frequent displacement as the result of erosion or bioturbation and associated structures are often reused over time making it difficult to ascertain their original function. This chapter discusses these, as well as other challenges which accompany efforts to interpret the material record of residentially mobile groups. In addition to tracing out these analytical difficulties, I outline the strategies used by archaeologists to resolve these issues and some of the ways I've sought to address these interpretive challenges.

The materiality of mobility

Chipped stone scatters

Chipped stone scatters are ubiquitous throughout the northern Rio Grande. These scatters range significantly in size, from small concentrations of a dozen or so flakes to large, dispersed carpets of hundreds of chipped stone tools and debris. Despite differences in size, these surface scatters typically contain relatively small numbers of formal tools and lack ceramics or associated rock features. Within the compliance and mitigation framework under which most archaeological survey work takes place on the Taos Plateau, the absence of culturally or temporally diagnostic materials at most chipped stone scatters, has resulted in their categorization as "insignificant." The guidelines for significance are outlined in the National Registry of Historic Places (NRHP). Under the NRHP criteria, archaeological remains representing high-density artifact clusters, particularly those including architecture or features, are more likely to be listed on the registry, thereby systematically excluding smaller and/or "undiagnostic" sites from further study.[2] As a result, chipped stone scatters remain a poorly defined "site" category and their fit within local and regional land-use systems continues to be understudied.[3] The sheer quantity of chipped stone scatters across northern New Mexico calls for more concerted attention to this site category.

The size of any given chipped stone scatter can reflect a myriad of factors including the skill of the manufacturer, the material being worked, and the type of tool being produced. For instance, scatters with small quantities of debitage may be the result of a skilled tool producer using high-quality materials. An individual of the same skill level may produce larger quantities of debitage if using poor-quality materials requiring continuous refinement to make a functional tool. Similarly, if the goal of the manufacturer is resharpening rather than tool production, smaller amounts of debitage should be expected.[4] Chipped stone scatters on the Taos Plateau are dominated by locally available dacite, suggesting that other factors, like the producers goals (e.g., tool resharpening versus production) rather than material type likely played a significant role in determining scatter size on the Plateau.

In addition to considering the role of individual tool producers in shaping the composition of chipped stone scatters, the distribution of lithic materials on the Plateau has been impacted by widespread deflation as the result of drought, seasonal runoff, bioturbation, and erosion associated with overgrazing and mining. These natural and human-induced processes have produced spatially inseparable distributions of chipped stone artifacts. Determining the boundaries of distinct scatters within this lithic carpet is often difficult and yet has direct implications for whether a chipped stone scatter is interpreted as a single intensive occupational episode or evidence of multiple distinct occupations.

As part of their standardized recording method, the Bureau of Land Management Manual H-8100-1 recommends that a site's boundaries be defined as encompassing a 20-meter distance in any direction from the center of an artifact concentration. However, this approach is largely inoperable on the Plateau given its light though continuous distribution of chipped stone artifacts.[5] Carving "sites" out of such a contiguous archaeological landscape requires a large degree of subjective subdivision on the part of the individual surveyor, resulting in different recording and sampling strategies across projects. While some surveyors may use a broad definition of artifact density, thereby creating fewer, but larger, chipped stone sites others may employ a more restricted set of criteria which divides the lithic landscape into smaller bounded units. The former tends to create a sense of technological consistency across time and space; the latter produces a more staccato picture of land use. Although imperfect, I adopted a "splitting" approach that used topographic features such as arroyos, playas, and significant changes in terrain to define the boundaries of otherwise continuous chipped stone scatters.[6]

Basic lithic refitting offers another method for distinguishing single occupations within the large dispersed scatters associated with the base camps of residentially mobile Indigenous people.[7] Refitting flakes to chipped stone tools can be used to address a range of questions around tool production and function as well as intra-site spatial dynamics.[8] Researchers working on the southern and northern Plains have used this method to enhance our understanding of inter-site movement patterns.[9] Although refitting studies offer detailed insights into the occupational logics of lithic carpets, this time-consuming approach becomes particularly daunting in study contexts like the Taos Plateau where scatters often contain hundreds and sometimes thousands of debris and which frequently lack formal chipped stone tools. Furthermore, the types of lab-based microscopic analysis and three-dimensional scanning methods used in lithic refitting are at odds with the in-field survey based analysis typically permitted on the Plateau and often preferred by Tribal Nations.

When refitting studies are not possible or practical, as in the study context discussed throughout this book, occupational episodes can be inferred based on the relative discreteness and density of the scatter. Distinguishing between dispersed scatters representative of multiple occupations and the redistributional effects of bioturbation and erosion, particularly on mountain slopes where much of this survey work took place, is more difficult. Excavation and subsequent comparison of the vertical and horizontal dimensions of chipped stone debris has traditionally been used to understand the formation of the archaeological record.[10] However, excavation was not allowed under the BLM permits issued for the fieldwork I conducted. Rather than attempting to impose subjective occupational sequences onto surface assemblages, I treated dispersed scatters as evidence of accumulative reuse of a given area. I then compared the content of these dispersed scatters to the materials in more discrete occupations to understand differences in how similar landscapes were used.

In addition to interpretive issues surrounding site size and occupational patterning, it is often difficult to assess with any clarity the temporal period in which chipped stone scatters were produced due to the lack of diagnostic tools or associated features. In those instances where chipped stone tools are present but are not "diagnostic," the relative proportion of formal and informal tools can offer insights into the mobility patterns of the scatter's producers. Broad divisions between formal and informal tools outlined by Lewis Binford in *Forager Collector Theory* suggest that higher levels of mobility are associated with higher frequencies of formal tools, which are transported to the site from a distance. In contrast, large numbers of informal tools reflect lower levels of mobility and greater task co-ordination.[11] Drawing on such ethnoarchaeological observations, I interpret the absence of formal tools within a scatter as indicative of production by a less residentially mobile Indigenous group.

In those instances where formal tools are completely absent, characteristics of the flake assemblage itself can be used to infer a scatter's relative chronology.[12] For example, there is a widely recognized shift from curated bifacial stone tool technologies and blade resharpening to more expedient forms of flake-based tools over time.[13] The former technological process results in smaller, thinner flakes and is associated with high levels of long-distance residential mobility, whereas the latter tool types were typically produced by Indigenous people practicing a diversified subsistence economy and more circumscribed forms of residential mobility.[14] Accompanying this shift from curated to expedient chipped stone tools was an increase in the use obsidian. This regional pattern suggests that we should see a general increase in the proportion of obsidian waste flakes in lithic scatters on the Taos Plateau over time.[15] With these criteria in mind, chipped stone scatters containing higher proportions of obsidian alongside larger flakes with fewer distinctive platform attributes can reasonably be attributed to Indigenous Peoples living in the region after 1800 BCE.

Patricia Hick's study of non-diagnostic lithic scatters from the Abiquiú, Reservoir and Albuquerque areas offer further insights into evolving patterns in raw material selection. Hick's research demonstrates a general shift over time from a reliance on non-local materials to the almost exclusive use of local materials and the incorporation of hard hammer reduction strategies.[16] She argues that "Pueblo" tool production areas are characterized by a preponderance of expedient tools, higher levels of heat treatment, smaller amounts of shatter, and less emphasis on bifacial reduction strategies.[17] These criteria can be applied to chipped stone scatters in order to differentiate "Pueblo" work areas dating from roughly 950 CE onwards from those of residentially mobile foragers.

Studies of surface artifacts from datable tipi encampments across the southern Plains also suggest that distinctions can be drawn between lithic scatters produced by residentially mobile groups before and after European colonization. Chipped stone assemblages associated with equestrian nomads have been shown to contain fewer bifacial tools following the introduction of metal trade items, which gradually replaced knives and projectile points as formal tools.[18] In addition to having smaller numbers of bifacial tools, Deni Seymour's work on lithic scatters associated with 18th- and 19th-century *Ndee* encampments indicates that these sites tend to have smaller and less diverse lithic assemblages.[19] While the temporal categories that can be assigned to lithic scatters through an assessment of waste flakes, material types, and the presence/absence of bifacial tools are inferential, these techniques offer non-invasive means of temporally refining non-diagnostic lithic scatters.

Rock piles, alignments, and circles

Stone features are a common facet of the archaeological record, associated with residentially mobile Indigenous groups living throughout the Southwest, Great Basin, and Plains. This rock complex is part of a "nomadic" landscape that is materially distinct from agricultural landscapes in the North American West and includes piles, cairns, linear alignments, U-shaped or semicircular structures, as well as stone rings.[20] Interpreting how and who used these features is complicated by morphological similarities across these features over time and space. Furthermore, diagnostic surface artifacts are often missing from these sites rendering the interpretive process yet more convoluted. The functional multiplicity of rock piles, cairns, and alignments challenges assumed connections between architectural form and use and defies archaeological efforts to assign them to singular explanatory categories. Instead, similar features often held multiple meanings and functions that were activated and altered in line with the cultural context and needs of the user.

Rock piles are concentrations of six or more rocks, which are not stacked like cairns but simply laid together. These features are found in a variety of contexts, including on mountain peaks or along trails. In contrast, a cairn typically has more rocks than are present in piles and include a clear upper rock supported by two or more lower ones.[21] Southern Ute elder Alden Naranjo notes that for residentially mobile groups, rock cairns served a wide variety of purposes, including as trail markers, indicators of seasonal change, memorials of events, or offering locations.[22] When synthesized with ethnographic information like that offered by Naranjo, the geospatial context of cairns and rock piles can help to narrow down their possible purpose. For example, cairns placed along trails are likely directional markers, whereas those constructed at high points may have served as offering locations. Excavations, off course, can also yield insights into how particular features were used. For instance, excavations of cairns in southern Alberta and Manitoba indicate that some of these features were used to cover human burials or as caches.[23]

Much like stone piles and cairns, rock alignments are abundant throughout the North American West and were constructed by both Indigenous and non-Indigenous people. Rock alignments are straight or slightly curving dry-laid masonry features that are not connected to other features. These alignments may be linear or curved but do not form formal enclosures.[24] Like rock piles and cairns, rock alignments have been documented in a variety of contexts, including along trails and ridges or on mountain peaks. Again, the location of these features plays a critical role in narrowing down their potential function. Consultations with Indigenous People suggest that rock alignments associated with "doings" are typically located in high places and in close physical proximity to other stone features recognized as prayer seats.[25] Within the Great Basin, comparable types of rock alignments have been interpreted as part of a sophisticated hunting landscape used to control the flow of medium-sized game across mountain slopes. For instance, linear rock alignments in the Colorado desert were historically used by Ivilyuqaletem (Cohuilla) and Tipai-Ipai (Kumeyaay) Peoples to channel bighorn sheep uphill to hunters concealed behind natural outcrops of rocks at the summit.[26] These drive lines take on a broad range of forms, including single, low-course alignments, which suggest a path for game as well as more substantial stacked rock walls and blinds.

Archaeologists have sought to place these features in cultural and temporal contexts, through a combination of methods, including archival research, ethnographic analogy, excavation, and typological comparisons. The geospatial positioning of piles and alignments can also be used to winnow down the possible cultural context in which a given rock feature was produced. For instance, modern cairn and piles used to mark boundaries or mine claims are typically associated with 20th-century artifacts like iron pipes, metal, or glass debris. In a similar vein, cairns or piles constructed by Indigenous farmers can be differentiated from those produced by residentially mobile groups based on their proximity to other agricultural features like mulch gardens or terraces. In contrast, cairns associated with Indigenous foragers are typically located on prominent points on the landscape—ideal locations for observing the movements of game and people across the landscape, close to sites with tipi rings and other stone alignments, or as part of other culturally modified features such as drive lines.[27]

Stone circles are also a part of the rock feature complex found throughout the region. Stone circles take on a variety of forms and sizes, including dry-laid stones stacked multiple courses high, rocks arranged in equal intervals or pairs to form a circle, or as a single layer of rocks arranged circularly with interior lines.[28] Much like the rock piles and alignments discussed previously, determining the precise function, cultural affiliation, and temporal period to assign stone circles to is complicated by the widespread use of this feature type and throughout time.

The excavation and subsequent carbon dating of ash and charcoal from subsurface hearths associated with stone rings offers the most direct and precise means of dating stone circles. Such excavations also have the potential to produce diagnostic projectile points or ceramics which can provide a relative means of dating surface and subsurface collections. Of course, excavation is not a silver bullet for such chronometric dilemmas, as many tipi rings lack hearths entirely. Indeed, over 90% of stone circle sites within the Archaeological Records Management System (ARMS) database for New Mexico as of 2014 did not contain hearths.[29]

In many instances excavations are simply not possible due to the nondestructive policies of Indigenous collaborators, time constraints, and permitting limitations. In these scenarios, archaeologists are left to examine the often sparse surface record to determine the possible temporal or cultural affiliation of stone rings. Interpretive issues often arise when trying to determine the spatial relationship between surface artifacts and rock features. Stone rings are often part of material palimpsests indicative of multiple different uses of the same space over time. The culturally and temporally layered nature of such sites can make it difficult to determine which occupational component rock features are associated with. These analytical issues are exacerbated by the fact that rock features are often situated in erosional areas in which potentially related artifacts are easily displaced over time.

Furthermore, studies of surface artifacts at stone ring sites are often analytically limited by the absence of diagnostic materials. As Waldo Wedel succinctly stated, "artifacts and camp rubbish are usually extremely scarce in and around the rings, so that their assignment to any specific time period, tribe, or culture is not easy."[30] A similar sentiment was articulated by George Frison: "Stone circles are noted for a lack of diagnostic cultural material...Most are associated with little more than a few flakes and an occasional broken point or tool...whatever their true function, stone circles will plague archeologists on the High Plains for some time to come."[31] Wedel and Frison's observations are particularly characteristic of small, single stone ring sites. While tipi ring sites in New Mexico range in size from short term occupations of a single tipi to medium-term aggregations consisting of up to 200 tipis, these large sites are quite rare. Instead, small sites dominate the archaeological record, with roughly 65% of tipi sites recorded within ARMS having only one or two tipi rings.

In the absence of datable hearths or diagnostic surface artifacts, some archaeologists have turned to chemical tests of the soil underneath rock rings to more precisely determine their antiquity. The effectiveness of this method, however, remains a subject of scholarly debate.[32] Other researchers have used differences in rock ring size to differentiate pre and post-horse encampments. Thomas Kehoe was the first archaeologist to pursue this relative means of dating stone rings, arguing that stone circles significantly increased in size after 1,600 CE when horses were reintroduced into the American West.[33] Subsequent studies have complicated Kehoe's findings by demonstrating, that stone ring size actually reflects a wide range of factors, including seasonality, wealth, status, and family size.[34]

Similar morphological studies have been used to identify differences in rock circles made by residentially mobile people prior to the development of agriculture. For example, a study by Laura Scheiber of over 250 stone rings in Wyoming suggests that stone circles made before and after 400 CE are morphologically distinct. According to Scheiber, "Archaic" period features are typically smaller, less variable in size, and have fewer total rocks in the ring. These sites also tend to have larger distances between circles.[35]

James T. Finnigan developed a similar set of morphological criteria characterizing the stone rings of equestrian groups which distinguishes them from rings used as shrines, corrals, or hunting blinds.[36] Finnigan used five criteria to identify tipi ring on the Great Plains: (1) the shape does not deviate significantly from a circle; (2) there are no interior stone features that would render the interior of the tipi ring uninhabitable unless they are clearly a post-use modification; (3) the inside diameter falls between 2.5 and 9 m—any rock ring with an interior diameter of 1 m or less would be too small to be used as a domestic shelter; (4) the slope of the ground is less than or equal to 5 degrees, and (5) the ground surface is dry and stable.[37]

Drawing on Finnigan's criteria, I developed a morphological profile for tipi rings in New Mexico. A comparative assessment of the site information recorded for roughly 1,400 stone circle sites in ARMS indicates that tipi rings in the state have an interior diameter between 1.7 and 12 m, but are on average around 4.3 m wide.[38] These features are rarely associated with internal features like storage pits or hearths and are typically found in a greater variety of topographic location and at a lower median elevation than other types of stone circles. These trends offer a rough if not definitive means of assessing the potential function of stone circles in the absence of or in concert with surface collections.[39] This criteria can also be compared with Schreiber's work as a means of distinguishing the encampments of "Archaic" mobile groups from equestrian ones.

While morphology offers a promising means of relatively dating rock features and assessing their function, this method relies on the surveyor's willingness to record such information. As discussed for chipped stone scatters, the absence of diagnostic artifacts associated with rock features often render them analytically unimportant under the NRHP criteria. This culture of archaeological recording has stymied the development of explicit criteria for locating and distinguishing between different types of ambiguous rock features in New Mexico. Ultimately, developing a more robust understanding of physical and contextual differences across rock piles, alignments, and circles in the region will require a concerted effort to record a broader and more detailed body of information at mobile sites.

In addition to interpretive issues around temporally affiliating stone circles, assigning these features to a particular cultural or ethnic group is, at best, difficult in the absence of directly associated diagnostic projectile points and ceramics. In these instances, the archival record offers one means of narrowing the list of possibly affiliated Indigenous Peoples. A letter sent by Juan de Onate to the viceroy of New Spain in 1,599 provides one such detailed description of Indigenous encampment patterns: "We have seen other nations such as the Querechos or Vaqueros who live among the Cibola cattle in tents of tanned hides. The Apaches, some of whom we also saw, are extremely numerous."[40] Such archival sources can be used as rough guides for determining which areas were most frequently inhabited by specific nomadic Indigenous Peoples and therefore the most likely peoples associated with particular stone circle sites.

Off course, documentary accounts are only snapshots of group configuration and territorial reach. The dynamic and fluid nature of residentially mobile societies suggests that camp configurations and mobility patterns were constantly changing. Furthermore, these archival accounts reflect Western perceptions of group identity that may not accurately represent the social-territorial structure of Indigenous People. Whether these accounts accurately represent Indigenous encampment patterns prior to or after the date they were written is often unclear, suggesting that such records should be used critically. In addition to "reading between the lines" of these accounts, conversations with Indigenous collaborators offer an important source of clarification regarding the observations preserved in the archival record and applied to archaeological assemblages.

▼▽▼

The archaeological record of the Taos Plateau is a lithic landscape comprised of chipped stone scatters and a variety of rock features. The widespread and long-standing production of similar tool and feature types by residentially mobile Indigenous groups points to a shared means of relating to and marking the landscape. We might think of these materials as the by-products of a "nomadic" logic rooted in an ontological commitment to malleability and mobility—a spiritual and physical mandate to move across space and adapt to the local environment.

Detailed documentation and assessment of the formal characteristics of rock features and chipped stone assemblages can help to unfurrow the interpretive conundrums associated with the archaeological record of mobile groups. This interpretive process continues to be complicated by the frequent absence of diagnostic projectile points, ceramics, or dateable features, the revisitation and reuse of particular areas, erosion, and bioturbation. It is also hindered by archaeological recording conventions, permitting structures, budgetary constraints, and work timelines. In order to address these interpretive issues. I draw on two analytical approaches. First, I employ a simple strategy of evidentiary convergence, in which trends across different artifact types and spatial patterns are synthesized with ethnographic, archival, and comparable archaeological evidence to develop inferences about cultural and temporal affiliation. Second, in Chapter 5-7, I present multiple possible explanations and interpretations of the material record rather than attempting to generate a singular narrative. Such epistemological fluidity, draws from Indigenous philosophy, which posits the existence of multiple "truths" and which understands knowledge production as a constantly evolving process.[41]

Notes

1 Deleuze and Guattari, 1986: 46.
2 Cain, 2017: 208; Dunnell and Dancey, 1983; Plog et al., 1978.
3 Cain, 2012: 207.
4 Reith, 2008: 2.
5 Dicks et al., 2017: I–63.
6 Dicks et al., 2017: I–64.

7 Cain, 2012: 215.
8 Hofman and Ryan, 2013: 69. Influential studies on refitting including Frison, 1968; Hofman, 1981; Jelinek, 1976.
9 For more recent examples of refitting studies, see Hofman and Ryan, 2013; Huckell, 2006; Jodry, 1992, 1999; Rose, 2011.
10 Morrow, 1996: 352–353. Excavations were not undertaken for this study under the non-collection permit issued to the surveyor.
11 Binford, 1980.
12 Binford, 1979; Cowan, 1999.
13 Vierra and McBrinn, 2017.
14 Ahler, 1989: 95; Cain, 2012: 214; Henry et al., 1976: 57.
15 Vierra, 2013: 153.
16 Hicks, 1994: 496–497.
17 Hicks, 1994: 514.
18 Smith, 2012: 99.
19 Seymour, 2009.
20 Haynal, 2000.
21 Chartkoff, 1983: 750.
22 McBeth, 2007: 119–127.
23 Brink et al., 2003: 214.
24 Chartkoff, 1983: 750–751.
25 Chartkoff, 1983: 752.
26 Schneider et al., 2014: 202.
27 Brink et al., 2003: 210, 214.
28 Chartkoff, 1983: 753.
29 Montgomery, 2015: 56.
30 Wedel, 1961: 262.
31 Frison, 1967:53.
32 Dormaar, 1976. For critiques of Dormaar, see Adams, 1978 and Brumley and Kooyman, 1978.
33 Kehoe, 1960. Following Kehoe's hypothesis, the work of Anthony Ranere (1969) in Idaho and Charles Mobley (1978) in north-central New Mexico have provided complimentary evidence that tipi rings dating from the 1600s onward tend to be larger.
34 Brumley, 1973; Davis et al., 1982; Finnigan, 1982; Roll, 1981: 81–84; Quigg, 1979; Wilson, 1983.
35 Kornfeld et al., 2010: 401; Schieber, 1993.
36 Hoffman, 1953; Kehoe, 1958, 1960, 1961; Malouf, 1960, 1961; Mulloy, 1960.
37 Finnigan, 1982: 4.
38 Montgomery, 2015: 48.
39 Montgomery, 2015: 58.
40 Hammond and Rey, 1953: 484.
41 Deloria et al., 1999.

Bibliography

Adams, Gary W. 1978. Tipi Rings in Southern Alberta The Alkali Creek Sites, Lower Red Deer River. Archaeological Survey of Alberta, *Occasional Paper* 9. Alberta Culture Historical Resource Division, Edmonton.

Adams, Gary W. 1983. Tipi Rings at York Factory: An Archaeological-Ethnographic Interface. *Plains Anthropologist* 28(102): 6–15.

Ahler, Stanley. 1989. Mass Analysis of Flaking Debris: Studying the Forest Rather than the Trees. In *Alternative Approaches to Lithic Analysis*, edited by D.O. Henry and G.H. Odell,

pp. 85–118. Archaeological Papers of the American Anthropological Association, No. 1. Washington, DC.
Binford, Lewis R. 1979. Organization and Formation Processes: Looking at Curated Technologies. *Journal of Anthropological Research* 35(3): 255–279.
Binford, Lewis R. 1980. Willow Smoke and Dogs' Tails: Hunter-Gatherer Settlement Systems and Archaeological Site Formation. *American Antiquity* 45(1): 4–20.
Brink, Jack W., Kristine Wrigh-Fedyniak, and Dean Wetzel. 2003. A Review of Certain Stone Alignments and Rock Cairns in Alberta Archaeology. In *Archaeology in Alberta: A View from the New Millennium*, edited by J.W. Brink and J.F. Drmaar, pp. 208–241. The Archaeological Society of Alberta, Medicine Hat.
Brumley, John H. 1973. Suffield Archaeological Project 1972: Preliminary Report. Press One, OFY Community Service Printing. Medicine Hat.
Brumley, John H., and Brian P. Kooyman. 1978. Excavations of Stone Circles at EhPB-1. Archaeological Survey of Alberta, Edmonton.
Cain, Daniel. 2012. Revisiting Lithic Scatters: A CRM Perspective. *Southeastern Archaeology* 31(2): 207–220.
Chartkoff, Joseph L. 1983. A Rock Feature Complex from Northwestern California. *American Antiquity* 48(4): 745–760.
Cowan, Frank L. 2017. Making Sense of Flake Scatters: Lithic Technological Strategies and Mobility. *American Antiquity* 64(4): 593–607.
Davis, Leslie B., Stephen A. Aaberg, Michael Wilson, and Robert Ottersberg. 1982. Stone Circles in Montana Rockies: Systematic Recovery and Culture Ecological Inference. Report to the Montana Army National Guard by Montana State University, Bozeman.
Deleuze, Gilles, and Felix Guattari 1986. *Nomadology: The War Machine*. Columbia University, New York.
Deloria, Barbara, Kristen Foehner, and Sam Scinta (editors). 1999. *Spirit & Reason: The Vine Deloria, Jr., Reader*. Golden: Fulcrum Publishing, New York.
Dicks, Merril, Arron C. Anderson, Jessical Mrstik, Peter Rogers, and Todd Scarbourgh. 2016. Rio Grande Del Norte National Monument Class III Cultural Resources Survey of the Cerro Montoso Project Area, Taos County, New Mexico. Bureau of Land Management, Taos.
Dormaar, John F. 1976. Effect of Boulderflow on Soil Transformation under Tipi Rings. *Plains Anthropologist* 19: 180–196.
Dunnell, Robert C., and William S. Dancey. 1983. The Siteless Survey: A Regional Scale Data Collection Strategy. *Advances in Archaeological Method and Theory* 6: 267–287.
Finnigan, James T. 1983. Tipi to Tipi Ring: A Transformational Model. *Plains Anthropologist* 28(102): 16–28.
Frison, George C. 1967. Archeological Evidence of the Crow Indians in Northern Wyoming: A Study of a Late Prehistoric Period Buffalo Economy. Unpublished PhD dissertation, Department of Anthropology, University of Michigan, Ann Arbor.
Frison, George C. 1968. A Functional Analysis of Certain Chipped Stone Tools. *American Antiquity* 33: 149–155.
Hammond, George P., and Agapito Rey. 1953. *Don Juan de Onate: Colonizer of New Mexico, 1595-1628*. University of New Mexico Press, Albuquerque.
Haynal, Patrick M. 2000. The Influence of Sacred Rock Cairns and Prayer Seats on Modern Klamath and Modoc Religion and World View. *Journal of California and Great Basin Anthropology* 22(2): 170–185.
Henry, D.O.C., Vance Haynes, and Bruce Bradley. 1976. Quantitative Variation in Flaked Stone Debitage. *Plains Anthropologist* 21: 57–61.

Hicks, Patricia. 1994. Dating the Undiagnostic Lithic Scatter Using Patterened Changes in Debitage Attributes. In *Archaic Hunter-Gatherer Archaeology in the American Southwest*, edited by B.J. Vierra, pp. 478–526. Eastern New Mexico University, Portales.

Hoffman, J.J. 1953. Comments on the Use and Distribution of Tipi Rings in Montana, North Dakota, South Dakota and Wyoming. *Anthropology and Sociology Paper 14*. Montana State University, Missoula.

Hofman, Jack L. 1981. The Refitting of Chipped-Stone Artifacts as an Analytical and Interpretive Tool. *Current Anthropology* 22: 691–693.

Hofman, Jack L., and Shannon R. Ryan 2013. Refitting the Great Plains: A Long Distance Stone Tool Refit from Western Kansas. *Plains Anthropologist* 58(226): 69–78.

Huckell, Bruce B. 2006. Clovis Lithic Technology: A View from the Upper San Pedro Valley. In *Murray Springs, A Clovis Site with Multiple Activity Areas in the San Pedro Valley, Arizona*, edited by C. Vance Haynes, Jr. and B.B. Huckell, pp. 170–213. Anthropological Papers of the University of Arizona 71. The University of Arizona Press, Tucson.

Jelinek, Arthur J. 1976. Form, Function, and Style in Lithic Analysis. In *Culture Change and Continuity: Essays in Honor of James Bennett Griffin*, edited by C.E. Cleland, pp. 19–33. Academic Press, New York.

Jodry, Margaret A. 1992. Fitting Together Folsom: REfitted Lithics and Site Formation Processes at Stewart's Cattle Guard Site. In *Piecing Together the Past, Applications of Refitting Studies in Archaeology*, edited by J.L. Hofman and J.G. Enloe, pp. 179–209. BAR International Series 578. British Archaeological Reports, Oxford.

Jodry, Margaret A. 1999. Paleoindian Stage Paleoecological Records. In *Colorado Prehistory: A Context for the Rio Grande Basin*, edited by M.A. Martorano, T. Hoefer III, M.A. Jodry, V. Spero, and M.L. Taylor, pp. 12–26. Colorado Council of Professional Archaeologists, Denver.

Kehoe, Thomas F. 1954. Stone "Medicine Wheels" in Southern Alberta and the Adjacent Portions of Montana: Were They Designed as Grave Markers?. *Journal of the Washington Academy of Sciences* 44(5):133–137.

Kehoe, Thomas F. 1958. Tipi Rings: The "Direct Ethnological" Approach Applied to an Archeological Problem. *American Anthropologist* 60(5): 861–873.

Kehoe, Thomas F. 1960. *Stone Tipi Rings in North Central Montana and the Adjacent Portion of Alberta, Canada: Their Historical Ethnological and Archaeological Aspects*. Bulletin Submitted to Bureau of American Ethnology, Washington, DC.

Kornfeld, Marcel, Georg C. Frison, and Mary Lou Larson 2010. *Prehistoric Hunter-Gatherers of the High Plains and Rockies*. Left Coast Press, Walnut Creek.

Malouf, Carling. 1960. Tipi Rings. *Southwestern Lore* 24(4): 3–5.

Malouf, Carling. 1961. The Tipi Rings of the High Plains. *American Antiquity* 26(3): 381–389.

McBeth, Sally. 2007. Native American Oral History and Cultural Interpretation in Rocky Mountain National Park. Report to Rocky Mountain National Park, National Park Service and Anthropology Program, University of Northern Colorado, Greeley. University of Northern Colorado, Department of Anthropology, Greeley.

Mobley, Charles. 1978. Ring Diameter as Criterion for Temporal Decimation at Tipi Ring Sites: Data from the Los Esteros Reservoir, Guadalupe County, New Mexico. Paper presented at the 1978 Plains Conference, Denver.

Montgomery, Lindsay M. 2015. Yndios Bárbaros: Nomadic Archaeologies of Spanish New Mexico. Unpublished PhD thesis, Department of Anthropology, Stanford University, Stanford.

Morrow, Timothy M. 1996. Lithic Refitting and Archaeological Site Formation Processes: A Case Study from the Twin Ditch Site, Greene County, Illinois. In *Stone Tools: Theoretical Insights into Human Prehistory*, edited by G.H. Odell, pp. 345–373. Springer, New York.

Mulloy, W.T. 1954. The McKean Site in Northeastern Wyoming. *Southwestern Journal of Anthropology* 10(4): 432–460.

Mulloy, W.T. 1960. Late Prehistoric Stone Circles. *Southwestern Lore* 25(4): 1–3.

Plog, Stephen, Fred Plog, and Walter Wait. 1978. Decision Making in Modern Surveys. *Advances in Archaeological Method and Theory* 1: 383–421.

Quigg, Michael J. 1979. Comments on the Significance of Stone Circle Excavations in Alberta. *Plains Anthropologist* 24(85): 261–266.

Ranere, Anthony J., Joan C. Rangere, and John Lortz. 1969. The Monida Pass Tipi Ring Site. Tebiwa, *Journal of the Idaho State University Museum* 12(1): 39–46. Pocatello.

Reith, Christina B. (editor). 2008. *Current Approaches to the Analysis and Interpretatio of Small Lithic Sites in the Northeast.* New York State Education Department, New York.

Roll, Tom E. 1981. A Re-examination of Tipi Ring Size-age Relationships. *Archeology in Montana* 22(2): 89–95.

Rose, Richard O. 2011. The Shfiting Sands Site: A Southern Plains Folsom-Midland Assemblage. *Bulletine of the Texas Archaeological Society* 82: 299–324.

Schieber, Laura L. 1993. Prehistoric Domestic Architecture on the Northwestern High Plains: A Temporal Analysis of Stone Circles in Wyoming. Unpublished MA thesis, Department of Anthropology, University of Wyoming, Laramie.

Schneider, Joan S., Robert S. Begole, Mark C. Jorgensen, Esther S. Rubin, and L. Louise Jee. 2014. Prehistoric Bighorn Sheep Procurement Tactics in the Colorado Desert: A Hypothesis for a Stone-Feature Complex in Yaqui Pass, Anza-Borrego Desert State Park, California. *Journal of California and Great Basin Anthropology* 34(2): 181–210.

Seymour, Deni J. 2009. Distinctive Places, Suitable Spaces: Conceptualizing Mobile Group Occupational Duration and Landscape Use. *International Journal of Historical Archeology* 13(3): 255–281.

Smith, Kathryn M. 2012. Lithic Activity Area Investigations at the Longhorn Site (41KT53) in the Upper Brazos River Basin, Western Texas. *Plains Anthropologist* 57(222): 91–108.

Vierra, Bradley J. 2013. Archaic Foraging Technology and Land Use in the Northern Rio Grande, New Mexico. In *From Mountaintop to Valley Bottom: Papers in Honor of Paul Williams*, edited by B.J. Vierra, pp. 145–160. University of Utah Press, Salt Lake City.

Vierra, Bradley J., and Maxine McBrinn. 2017. The Southwest Archaic. In *The Oxford Handbook of Southwest Archaeology*, edited by B.J. Mills and S. Fowles. Oxford University Press. DOI: 10.1093/oxfordhb/9780199978427.013.12.

Wedel, Walter 1961. *Prehistoric Man on the Great Plains.* University of Oklahoma Press, Norman.

Wilson, Michael Clayton. 1983. A Test of the Stone Circle Size-Age Hypothesis: Alberta and Wyoming. *Plains Anthropologist* 28(102): 113–137.

PART II

Persistent places on the Taos Plateau

IN SEARCH OF MOBILE PLACES

In 1599, Vicente de Saldivar Mendoza penned the first written account of a nomadic encampment on the plains to the east of New Mexico: "Fifty tents made of tanned hides very bright red and white in color and bell-shaped, with flaps and openings, and built as skillfully as those of Italy and so large that in the most ordinary ones four different mattresses and beds were easily accommodated."[1] Mendoza's diary entry offers a remarkably detailed description of the hide tipis used by Indigenous people during the late 16th century. The discourse of Indigenous barbarism and simplicity, so often applied to such "wandering nomads" by European settlers is entirely absent from Mendoza's account. Instead, he speaks of a sophisticated desert metropolis which would seem more at home in the bustling trade centers of colonial metropoles than the frontier. While such archival accounts clearly indicate that residentially mobile Indigenous Peoples constructed large-scale encampments, the question I asked myself was "where exactly were these mobile households"?

5

PLAYA LANDSCAPES

The playas surveyed for this project are persistent places containing material evidence of long-term human use. These playas operated as resource nodes within a broader land-use pattern that emerged on the Plateau around 5500 BCE. Although the types of technologies and mobility patterns employed by Indigenous Peoples using the Plateau shifted over time, the role of playas appears to have remained largely consistent. Accompanying each successive use of these sites were new modes of conceptualizing space and place, a process that Arjun Appadurai has called the "production of locality."[2] Producing locality entails a back and forth between individuals and specific "neighborhoods" or places and is intimately shaped by preconceived notions of appropriate land-use practices (e.g., residential versus logistical activities, localized versus long-distance mobility, pastoralism versus pedestrianism).[3] Punche Lake, Arroyo Punche, and Three Basins contain material evidence for the production of locality by a variety of groups, including through their use as logistical activity areas by Indigenous foragers between 5500 BCE and 400 CE, residential base camps constructed by Numic- and/or Athabaskan-speaking peoples sometime after 1300 CE, and ranching and homesteading settlements made during the late 19th and early 20th centuries. Each of these occupational episodes is materially marked in similar, although distinct, ways within each playa.

Punche Lake, Arroyo Punche, and Three Basins contain discrete chipped stone scatters with varying numbers of formal and informal tools, including diagnostic projectile points (Figure 5.2).[4] These three playas also contain a variety of rock features, including stone rings, rock piles, and linear alignments, which offer evidence for consecutive and consistent human modification to the landscape. The material and occupational similarities across these places suggest that playas are a specific "type" of persistent place. Through an investigation of the surface record

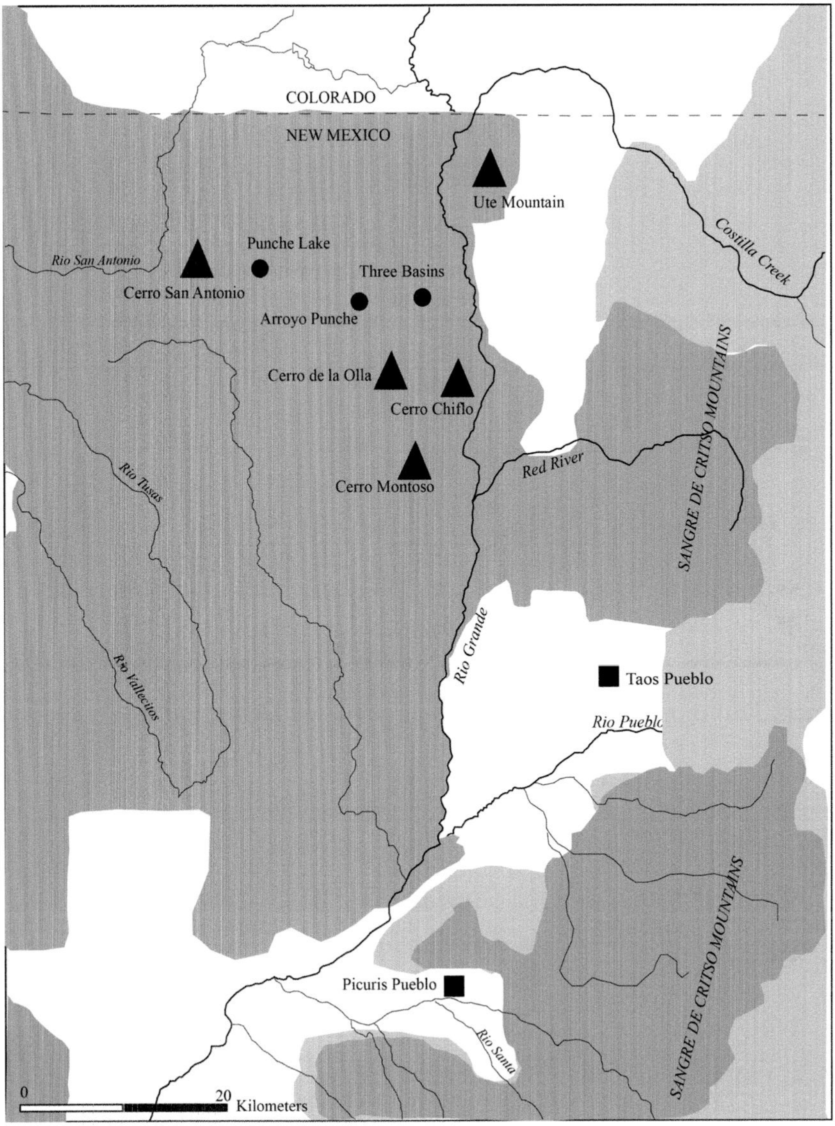

FIGURE 5.1 Overview Map of Punche Lake, Arroyo Punche, and Three Basins.

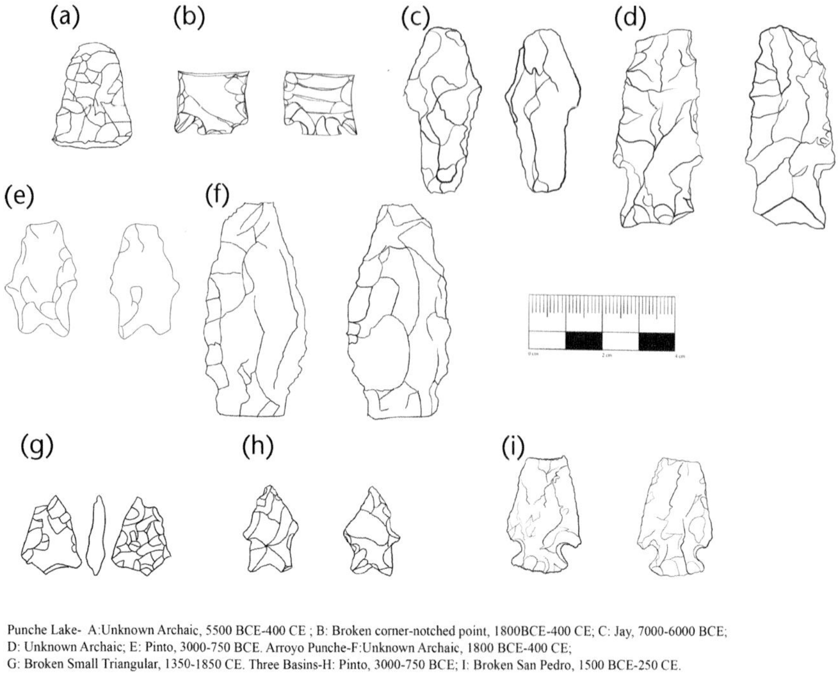

FIGURE 5.2 Diagnostic Projectile Points from Punche Lake (a–e), Arroyo Punche (f–g), and Three Basins (h–i).

at these playa sites, I discuss patterns in mobile land-use practices and settlement logics over time.

▼▽▼

Punche Lake

Punche Lake is a kidney-shaped playa enclosed by vesicular basalt embankments at the base of Cerro San Antonio. Standing at the towering height of 10,908 feet, Cerro San Antonio is the highest peak on the Taos Plateau and serves as the largest source of dacite—a "glassy andesite" material used to produce stone tools—in the region.[5] John Marshall Gettys first recorded the archaeological materials at Punche Lake in the 1970s as part of his unpublished master's research at Eastern New Mexico University.[6] Gettys identified two distinct archaeological areas within the playa: Area 1, located along the northwestern embankment that contained 30 stone circles and Area 2, situated along the southern ridge that contained around 15 rock rings. He also recorded a large number of isolated projectile points on the rim of Punche Lake, representing a distinct use of the playa from the stone circles within the basin.

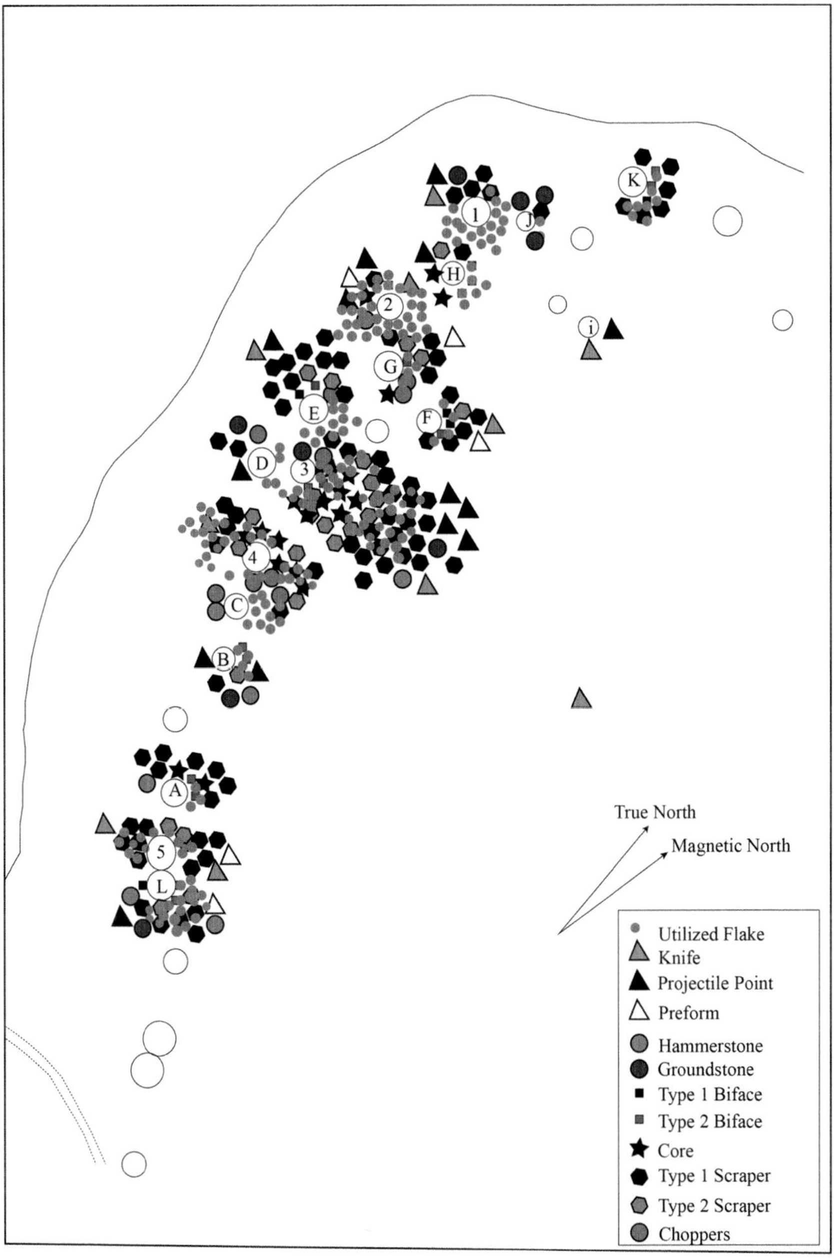

FIGURE 5.3 Area 1 of Punche Lake Based on John Gettys's Research.

In 2013, I undertook a non-collection-based survey of Punche Lake in order to document how the surface record of the playa had changed over the intervening period. This survey work produced several notable differences between

Gettys's fieldwork and the archaeological record of Punche Lake in the 21st century. Perhaps the most significant of these differences was the presence of 34 previously undocumented stone features, including additional stone rings as well as rock piles and linear alignments (Figure 5.3).

Addition to recording a larger number of rock features, in 2013 there were significantly fewer bifacial tools, including projectile points present on the surface of the playa, as well as approximately half the number of chipped and ground stone tool debris. This discrepancy reflects several factors, including the fact that Gettys collected a representative sample of roughly 40% of all chipped and ground stone tools arti from Areas 1 and 2 that are now housed at the Laboratory of Anthropology in Santa Fe. Since his initial survey, nearly 40 years earlier, there have also been significant changes to the Plateau landscape, including increased soil erosion and decreasing moisture levels. These natural processes, along with cattle grazing in the playa has created a significant degree of artifact displacement.

The "old" mobility model: Indigenous activity areas

A stylistic analysis of the 24 isolated projectile points identified by Gettys along the rim of Punche Lake indicates that Indigenous Peoples were visiting this area from 5500 BCE to 400 CE. Roughly 86% of these points had missing or fragmentary tips, a breakage pattern typically caused by contact after striking an animal during a hunting event.[7] The accumulation of broken projectile points along the playa's rim, suggests that Punche Lake was used multiple times as an intercept hunting site. In contrast to wooded settings, in which Indigenous groups often employed an encounter strategy for hunting game, the intercept technique was more successful in open settings.[8]

Punche Lake was likely one important resource node within a broader mobility system, in which small groups undertook logistical trips to and from base camps in order to locate food caches and hunt game like antelope, deer, and elk. These intercept hunting episodes likely followed a seasonal logic. Historic reconstructions of game migration patterns indicate that elk typically aggregated into large herds on the Taos Plateau in the early winter, suggesting that the area surrounding Punch Lake would have been particularly rich in large game during this season. The use of Punche Lake as a logistical hunting site during the winter or early spring is supported by climatic reconstructions of precipitation patterns for northern New Mexico over the past 1,000 years which indicate that water levels across the region are highest between November and April.[9] The 18 broken projectile points (5500 to 1800 BCE) documented along the rim of the playa, offer material evidence for a logistical use of the site during a period when water levels at the lake were high and large game were aggregating on the Plateau.[9]

Archaeological evidence from elsewhere in the region suggests that Punche Lake was part of a north-south residential mobility pattern in which small family groups migrated between the San Luis Valley in southern Colorado and the and Rio Grande.[10] Such large-scale residential mobility, between roughly 5500 and

1800 BCE, encouraged a *replacement when exhausted tactic* for projectile points. This tactic involved the creation of durable tools that could be continuously re-sharpened, since access to new raw materials was often unpredictable. This preference for tool reuse required the selection of robust raw materials and bulkier point designs, allowing for several episodes of blade resharpening and base refurbishment.[11]

There are seven points dating from 1800 BCE to 400 CE at Punche Lake which signal a later, and perhaps less frequent, use of the playa. These points are distributed across the playa's rim (n = 3) and within the playa (Area 1 = 4), offering preliminary evidence for increasing seasonal variability in when the site was visited. The smaller total number of points dating to this period may also reflect broader shifts in subsistence strategies and mobility practices in the region after 1800 BCE. During this period, conditions became moister overall, leading to an expansion in piñon-juniper woodlands across the northern Rio Grande. In response to these changing environmental conditions, Indigenous groups gradually shifted toward a more intensive and varied use of smaller territories.[12]

A comparative study of stone tools from the Santa Fe, Trés Piedras, and San Luis Valley areas by Bradley Vierra, indicates that after 1800 BCE, long-distance north-south travel became less frequent as Indigenous Peoples increasingly engaged in a more localized movement pattern between upland and lowland resource nodes within the Rio Grande Valley.[13] Vierra's work demonstrates that during this period, Indigenous groups developed a bimodal settlement pattern involving wintering in the Rio Grande Valley followed by a move into nearby uplands during the summer and fall.[14] This seasonal settlement pattern strategically exploited a diversified set of resource niches: (1) spring and early summer movement into the juniper savanna to harvest rice grass; followed by (2) a mid-late summer movement upland into the ponderosa pine and conifer forests for wild onion, potato, and berry gathering; (3) a fall-time movement down into the piñon-juniper woodlands for collecting pine nuts, acorns, and broadleaf yucca; and, finally, (4) a movement into riverine valleys during the winter.[15] Punche Lake is situated within the broader survey area investigated by Vierra, suggesting that after the 2nd-century BCE it likely functioned as one hunting site within a more diversified set of established intercept hunting sites, visited by Indigenous groups as they moved into higher elevations during the summer and early fall.

The Punche Lake point assemblage reflects previously documented shifts in tool morphology, as resource procurement ranges decreased and upland plant resources, particularly piñon nuts harvested during the late summer and early fall, were increasingly integrated into Indigenous subsistence practices. Changes in the mean width and length of points over time, reflect increased attentiveness to penetration efficiency rather than durability. This transition is reflected in the archaeological record at Punche Lake, in which the mean length and width of points dating to 5500-3200 BCE is 32.1 × 20.3 mm whereas points dating from 1800 BCE to 400 CE have noticeably smaller mean dimensions (29.6 × 17.5 mm).

This morphological shift suggests that the Indigenous occupants of Punche Lake were more frequently replacing, rather than refurbishing, projectile points after 1800 BCE.

This evolving subsistence strategy also involved a corresponding diversification in the types of wild game being hunted. Archaeologically, these new hunting and gathering practices are signaled by a proliferation of specialized point types, including corner-notched, side-notched, wide and narrow stemmed, contracting-stemmed, and leaf-shaped varieties.[16] At Punche Lake, similar point types were documented, including several side-notched (n = 2), corner-notched (n = 4), and stemmed (n = 1) types dating to 1800 BCE–400 CE. All of these points have fragmentary tips, suggesting that they likely broke on impact during hunting expeditions. The fracture pattern exhibited by this subset of projectile points is particularly common for tools from this time period, which were designed to stay attached to the fore shaft of the arrow, and therefore were more likely to break and stay in the animal.[17]

Notably, 83% of isolated projectile points dating from 5500 BCE to 400 CE were made from dacite, which is mostly commonly found at Cerro San Antonio, roughly 10 kilometers to the north. The remaining points associated with this broad period were made from obsidian (n = 3) and chert (n = 1) and are stylistically similar to points dating from roughly 1550 BCE to 400 CE. The increased representation of obsidian within the sample of points dating after 2000 BCE is consistent with an increased emphasis on point efficiency. These obsidian points offer preliminary evidence for a shift in raw material procurement patterns over time as non-local materials were increasingly incorporated into tool assemblages.

The "new" mobility model: temporary residential encampments

A large number of stone circles cover the interior of Punche Lake, indicating that the playa was used a temporary residential base camp likely used by Numic- and/or Athabaskan-speaking peoples. Specifically, during the 2013 survey, I documented 38 stone circles in Area 1 and 24 circles in Area 2 (Figure 5.4). Based on the morphological criteria laid out in Chapter 4, these stone rings fit the general typological profile for domestic structures or "tipi rings" in New Mexico. These domestic features are clearly different from the pit structures, ash pits, and milling stone concentrations typically associated with longer-term base camps used by Indigenous People between 5500 BCE and 400 CE in the region.[18] The material record within the playa basin signals an important shift in the role of playa sites within Indigenous mobility circuits in the region. Rather than operating as a logistical hunting node as in previous periods, Punche Lake also served as an intensively and likely seasonally occupied domestic site within a broader residential mobility circuit.

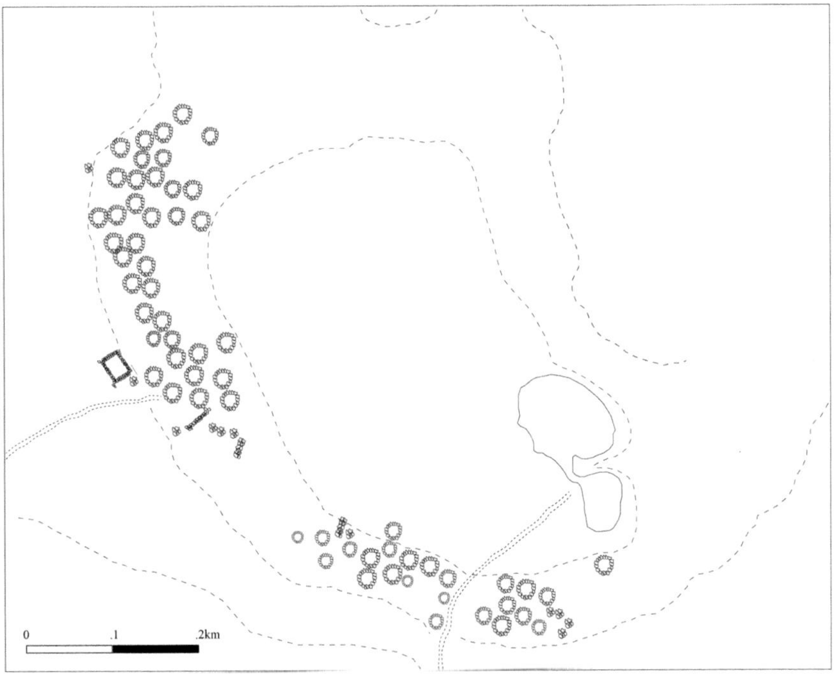

FIGURE 5.4 Area 1 of Punche Lake, Based on 2013 Survey.

Punche Lake is situated near strategic routes of travel within the Taos Plateau, making it an attractive area to establish a larger encampment. Specifically, the playa is located directly west of one of the few traversable locations across the Rio Grande, making this site a desirable stopping place for Indigenous groups moving east-west across region. A similar spatial patterning for tipi sites has been documented on the northern Plains by Thomas Kehoe, who has recorded some 170 stone rings overlooking the "Old Whoop-up Trail," which was frequently used by traders and war parties moving through *Siksika* (Blackfoot) territory in Montana and Alberta.[19] Punche Lake is also strategically located within 10 kilometers of a source of flakeable dacite and is situated within elk migration corridor, making it a highly desirable location for hunting and associated tool production.

Although it is difficult to determine with any certainty which Numic- or Athabaskan-speaking community would have resided at Punche Lake and when this occupation occurred, there is some preliminary evidence to suggest that the stone circles at the site are associated with an ancestral *Ndee* presence. This connection is linguistically signaled by the Jicarilla Apache term *nahkeyaa*, translated literally as "our footprints are there," which they use to refer to the Taos area.[20] This connection is also archived within the Jicarilla's origin story. According to the narrative recorded by Morris Opler in the 1930s, after the Jicarilla emerged from the underworld, White Shell Woman (an ancestral mother figure) was created and eventually gave birth to two sons.[21] One was the offspring of the sun named the Killer-of-the-Enemies; the younger son's father was the moon and was named Child-of-the-Water. The story maps out a number of significant geographic places linked to these culture heroes, who undertake a series of challenges to rid the northern Rio Grande landscape of monsters and troublemakers. After accomplishing these feats, Killer-of-the-Enemies prepares to leave the physical world but before doing so travels to the Taos area to counsel the Jicarilla people one last time. During this visit, he remade the northern Rio Grande in the form of his mother, White Shell Woman. Her heart was placed near El Prado marsh and the four sacred rivers, the Arkansas, the Canadian, the Rio Grande, and the Chama, flow from there. The Rio Grande Gorge became her backbone and her head was placed at Pikes Peak. The Sangre de Cristo Mountains formed one of her legs and the other was located along the San Juan and Jemez Mountains. White Flint Mountain (Pedernal Peak) and Rock Bell Mountains are her nipples. The two moieties that make up Jicarilla society, the Gołgaihėń and Saidindėh, occupy the eastern and western halves of White Shell Woman's body, respectively. This rich cosmogeography physically documents the historical connection between the Jicarilla People and the northern Rio Grande and situates Punche Lake within the traditional territory of the Saidindėh.

In addition to this oral historical evidence, there are particular elements of the archaeological record at Punche Lake that suggest these stone rings were associated with a *Ndee* community rather than a *Nuutsiyu* group. Archeological investigations in southern Colorado indicate that ancestral *Nuutsiyu* almost exclusively used temporary brush structures, referred to as wickiups, prior to the 18th century.[22] The presence of large, well-defined stone rings at Punche Lake seems to conflict with the predominant use of wickiups by mountain-adapted *Nuutsiyu* communities for the period when the playa was likely occupied. Furthermore, the absence of Uncompahgre brownware ceramics as well as diagnostic desert side-notched points typically found at longer-term *Nuutsiyu* encampments in the region strongly suggests that the Punche Lake tipi rings are not associated with this particular Indigenous community.[23]

Although the diagnostic tools or ceramics typically associated with *Nuutsiyu* encampments are missing from the playa, there are 16 projectile points surrounding the stone rings in Areas 1 and 2. Half of these points were too

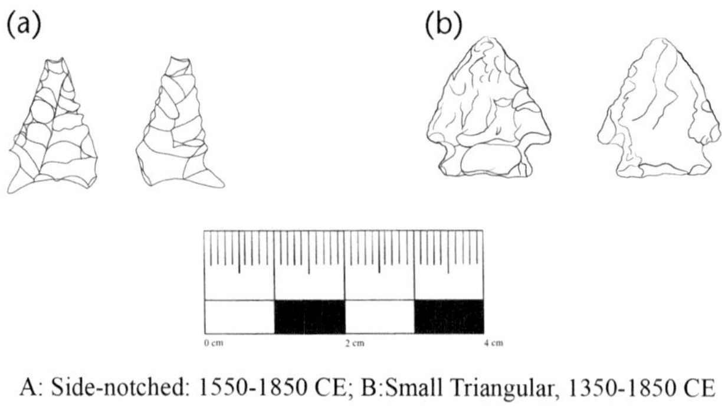

FIGURE 5.5 Diagnostic Projectile Points from Punche Lake, 1800 BCE–400 CE.

fragmentary to type. Of the remaining diagnostic points, six were Plains side notched (1250–1750 CE) and two were simply small triangular points. These point styles resemble artifacts found at ancestral *Ndee* sites in northeastern New Mexico and southern Colorado (Figure 5.5).[24] James Gunnerson described *Ndee* points as

> Small, delicate, and well made. The most common are triangular with side notches a third or fourth of the way from the base. These points are 20 to 28 mm long with widths about half to two thirds the lengths and are all about 3 mm thick. The bases are thinned and, on all but one, concave.[25]

These small, sharp-angled, triangular-notched points reflect a transition in lithic hunting technology associated with an explosion in the bison population on the northern and southern Plains during the 14th century.[26]

Over half of the projectile points associated with stone rings had broken tips as well as fragmentary bases, suggesting that they were refurbished before being left at the playa. These points also have a high thickness-to-length ratio, indicating that durability was a primary concern for their producers.[27] These trends, along with large numbers of tertiary flakes across the playa, indicate that the Indigenous inhabitants of these stone rings were using a tool exhaustion strategy typically employed by community's engaged in relatively high levels of residential mobility. The stylistic and morphologically characteristic of the points directly associated with tipi rings at Punche Lake strongly suggest that the playa was inhabited by *Ndee* groups; perhaps the Manansas or Quinías, identified by Spanish explorers as living on the west side of the Rio Grande along the Chama River and 10 leagues north and east of Taos.[28] As Sunday Eiselt has documented in *Becoming White Clay*, the Quinías and Manansas are likely the ancestors of both *Diné* and Jicarilla peoples, and regularly moved between the mountains and the Plains in order to hunt bison.[29]

In addition to small triangular projectile points, archaeological evidence from Rio del Oso in northern New Mexico indicates that a distinct type of thin, lipped-rim micaceous pottery is often found at *Ndee* sites in the region. While scholars continue to debate whether this ceramic type was developed by *Ndee* artisans independently or through trade relationships with northern Tiwa-speaking people, it is clear that Athabaskan-speaking groups were producing and trading micaceous pots from the 17th century onward, if not earlier.[30] At a site with significant evidence of domestic activities and large numbers of features, the lack of micaceous ceramics is notable. This trend offers some preliminary evidence for a pre-1600 *Ndee* occupation of the playa.

Several additional material and spatial lines of evidence support an occupation date sometime between 1300 and 1600 CE. The Punche Lake tipi rings are not directly associated with metal or glass artifacts as are often found in Indigenous encampments dating to the 18th and 19th centuries.[31] In addition to such shifts in Indigenous artifact assemblages following European colonization, there is some evidence that *Ndee* encampment practices also changed during the 17th and 18th centuries. In response to increased pressure from Indigenous groups competing for resources on the southern Plains as well as the threat posed by colonial settlers, defensive concerns came to play a critical role in determining camp layout. According to a study by Deni Seymour, some *Ndee* communities shifted their encampments away from open grasslands and towards elevated locations and rugged terrain. At some of these sites, work areas were located at significant distances, up to 200 meters away, from the dwellings themselves.[32] Punche Lake's location on the open expanses of the Taos Plateau, the size of the encampment, and the large number of directly associated chipped stone tools all suggest that these stone rings were constructed prior to an intensive settler colonial presence in the region.

Compared to the stone rings at Arroyo Punche and Three Basins , the Punche Lake features were significantly larger both in terms of the number of rocks associated with each ring (around 40 rocks on average) and in terms of their median interior diameter, which was approximately 6 m. Estimates of residential group size using ethnographic population numbers along with floor area calculations based on ring diameter indicates that the tipis in Area 1 could house an average of 3.7 people, for a total of approximately 107 occupants.[33] The Area 2 tipi rings are slightly smaller, housing an average of 2.5 people, for an estimated total occupation of around 64 people. While most tipi sites on the northern and southern Plains consist of one to three stone rings, large aggregated sites of 50 or more structures, as seen at Punche Lake, are not unprecedented, as the account by Vicente de Saldivar Mendoza that introduced this chapter shows. A rough estimate based on this account suggests that Mendoza had encountered an encampment of between 200 and 400 people, indicating that Indigenous groups were camping in large numbers within the modern boundaries of New Mexico during the late 16th century. A similar account written by Don Joaquin Codallos y Raba indicates that Jicarilla people continued to camp in "houses, palisade huts and other shelters" in large numbers north of Taos into the 18th century."[34]

Thirty percent of the stone rings at Punche Lake contained central rock clusters, which likely served as internal hearths. The presence of hearths at many of these features is suggestive of a more intensive domestic use of the area compared to smaller, short-term encampments identified elsewhere in New Mexico that contain fewer features, lack hearths, and have small amounts of chipped stone debitage.

Plains archeologists believe that external hearths were primarily used for cooking, whereas internal hearths provided warmth, repelled insects, and were occasionally used for cooking.[35] The pronounced absence of external hearths at Punche Lake suggests that these features were likely used for cooking as well as heating sources. While scholars previously believed that internal hearths were a marker of wintertime use, subsequent investigations using timestamped historic photographs by Gary Adams of tipi rings at York Factory along the Hudson Bay demonstrates that internal hearths were also used at summertime encampments.[36] Based on this evidence, the tipi rings at Punche Lake may have been occupied sometime during the summer or fall before water levels typically rose in the lake and when Spanish colonial documents note the presence of such "nomadic" groups in the region. For example, an account of trade at Abiquiú from 1776 states that "every year, between the end of October and the beginning of November, many heathens of the Ute Nation come to the vicinity of this pueblo."[37] Although the rings at Punche Lake predate such accounts, the documentary record gestures towards a seasonal mobility pattern in which residentially mobile groups regularly moved into the region for the purposes of trade with village-based Indigenous communities.

The large number of tipi rings at Punche Lake represent two possible encampment logics. In one scenario, all the rings in each area were occupied simultaneously for several months. Alternatively, these features could represent distinct occupations of several smaller family groups who revisited the site seasonally, establishing their tents in areas adjacent to previously used rings. Studies of encampments on the Great Plains have demonstrated that tipis in aggregated camps typically clustered into clear groupings of five to seven rings spaced 1 to 3 m apart.[38] Based on the current distribution of stone rings in the playa, there is no clear spatial clustering to support a seasonal revisitation logic within Areas 1 and 2, respectively. Furthermore, while nomadic groups would often return to specific sites, they rarely reused the same exact camping areas. Excavations conducted by Gettys's at five of these stone rings revealed that there were no living floors or caches below the surface, confirming that these features were likely not reused over time. This comparative and subsurface evidence, along with the large distance, some 120 m, separating Areas 1 and 2 point to an asynchronous occupation of the playa.

While Areas 1 and 2 both appear to represent large, single-use domestic encampments, there is evidence to suggest that these areas were occupied by groups with similar family structures. A kernel density estimation (KDE) statistic was used to assess differences in the number of rocks in each tipi ring and its diameter across Areas 1 and 2. The KDE statistic provides a means of comparing two similar distributions in a single graph and has the potential to produce one of two distributional curves, a unimodal or a bimodal curve. In this context, a unimodal curve indicates that the tipi rings are statistically consistent across Areas 1 and 2, whereas a bimodal curve would indicate that tipi morphology varies significantly between areas. The KDE for both parameters follows a unimodal normal distribution, indicating that there is no statistically significant difference in morphology across these two occupational areas. This comparison suggests that both occupational areas were inhabited by groups with similar familial size and encampment patterns.

Notably, seven rings from Area 1 and nine from Area 2 were modified to include linear lines of stone (Figure 5.6). These spaced stone rings were slightly smaller than those without interior rocks, with an average diameter of roughly 5 m. These modified features do not correspond with those excavated by Gettys. Futhermore, the linear nature of these alignments, along with the fact that this feature type is repeated in both parts of the playa, suggests that they were deliberately created.

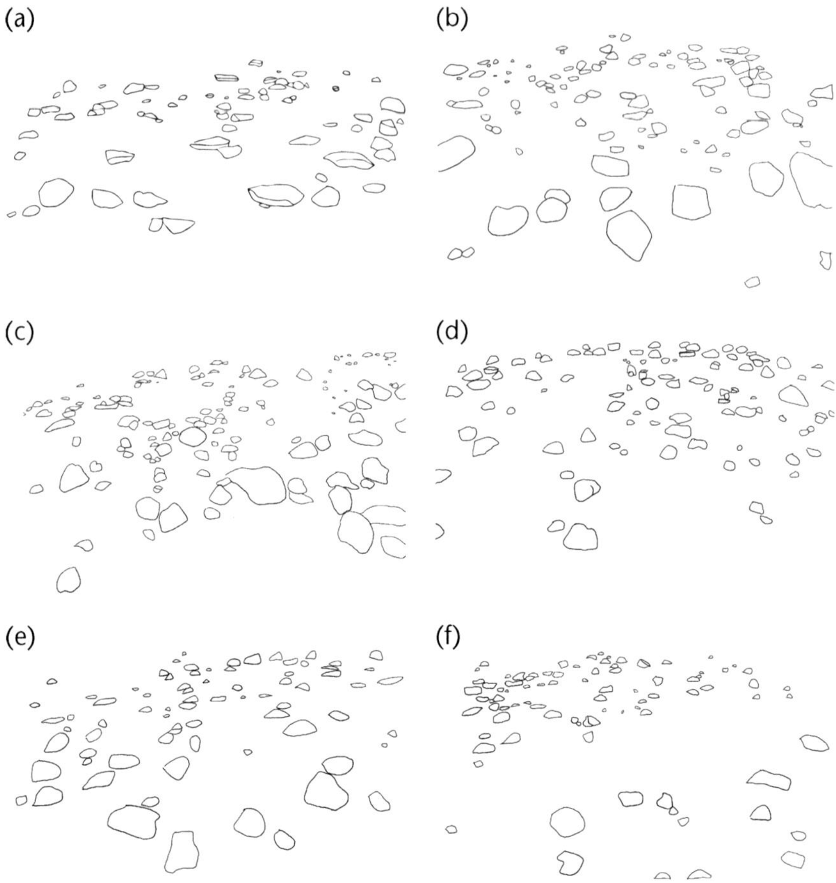

FIGURE 5.6 Modified Rock Ring Features at Punche Lake.

Ethnographic evidence drawn from across highly mobile Indigenous communities living across the Great Basin and Plains indicates that the ceremonial and cosmological importance of the lodge is inextricably linked with the structures domestic function and use.[39] This entangled approach, suggests that ritual structures often exist alongside domestic structures and that in some instances these features are one and the same. For example, according to the *Ndee* worldview, four is an important number linked to Jicarilla origins; the universe was created in four days, bounded by four sacred rivers and peaks, and oriented along the four cardinal directions.[40] Each direction is associated with a series of colors, celestial bodies, seasons, geographical referents, animals, and stories. Within this framework, the modified stone features, which are roughly oriented in a north-south and east-west direction, may be material markers of abstract ideas associated with the cosmos and communal origins.

Alternatively, these features may have been part of a material tradition associated with acts of *doing*. In reference to stone circles in Colorado, Clifford Duncan (Northern Ute) noted that, "One common ingredient in many ceremonies was stone laid upon the ground in a circle…they were not used in a uniform, structured manner. Each medicine man or spiritual person who practiced shamanism had his own ritual. Generally, the circles were used for ritual benefiting the immediate family or band."[41] Drawing on Duncan's description, the stone features at Punche Lake may have been modified as part of individually undertaken ceremonial doings oriented towards ensuring the collective well-being of the community.

Similar evidence from the northern Plains suggests that stone rings were often modified as part of communal mourning practices. For example, among the *Siksika*, when a notable person died, their body was deposited within their lodge in the place where it was last erected.[42] A circle or circle of stones were placed around the lodge along with radiating stone lines, which were said to represent aspects of the individual's life.[43] Although the exact meaning evoked by the Punche Lake spaced stone rings is currently unclear, these modified domestic structures offer compelling evidence for the entanglement of the domestic and ceremonial among residentially mobile Indigenous People. These modifications also point to the very materials ways in which locality is constantly being remade.

▼▽▼

Areas 1 and 2 contained a diverse chipped stone assemblage including large (choppers and type 2 bifaces) as well as smaller bifacial tools (knives, type 1 scrapers, and type 1 bifaces) used in more precise cutting tasks. Gettys's documented over 3,000 pieces of lithic debitage identified within Area 1, along with 172 chipped stone tools, 6 hammerstones, 9 pieces of ground stone, and 1 drill. Over 400 pieces of debitage were documented in Area 2, along with 34 chipped stone tools and a hammerstone. Cores were also recorded in association with the Area 1 and 2 features, indicating that both primary and secondary forms of tool construction were occurring. Overall, the chipped stone assemblage—particularly the high number of scrapers, which are informal tools intended for short-term use—points to the expedient construction and use of tools on-site in both areas. Comparative evidence from the central Plains suggests that these informal tools were likely produced by both men and women, who made and resharpened their own tools for hide processing .[44]

There are two types of bifaces at Punche Lake, distinguished based on edge angle and bifacial ware as well as two scraper types—one associated with scraping and another with cutting.[45] Both areas contained a larger number of scrapers relative to bifaces, indicating that the inhabitants were undertaking more fine-grained cutting tasks. The general absence of faunal remains, particularly long bones, at the site along with the high number of scrapers in both areas suggest that the initial butchering of animals occurred off-site.[46] There is also a strong statistical correlation (r-squared = .75) between the presence of type 2 scrapers used for general cutting and utilized flakes used in finer-grained tasks, suggesting that these tools may have been used together as part of a toolkit used during different phases of hide working. Variability in the mean length and width of bifaces and scrapers, also points to the use of a specialized toolkit (biface 1 standard deviation = 15.2 mm; biface 2 standard ; deviation = 17.7 mm; scraper 1 standard deviation = 20.6 mm versus scraper 2 standard deviation = 21.6 mm). The considerable variability across formal tools offers additional evidence that Punche Lake was part of residential mobility rounds rather than a logistical mobility base camp, where we would expect to see a larger proportion of simple expedient tools.

Within Area 1, there is also evidence that households may have engaged in different types of tasks. For example, several tipis are associated with larger numbers of processing rather than cutting tools (Tipi 5, 3, 1, and E in Figure 5.4), suggesting that these households may have undertaken more specialized hide working activities. Tipi 3, one of the larger features at the site (diameter = 7.5 m), was associated with a particularly dense concentration of tools and chipped stone debris. This residence was surrounded by over 800 artifacts, including a significant number of cores (n = 7) and flakes (n = 727). There were also a large number of types 1 and 2 scrapers associated with Tipi 3 (n = 28). The density of artifacts, along with its location in the middle of Area 1, suggest that this residence may have served as a centralized work area for intensive stone tool production and refurbishment.

The spatial distribution of tools across Areas 1 and 2 suggests that tool production may have been a communal activity. Such collective labor practices are documented ethnographically among Numic-speaking communities, including the *Nuutsiyu*, *Newe*, and *Nuwuvi*, in which leading households would direct logistical activities such as piñon-nut-gathering activities and pronghorn hunts.[47] A similar pattern of task leadership may be present at Punche Lake, with the leading household signaled by tipi size and artifact density. Based on these criteria, Tipis 1, 3, 5, and E in Figure 5.4 may have been important households inhabited by individuals holding a particularly important labor role within the community.

While the material assemblages from Areas 1 and 2 share many similarities, there are also some notable differences between these areas. Area 1 contained significantly more artifacts overall and six times the amount of chipped stone debitage as Area 2. This trend in part reflects the larger number of tipi rings and associated inhabitants within Area 1. However, if residential size was the only relevant factor, we might expect to see a smaller but proportional number and type of artifacts in each area, which is not the case. This discrepancy suggests that Area 2 was likely inhabited by a smaller group of *Ndee* families for a shorter period of time.

In addition to the larger quantities of debitage in Area 1, Gettys's recorded significantly more dacite cores (n = 18 vs. n = 3) in association with this encampment. A variety of core types were identified in Area 1, including "true blade" cores, more than half of which were complete, as well as resharpened and less modified pieces.[48] The three cores identified in Area 2 were not fully exploited, pointing to lower levels of primary tool production as well as offering some evidence for their use as choppers and scrapers. While the occupants of Area 2 appear to have been engaged in tool maintenance activities over a shorter duration, the greater number of cores, along with the presence of several preforms (n = 5) in Area 1, indicates that the inhabitants of this area were undertaking significantly more primary tool production; a production pattern consistent with a longer-term residency.

Furthermore, there are notably higher numbers of expedient tools in Area 2 compared to Area 1. Utilized flakes make up a greater proportion of the Area 2 assemblage and there is a higher ratio of scrapers to bifaces in Area 2 (8:1) when compared to Area 1 (4:1). These patterns reflect the expedient production of tools on-site rather than formal and more time-consuming biface reduction. The Area 2 bifacial assemblage is also less diverse overall, indicating that the Area 1 inhabitants were undertaking a greater variety of domestic tasks around hunting, gathering, and food processing.

As would be expected for a smaller encampment, Area 2 (n = 4) also contains fewer projectile points than Area 1 (n = 20). In Area 1, 85% of the points are associated with a tipi ring. As with other bifacial tools, Tipi 3 was directly surrounded by a large number of points (n = 5), offering additional evidence that this household was a central tool production and refurbishment area within the encampment. Unlike many of the projectile points in Area 1, the Area 2 points were too fragmentary to accurately type and only two of these tools were directly associated with a tipi ring. The lack of diagnostic tools in Area 2 makes it difficult to determine when this part of the playa was occupied relative to Area 1.

That the Area 1 inhabitants were undertaking a more intensive and varied set of domestic practices is further supported by the presence of groundstones (n = 9), several pieces of which appear to be portions of heavily used simple cobble manos.[49] These tools are concentrated around eight tipis (Tipi 1, 3, A, B, C, D, J, and L) and were most densely clustered around Tipis 3, L, and J, suggesting that these residences served as designated activity areas associated with stone, seed, and plant grinding. In contrast, there is no material evidence to suggest that the residents of Area 2 were engaged in similar types of food processing activities. In contrast to the robust evidence for plant and animal processing tasks in Area 1, the archaeological record in Area 2 appears to represent as a shorter-term residential encampment whose inhabitants were engaged primarily in tool refurbishment activities.

The types of raw materials used to produce stone tools at Punche Lake offer additional insights into the encampment logics of the playas' inhabitants. The lithic assemblage at Punche Lake is dominated by dacite. A sample of nine dacite artifacts were assayed by Steven Shackley using thermoScientific *Quant'X* EDXRF spectrometry, all of which sourced to the San Antonio Mountain A complex. The San Antonio Mountain A dacite source is a late Pliocene basalt shield that dominates the western portion of the Taos Plateau.[50] This raw material source is present in large nodules and was frequently used to produce bifacial tools as well as projectile points throughout the Rio Grande basin from 5500 BCE onwards.[51] As a prominent feature on the Taos Plateau, Cerro San Antonio would have been a highly visible and well-established source of raw materials. While the total number of dacite tools sampled is small this sourcing data indicates that at least some, and perhaps a significant amount, of the dacite at the site was acquired from Cerro San Antonio. This pattern of local raw material use appears to have remained consistent over a 5,000-year period, despite changes in residential mobility and subsistence strategies.

Approximately 20% of projectile points recorded at the site were made from obsidian and non-basalt flakes made up less than 2% of all the chipped stone debris at the site. A sample of 12 obsidian artifacts (7 from Area 1 and 5 from Area 2) were also assayed by Shackley.[52] A variety of local and non-local sources were identified by this analysis, including Cerro del Medio, El Rechuelos, and No Agua Peaks (Figure 5.7). El Rechuelos and del Medio are part of the pre-caldera and caldera sources of archaeological obsidian found within the Jemez Mountains. El Rechuelos obsidian was the most common material represented within the sample (n = 7) and erodes into the Chama River, the closest source for the materials used to produce projectile points at Punche Lake.[53]

In contrast, only two artifacts were made from obsidian derived from the Cerro del Medio source. This source has not eroded outside of the caldera, indicating that the Punche Lake artifacts were most likely acquired at the primary source, located over 100 km to the southwest of the playa.[55] Finally, three artifacts sourced to the No Agua Peaks West obsidian source, which lies within 5 km of Punche Lake, offering an easily accessible form of obsidian to groups residing in the area over several months. Only seen at sites on the Taos Plateau, this source is generally vitorphyric and was primarily used to produce more expedient cutting and scrapping tools.[56] Although the sample size is small, this sourcing analysis suggests that *Ndee* people residing at Punche Lake were engaged in a nested raw material procurement pattern. On the one hand, these groups were traveling over significant distances or had established trading networks, up to 100 km away, to directly procure obsidian from sources in the Chama River and Jemez Mountains. The absence of obsidian cores or large numbers of flakes in the Punche Lake assemblage indicate that this raw material was primarily entering the site in the form of finished bifacial tools. These obsidian tools signal an increasing diversification in Indigenous procurement practices linked to either long-distance mobility or trade. On the other hand, the inhabitants of the playa appear to have been largely using dacite within a day's walk from their base camp to produce tools on-site.

Mobility in the 20th century: ranching on the plateau

Gonzalez, 2011. Atencio, 1939. Ortiz, 1930. Archuleta, 1909. Marques, 1892.

These are the names pecked and incised into the basalt boulders, which encircle the western embankment of Punche Lake (Figure 5.8). To the left of these petroglyphs, beneath a small overhang, are the remnants of a temporary field camp, containing chert flakes and 50 thick black ceramic Manzano Coarse ware

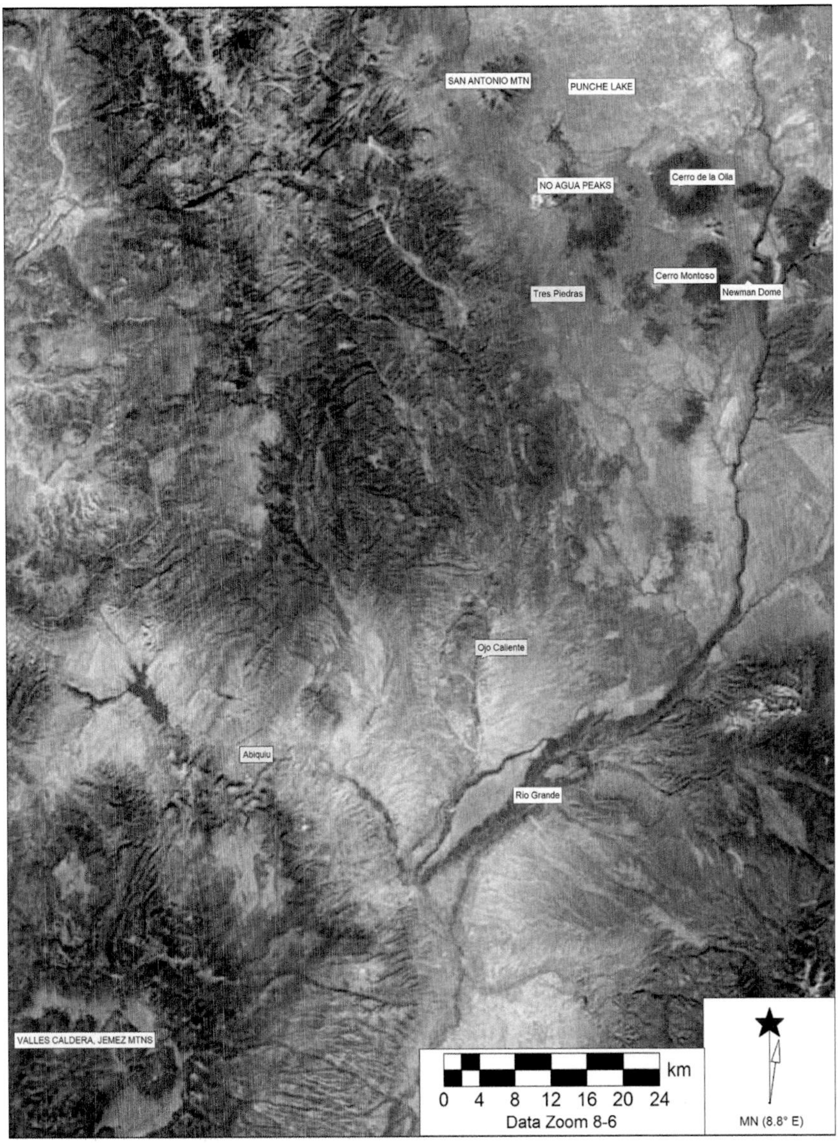

FIGURE 5.7 SPOT Image of Northern New Mexico of Dacite and Obsidian Sources Identified at Punche Lake.[54]

sherds.[57] These ceramics are part of a material assemblage that is distinct from earlier occupations of the playa marked by chipped stone tool technologies overwhelmingly made from locally available dacite. Whether these ceramics were produced by "Indigenous" people or "settlers" however, is less clear. As Jun Sunseri has argued in relation to Manzano culinary wares at Casitas Viejas, the ethnic identity of the consumers and producers of this ceramic type

FIGURE 5.8 Pecked Petroglyphs at Punche Lake.

is somewhat ambiguous. Communities on the northern frontier often blurred the boundaries between "Indio" and Hispano," obscuring simple one-to-one correlations between ethnicity and material culture.[58]

The foundations of three-square wooden corrals are located on the southwest wall of the playa. These structures along with numerous bottles, rusted buckets, and lightweight metal fragments offer additional evidence for a 19th or early-20th century occupation of the playa. These materials signal a new occupational logic likely associated with the presence of *Taoseño* herders moving sheep, goats, and cattle across the Taos Plateau.[59] Ethnographic interviews with New Mexican herders along with comparable archaeological evidence from southern Colorado suggest that it was common for young men and boys to create these types of penning structures over the course of seasonal summer herding of livestock.[60]

Hispano settlers referred to the west side of the Gorge as *La Otra Banda*, translated loosely as "the other side"—an area which remained relatively "unsettled" for much of the 18th and 19th centuries.[61] During this period, seasonal transhumance on the Otra Banda gradually expanded as sheep herding became a viable and exportable industry.[62] A report written by Governor Fernando de Chacón in 1803 conveys the increasing importance of herding to New Mexico's economy:

> Although the Province possesses sufficient oxen for farming, what is most in abundance is sheep. Without counting what is consumed locally, there is exported to Vizcaya and the lesser presidios from one year to the next twenty-five to twenty-six thousand head of sheep. Of swine there exists no great number because the natives of this country are more accustomed to the use of fat from beef than from hogs, and there is no one dedicated to the manufacture of soap. The raising of horses and mules is little encouraged because of the continual raids by the enemy [Indians].[63]

By the 1820s, the sheep population in New Mexico had grown to over 200,000 and rancher-merchants had expanded their ranges out of the Rio Grande Valley to the north and east.[64]

Sheep pastoralism shifted human engagements with playa landscapes, like Punche Lake, and movement across the Taos Plateau. The Spanish land grant system introduced a distinctive way of legally dividing up land. This system created proprietary grants allotted to individuals or communities of ten or more families. This land-use system led to the formation of small, isolated villages within micro-basins, transforming the northern Rio Grande into bundled territories centered on "the community."[65] The territorial extent of a community's land holdings was largely defined by local topography, creating boundaries that appeared jagged and dispersed. In addition to small-scale community grants, Spanish colonial officers also administered sitios, or ranch grants, which significantly varied in size. Sheep herding encampments associated with these ranching grants were environmentally low-impact and distributed across the landscape.

Accompanying this emergent herding economy was a unique pattern of movement which entailed year-round residency in permanent settlements to the east of the Rio Grande Gorge and short-term movements onto the Plateau during seasonal grazing rounds. As the petroglyphs and penning structures demonstrate, Punche Lake likely served as a natural source of seasonal water for herders moving across the landscape as part of this transhumance pattern. Within this model, *La Otra Banda* was not a place "to live" per se, but rather a natural resource to be used intermittently. Indeed, as of 1897, no Spanish land grants had been issued on the Plateau and no homestead plots had been confirmed or reserved in the area despite having been surveyed by US government officials.[66]

There are several rock-lined features across the playa, which point to a more intensive occupation sometime during the early 20th century in association with cattle ranchg. For example, a 4 × 4 m square rock-line foundation is perched on top of the southern rim of the playa and is surrounded by a variety of metal objects dating to this period. Within the basin itself there are three linear rock alignments oriented in a north-east direction. These alignments range in length from 6 to 19 m and are comprised of anywhere between 40 and 80 small to medium-sized rocks. There are also 12 other rock piles at the site, ranging in size from 15–100 rocks, some of which are associated with purple glass. BLM records indicate that a patent was never formally filed under the Homestead Act for the Punche Lake area, suggesting that these structures likely date to the late 20th century once the area had become public lands leased to ranchers. These linear and circular rock features may have served as boundary markers, supports for fence posts, or the remains of former structures made by cattle ranchers using the area.[67] As will be discussed in greater detail in the following section, cattle ranching was associated with a intensive pastroal land-use pattern which included the construction of more durable architectural structures and distinct modes of dividing space.

Arroyo Punche and Three Basins

Arroyo Punche and Three Basins both have a layered occupational history that resembles the cultural palimpsest discussed above. Arroyo Punche is a now-desiccated playa situated on the open grasslands of the Plateau, approximately 14 km east of Cero San Antonio and roughly 11 km west of the Rio Grande Gorge. The basin is bounded on the west by an arroyo, which connects together a series of small basins running from the base of La Segita Peak across the Plateau. A non-collection-based survey of the playa and its surrounding areas revealed three overlapping activity areas representing discrete uses of the playa over time (Figure 5.9).

As at Punche Lake, the earliest component at Arroyo Punche is marked by isolated diagnostic projectile points associated with an Indigenous use of the area sometime between 1800 BCE and 400 CE. Five small rock rings loosely clustered into two groupings indicate that Numic- and/or Athabaskan-speaking peoples visited this playa sometime after the 15th century. Finally, the playa also contains material evidence of 19th or early 20th century ranching, including two rectangular rock-lined structures associated with cans, nails, glass, and metal debris.

The Three Basins playa is located approximately 20 km to the east of Cerro San Antonio and 6 km west of the Rio Grande Gorge. The site covers a roughly 1,000 × 600 m area bounded on the northwest side by three playas (Figure 5.10). This expansive area is broadly divided into two activity centers. Area 1 is located in the northwest portion of the survey zone and consists of 12 loosely clustered rock rings likely made by Numic- and/or Athabaskan-speaking groups moving through the area. Situated to the southeast, Area 2 is associated with a single tipi ring as well as two rock cairns, and a semicircular rock pile. Both areas contained discrete lithic scatters comprised predominantly of dacite flakes. A large rock-lined structure within the Three Basins survey area indicates that this playa was also occupied during the early 20th century.

The "old" mobility model: the logic of playa lithic scatters

The archaeological record at Arroyo Punche and Three Basins indicates that playa landscapes were used by residentially mobile Indigenous Peoples in distinct ways. While Punche Lake appears to have been used exclusively as an intercept hunting location, the archaeological record at Arroyo Punche suggests that Indigenous groups were both hunting and producing tools on-site. At Arroyo Punche, two

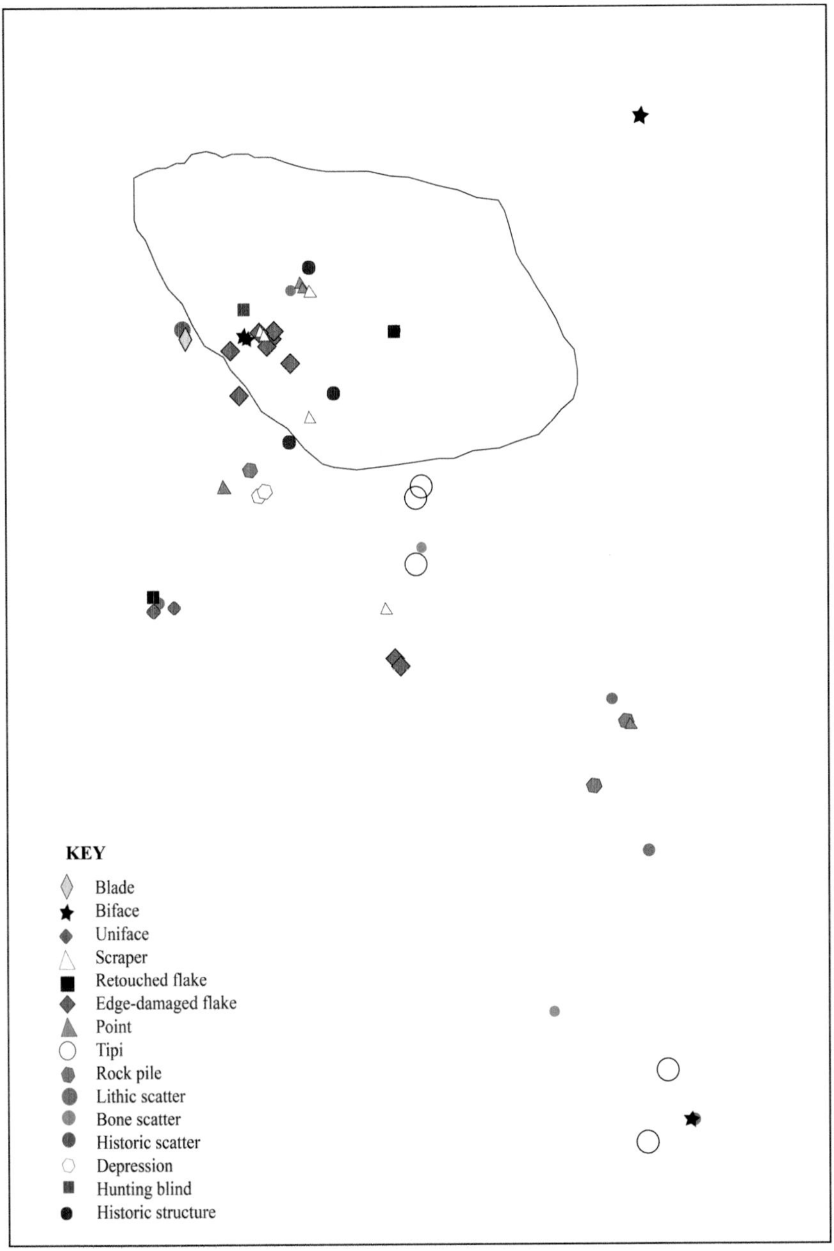

FIGURE 5.9 Map of Arroyo Punche.

stemmed dacite points produced between 1800 BCE–400 CE were recorded along the northwest rim of the playa (Figure 5.2f and g). Both of these points had fragmentary bases, a breakage pattern caused by either missing the intended target or fracturing upon contact during intercept hunting.[68]

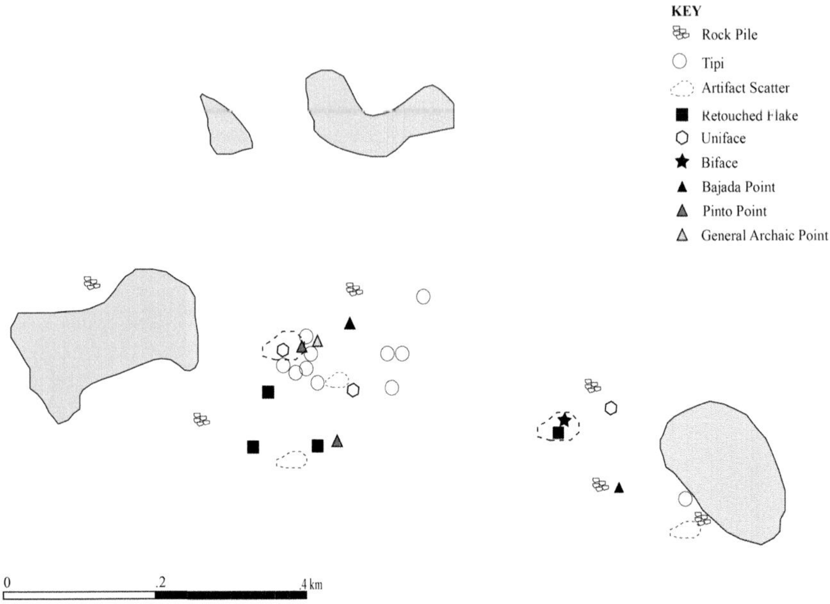

FIGURE 5.10 Map of Three Basins.

These two points are located between the playa's edge (approximately 40 m away) and a series of rock features, including three rock cairns (1–2.8 m in diameter) and a U-shaped alignment comprised of 30 medium-large basalt rocks (Figure 5.9). A similar communal hunting complex documented by Jason LaBelle and Spence Pelton in Colorado, suggests that the Arroyo Punche structure may have been used as part of a cooperative intercept hunting strategy. At the Olson site, LaBelle and Pelton recorded cairns and rock walls used by Indigenous hunters to drive mountain game downslope along the alpine tundra towards hunting blinds.[69] These sorts of communal hunting practices have also been documented ethnographically among the Panamint Shoshone who took advantage of the herd-centered nature of bighorn sheep by startling animals so they would run upslope to hunters hiding behind rock-lined hunting blinds at the top of hills or along game trails.[70] Similar types of communal hunting strategies have also been documented ethnographically by Omar Steward among the *Nuutsiyu*, *Nuwuvi*, and *Numu* who used a variety of strategies including pitfalls, ambushing, running sheep past hidden hunters, and driving sheep into V-shaped enclosures.[71]

Not all game drives were as intensively used or as complex as those recorded in the Great Basin. Indeed, medium-sized game, like elk and deer, tend to aggregate in small groups, facilitating slow, controlled hunts during which few animals were selectively taken.[72] On the open expanses of the Taos Plateau, hunting blinds, which are typically between 1.1 and 2.7 m in interior diameter, rather than game drives, would have been particularly effective.[73] The construction and size (2.3 m in diameter) of the u-shaped alignment at Arroyo Punche suggests that it was likely used as a hunting blind. This U-shaped alignment has an opening which faces away from the playa's edge, suggesting that it was used to hide one or two hunters from medium-sized game approaching the lake bed from the east.

In addition to these projectile points, several isolated formal tools were documented across the site, which show evidence of deliberate bifacial or unifacial working over more than 50% of the tool's edges.[74] Despite differences in tool function, the 6 bifaces and 4 scrapers documented at Arroyo Punche were consistently sized (approximately 5.37 × 4 cm). Scholars have argued that the importance of portability for hunting-gathering groups places some basic limits on both the total number and diversity of artifacts these groups used while encouraging tool standardization—assessed using the ratio of length-width-thickness of an artifact.[75] Based on this logic, the high levels of tool standardization at Arroyo Punche suggest that the producers of these tools were practicing comparatively high levels of mobility.

There is a notable absence of evidence for primary stage tool production in the form of cores or evidence of cortex on 80% of the stone tools at Arroyo Punche. Rather than a site for tool production, Arroyo Punche was likely part of a broader logistical mobility pattern linked to the seasonal acquisition of different wild game and plant resources within the piñon-juniper woodlands of surrounding mountains. Unlike residential mobility, logistical mobility entails frequent forays mounted from residential locales to conduct specialized tasks, such as raw material procurement, hunting, or gathering specific plant resources.[76]

Similar isolated projectile points were identified at the Three Basins site, suggesting that this playa was also part of a logistical mobility circuit. Specifically, five points were identified across the site, four of which were complete enough to be identified typologically: two Bajada points (4800–3200 BCE) and two Pinto points (3200–1800 BCE). The Bajada points both had cleanly fractured tips and lacked evidence of reworking suggesting that they were likely broken upon impact during an intercept hunting event. In contrast, the Pinto points each had distinct breakage patterns. One of the Pinto points was complete and made from dacite. Due to the large quantities of easily accessible workable dacite on the Plateau, Indigenous Peoples using the area may not have been particularly concerned about raw material accessibility, suggesting that this particular point may have simply been discarded on-site after serving its purpose. Alternatively, it could have been left behind, following a variety of activities associated with hunting, including a missed shot, an incident where the point traveled through the animal completely, or the point may have simply fallen from its haft after being removed from the animal.[77]

The other Pinto point was made from a white-pink banded chert resembling materials from Pedernal Peak described by Kirk Bryan as

> ...commonly white to pearly gray in color though in places the color may vary considerably. Near the base and sometimes near the top the chert shows

> bands ¼" and ½" thick and is black in color. In places near the op weathering has changed the color to pink, red, or yellow.[78]

Pedernal Peak, also referred to as *Tsiping,* or "flaking stone mountain," by the Tewa, is the primary source for this type of chert, and is located some 160 km south of the Taos Plateau.[79] Secondary sources of Pedernal cobbles can also be found within the Rio Puerco, Rio Jemez, and Rio Grande.[80] Preliminary observations from the middle Rio Grande Valley suggest that the more colorful varieties of Pedernal chert, such as red-spotted, yellow, pink, and purple, are found in greater numbers at primary outcrops, offering some evidence for a long-distance north-south residential mobility pattern.[81]

The ears of the chert Pinto point at Three Basins were retouched; evidence of a tool curation strategy. This reuse pattern differs from the dacite Pinto point, suggesting that the accessibility and quality of raw materials played an important role in shaping tool discard patterns. While non-local resources like Pedernal chert are more likely to be curated and reworked, dacite is ubiquitous on the Plateau suggesting that dacite tools were more likely to be discarded prior to exhaustion. Of course, Three Basins is simply one site. A more robust understanding of the relationship between raw material accessibility and tool discard will require a broader study examining similar isolated tools across the northern Rio Grande.

Research by Bradley Vierra and Teralene Fox suggest that from roughly 4800 and 1800 BCE Indigenous Peoples in the region were engaged in a residential mobility circuit that moved in a north-south direction between the San Luis and Rio Grande Valleys. Around 1800 BCE, this residential mobility circuits contracted.[82] The isolated points from Arroyo Punche and Three Basins suggests that these playas were used as logistical activity areas associated with intercept hunting, rather than residential sites, within this localized seasonal mobility pattern. Playas were most attractive to wildlife, particularly during the early spring when water levels would be at their highest and during the late summer/early fall when residual salts would accumulate in the dry-lake bottoms. Although there is no direct means of pinpointing the seasonality of such logistical visits from surface assemblages, the predictable ebb and flow of intermittent water sources like playas likely played an important role in shaping Indigenous use patterns in this high desert climate.

▼▽▼

In addition to evidence of intercept hunting, the archaeological record at Arroyo Punche and Three Basins indicates that Indigenous Peoples were refurbishing tools on-site. There are six non-diagnostic lithic scatters with high frequencies of shatter (i.e., angular debris) at Arroyo Punche. The preponderance of dacite shatter at the site suggests that its occupants were using a technique focused on expedient flake production, rather than more intensive forms of bifacial reduction. The Arroyo Punche scatters resemble assemblages in northwestern New Mexico assigned by

Patricia Hicks to the "Late Archaic", roughly 1800 BCE–400 CE.[83] These trends suggest that Arroyo Punche may have been used by Indigenous activity groups during the transition towards a more localized pattern of residential mobility centered on the northern Rio Grande.

The scatters at Arroyo Punche fall into two broadly defined categories: small, discrete scatters of 5 to 18 flakes (n = 3), and larger, more dispersed scatters of between 60 and 160 pieces of chipped stone debitage (n = 3). The three smallest chipped stone concentrations represent isolated temporary occupations of the site and were comprised exclusively of dacite debris produced during tool refurbishment. The predominance of dacite within these scatters provides evidence for the intensive use of local raw materials linked to a more concentrated mobility pattern focused on upland-lowland movement.[84]

The larger scatters at Arroyo Punche had a more diverse assortment of raw materials. For example, Scatter 3 contained over 100 dacite flakes, 20 chert flakes of various colors, and several obsidian flakes. These large scatters are also associated with small numbers of formal dacite tools, such as blades (Scatter 2) and scrapers (Scatter 3), as well as more expedient tools, including retouched flakes and unifaces (Scatter 1). The low ratio of tools to flakes at these scatters (0.013, 0.006, and 0.044, respectively) suggests that these areas were associated with tool maintenance, rather than on-site use.

While making up a small proportion of the total assemblage at large lithic scatters (approximately 6.5%), chert was more common than obsidian (only 1%) in these assemblages. When compared to obsidian, chert is a stronger, more versatile material that can be used to produce expedient all-purpose tools rather than more specialized bifacial tools. The absence of finished chert tools associated with these large scatters suggests that such all-purpose tools were likely curated rather than discarded after use. This curation strategy is consistent with complimentary evidence that Indigenous people at Arroyo Punche were participating in a long-distance mobility or trade network associated with the acquisition of chert from Pedrnal Peak.[84]

To summarize, the chipped stone assemblage at Arroyo Punche offers evidence for two distinct activity patterns. The small scatters are spatially discrete and comprised primarily of dacite debitage, suggesting that they were single-use activity areas associated with tool refurbishment. In contrast, the large scatters at Arroyo Punche are dispersed, suggesting that they were produced over the course of multiple visitations to the site. These areas also contain non-local materials including obsidian and Pedernal chert, offering evidence for a more diversified set of procurement patterns associated with long-distance travel or trade. Whether representing accumulative visitations by Indigenous foragers as part of a long-distance travel circuit or isolated activity areas by individuals engaged in a more localized mobility network, playas appear to have been considered advantageous stopping places associated with water and potential game resource.

Similar to the Arroyou Punche scatters, the five lithic scatters at Three Basins primarily consist of tertiary flakes associated with tool refurbishment, suggesting that this location was also used as a logistical activity area. All of the Three Basins scatters are relatively discrete and include small concentrations of between four and 40 pieces of chipped stone debris (Figure 5.11).

The Three Basin lithic scatters are primarily associated with informal tools, including three unifaces and four retouched flakes that show minimal levels of bifacial or unifacial working. These expedient tools were likely used on-site as part of coordinated task-group activities before being discarded. These scatters were also more materially diverse than those at Arroyo Punche, each containing obsidian, chert, and quartzite flakes. Notably, obsidian made up 32% of the chipped stone assemblage at Three Basins overall, a significantly greater quantity when compared to both Punche Lake (22%) and Arroyo Punche (1%). Without additional raw material sourcing studies, it is difficult to assess whether the obsidian at Three Basins reflects an increased use of local raw materials or long distance mobility or trade.[85] However, the higher frequency of obsidian within this playa does suggest that the occupants of the site had integrated obsidian into their raw material procurement pattern to a greater degree.

The lithic assemblages from Arroyo Punche and Three Basins draw attention to the various ways in which surface collections obscure correlations between tool type and human behavior. Instead of representing clearly defined patterns of mobility, these undiagnostic scatters reveal similarities in how Indigenous groups were using playa landscapes over time. Over a roughly 6,000-year period, both playas appear to have been used by different groups of Indigenous foragers as logistical activity areas rather than as base camps. The general paucity of faunal remains at these sites suggests that if hunting did occur nearby, the carcasses were likely removed intact or in pieces to a nearby longer-term campsite.[86] This hunting-butchering strategy would have been particularly feasible when targeting medium-sized game, such as mule deer or antelope, both of which are commonly found across the Plateau.[87]

The reason why these playas may have been such attractive activity sites over time in part lies in their unique ecology. Playas contain biotic communities of water-tolerant bulrushes, sedge, and cattails that are distinct from the surrounding piñon-juniper forests of the Upper Sonoran life zone (7,500 ft).[88] As a seasonal source of water, salt, and plant life, these playas would have consistently attracted a variety of fauna as well as humans to the area. As unique natural resource niches playas have functioned as persistent and specialized resource procurement places despite shifts in Indigenous mobility patterns over time.

The "new" mobility model: short logistical camps

Much like Punche Lake, there is archaeological evidence that Arroyo Punche and Three Basins were occupied by Indigenous groups using hide tipis sometime after the 16th century. The "new" Indigenous use of these playas was significantly less intensive than the encampments at Punche Lake, indicating that Numic- and/or Athabaskan-speaking groups engaged in a variety of residential mobility strategies on the Taos Plateau.

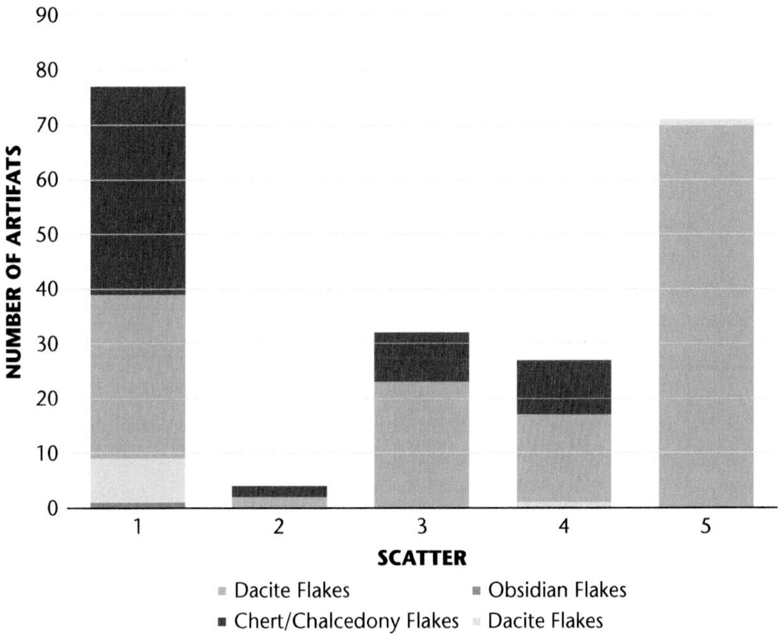

FIGURE 5.11 Distribution of Flakes and Tools by Raw Material Type at Three Basins.

Several of the scatters at Three Basins were directly associated with rock alignments and piles clustered around the central playa (Figure 5.9). The largest of these features is located on the north side of the basin near the playa's edge and is comprised of 40 piled rocks. The other two smaller rock piles are situated on the south side of the same basin. Although similar types of rock features were made by Tiwa-speaking people in the northern Rio Grande, the features documented at Three Basins more closely resemble rock alignments, piles, and cairns documented in the Great Basin.[89] Specifically, comparable features from the California area indicate that Algonkian- and Athabaskan-speaking peoples began constructing rock complexes sometime after their arrival to the area around 900 CE.[90] Parallel evidence of cairns, stonewalls, and semicircular rock features from the Colorado indicate that these types of features were used by mountain-adapted Numic-speaking peoples sometime after the 10th century.[91] These regional studies suggest that many of the rock piles and alignments identified on the Taos Plateau were likely made by Numic- or Athabaskan-speaking activity groups moving through the northern Rio Grande area sometime after the 10th century.

The location of these features within or surrounding one of the low-lying playas at Three Basins, rules out their use in power or "vision" quests, which occur in high spaces throughout the American West.[92] Furthermore, these three cairns do not appear to have been used in hunting or trapping activities or as burial markers as identified in the Great Basin. Alternatively, evidence from the northern Plains suggests that cairns can mark areas where lithic raw materials were available or where materials had been cached in rock piles for future use.[93] Drawing on this evidence, the rock cairns at Three Basins may have been used by Numic- and/or Athabaskan-speaking groups as landscape markers identifying this playa as an important source of water or to signal the storage of raw material.

The Three Basins site also contained ten stone ring features clustered into three groupings within a large open area separating two of the playas. The large spatial divisions between these stone rings suggest that they likely represent distinct occupational events. Each of these occupational events follows a slightly different encampment pattern, which may map onto distinct territorial rounds and mobility circuits. Tipi Cluster 1 is the largest encampment with five stone rings arranged in a somewhat U-shaped pattern (Tipi Cluster 1 in Figure 5.9). This tipi cluster is associated with a dispersed scatter of over 70 pieces of chipped stone debris dominated by obsidian and chert secondary and tertiary flakes pointing to the refurbishment of bifacial tools manufactured off-site. The presence of chert and obsidian flakes from the south along with the size of this encampment suggests that this encampment was likely inhabited for a short period by a group of extended family members traveling together as part of a larger residential mobility north-south circuit across the Plateau.

Tipi Cluster 2 consists of a roughly linear alignment of three tipis. Two of these features are similarly sized while one appears to be significantly larger (4 m), perhaps a reflection of individual status or a larger family size, often these were linked. These features are associated with a smaller quantity of obsidian and chert flakes (n = 4) compared to Tipi Cluster 1 (Tipi Cluster 2 in Figure 5.9). The presence of obsidian and chert, suggests that the residents of both Tipi Clusters 1 and 2 were engaged in similar north-south mobility circuits. While the small number of flakes in Cluster 2, partially reflects the size of the encampment, it also suggests that its inhabitants where moving more quickly across the landscape, perhaps in association with raiding or trading activities rather than seasonal domestic activities.

A third grouping of two rocks rings (3.2 m in diameter) was identified at Three Basins and was not directly associated with any artifacts (Tipi Cluster 3 in Figure 5.9). The small size of this encampment along with the lack of associated artifacts suggests that these features may have been part of a "cold camp" associated with task-specific activity groups rather than extended families.[94]

Arroyo Punche also contains several rock features, including, five small rock rings clustered into two discrete groups: a cluster of three rings roughly 50m from the playas edge and a group of two rings located 500 m south (Figure 5.8). Although it is difficult to determine fine-grained sequential occupations from surface collections alone, the significant spatial divide between these two clusters of stone rings offers preliminary evidence for two temporally distinct occupations of the playa. Overall, these features shared similar morphological traits and were comprised of evenly spaced medium-sized rocks with an interior diameter of 2.4–2.9 m.

Although tipi size may reflect a myriad of social factors, including wealth and status, it can also serve as a proxy for the number of individuals present at the site.[95] The dimensions of the tipi rings at Arroyo Punche suggest that they could hold between one and two people comfortably, signaling to a relatively short-term small-group occupation.[96]

Some additional insights into the encampment logics of playas is found in the small scatter of dacite secondary and tertiary flakes and bifacial tools associated with the Area 2 tipis at Arroyo Punche. In addition to providing evidence of tool refurbishment by the inhabitants of these tipis, the Area 2 assemblage fits a discard prior to exhaustion pattern. In contrast, there were no artifacts directly associated with the three tipis in Area 1 of the playa. The general absence of artifacts around these rings mirror archaeological site patterns on the northern and southern Plains, offering some insights into occupational length or at least occupational intensity at the site. The lack of evidence for formal domestic activities suggests that these structures are likely short-term encampments associated with logistical activities rather than a large-scale encampment, like Punche Lake, typically occupied for several months.[97]

Unlike the evidence from Punche Lake, there were no diagnostic artifacts associated with the stone rings at Arroyo Punche and Three Basins. This pattern is typical of temporary encampments made by residentially mobile groups and indicates that these playa sites were used as short-term stopping places associated with logistical trips into the area rather than as base camps within an annual mobility cycle of seasonal dispersion and aggregation. Overall, the diversity of stone circle arrangements and associated assemblages across playa sites on the Plateau obscure attempts to create a definitive "site type" for such mobile communities. Instead, this evidence draws our attention to the decentralized structure of Numic- and/or Athabaskan-speaking communities, in which individuals and family groups moved autonomously across the landscape, engaging in a wide variety and intensity of activities.

Mobility in the 20th century: grants and parcels

Typically, from the well-watered coastal areas in the North American East, the Anglo-American settlers that entered the Plateau during the mid-19th century were in many ways unprepared for the constraints of New Mexico's environment.[98] Unlike, the more ephemeral encampments left by Hispano sheepherders, Anglo-American settlers brought with them a model of land use based on occupation and ownership.[99] The Homestead Act codified these notions and imposed a new cartographic logic onto the Taos Plateau, carving the landscape into linear and clearly defined grids. Under this law, land was granted to claimants who could prove that they had "occupied" and/or "improved" the land continuously for 5 years. Although originally focused on cultivation, later versions of the Homestead Act expanded the criteria to include timbering and ranching.[100] Unlike community-centric Spanish land grants, these parcels were alloted to individuals and imposed over top of existing topographic features rather than shaped around them.

Federal surveyors tasked with implementing this new settlement system arrived in New Mexico as early as 1855. These men typically neglected homesteading, instead promoting cattle ranching and land speculation through silent partnerships with politicians known as the Santa Fe Ring.[101] Beginning around 1920, there was a sudden surge in land-claim filings on the Taos Plateau by Taoseño and non-Hispano immigrants with the Government Land Office. Spurring this shift was a cycle of wet years that made the open grasslands particularly appealing to young men, returning from World War I in search of employment and a new beginning.[102] While the northern borderlands of New Mexico never became intensively settled, late-19th- and early-20th-century efforts at homesteading and ranching have had long-lasting and deleterious effects on the landscape.

The material residues of this settlement boom and cartographic logic are signaled by corner boundary markers, barbed wire fence lines, and the matrix of two-track roads which now crisscross the Plateau.[103] For example, across the north side of Three Basins are a series of rock piles placed in a semicircular arrangement around the eastern edge of the southern basin. These rock piles are evenly spaced, separated by about 100 m each, with barbed wire remnants strewn in between. Patented in 1874, in DeKalb, Illinois, barbed wire became a staple of the American ranching landscape, carving up large tracks of space into visually identifiable and legally defined territories based on orthogonal grids.[104] The remnants of this fencing system are interrupted by ATV tracks and the traces of a once-used dirt road lined with basalt rocks. These modifications and boundary markers were likely put in place by the state of New Mexico, which purchased this track of land (Township 30N, Range 11E, Section 15) in July 1933.[105]

The Three Basins site also contains material evidence of permanent residency in the form of a large, roughly rectangular rock structure accompanied by metal can fragments. These durable material markers are juxtaposed to the more ephemeral traces left by Hispano sheepherders which typically went unrecognized by American settlers who viewed "land use" in terms of permanent architecture and commercial agriculture. The archaeological record of Arroyo Punche also contained scatters of metal can fragments and glass bottles (e.g., a Dacars Breakfast cocoa can). "Breakfast cocoa" was an official term used to refer to high-fat mass-produced cocoa powder, which would have served as an easy morning meal.

The reliance on store-bought canned food is a distinctive feature of 20th century life on the Taos Plateau. In contrast to settlements in the Rio Grande Valley at which gardening and canning appears to be more common, there is a notable lack of evidence for food production on the Plateau. This pattern partially reflects the harsh realities of life in a high-altitude desert scrub environment, unhospitable to subsistence gardening or agriculture.[106] The already denuded vegetation and unforgiving climate of the area also made large-scale commercial ranching difficult, forcing many homesteaders to take up alternative jobs, like cutting fence posts or shaping cross ties for the Denver and Rio Grande Railroad. As a result, many homesteaders chose to purchase their food rather than attempt to grow their own.[107]

Despite these challenging conditions, settlers did file claims on the Plateau. A claim was filed with the US government for the area encompassing Arroyo Punche by Antonio C. Pacheco in June of 1940. Pacheco's patent was made under the 1916 Homestead Entry-Stock Raising Act (39 Stat. 862), which gave settlers 640 acres of public land explicitly for cattle ranching.

Two rectangular rock-lined foundations located along the edge of the basin may have been built and inhabited by Pacheco and offer material evidence of homesteading and ranching at the site. These structures were associated with a range of construction and building materials, including plaster and wire nails, as well as ceramics, metal cans, and various pieces of colorless, blue, and amethyst glass. While Pacheco may have used these structures following his patent claim, these materials suggest that they were more likely built and occupied during New Mexico's "territorial period," which lasted from 1850 to 1912. For example, amethyst-colored glass was particularly popular during the 1840s and early 1880s.[108] Furthermore, the remnants of plaster associated with these rock foundations was most commonly used in house construction prior to the 1930s and 1940s, after which time drywall became the preferred building material.[109] Finally, there were several bullet casings, including a .44 Winchester shell associated with these structures. The .44 Winchester was introduced to Euro-American consumers in 1873 by the Winchester Repeating Arms Company. This gun became so popular over the course of the next 20 years that it was affectionately referred to as "the gun that won the West" by settlers of the period.[110]

Regardless of who the structures at Arroyo Punche and Three Basins, these materials signal an important transition in land-use logics from the Indigenous inhabitants of these playas. While playas appear to have remained important sources of freshwater access and attractive hunting locations, as evidenced by the bullet shells at Arroyo Punche, they also became sites of permanent occupation. This transition marks a move from an extensive ephemeral land-use pattern to an intensive one.

▼▽▼

The material records at Punche Lake, Arroyo Punche, and Three Basins reveal some of the challenges that accompany the archaeology of mobility. As was outlined in Chapter 4, assigning a cultural and temporal affiliation to lithic scatters that lack diagnostic artifacts poses a significant interpretive hurdle to understanding the evolving nature of raw material procurement, stone tool production patterns, and associated mobility circuits. However, differences in the proportion of material and flake types provide a rough means of lumping sites into broad temporal categories. When diagnostic projectile points are present, we can make more precise arguments about what time frame a particular playa may have been used; however, these categories remain broad. Interpreting isolated tools is further complicated by the tendency for Indigenous groups to revisit particular sites over time. While spatial analyses of these surface artifacts provide one means of differentiating between occupational episodes; these patterns are skewed by processes of displacement, which create the impression of a single large event.

A similar set of issues bely the analysis of stone circles and associated materials. Determining occupational sequences and assigning these features to a temporal and/or cultural group are complicated by the often-broad temporal categories assigned to chipped stone tools, similarities in tool types across groups, and the effects of erosion and displacement. For stone rings, as with other rock features, the ethnographic and oral historical record offer one culturally grounded method for developing hypotheses about these enigmatic structures which often held multiple meanings and functions. Despite these limitations, the archaeological record at these playa sites can and does offer some insights into how human communities engaged with these seasonal water features over time.

From roughly 5500 BCE to 400 CE Indigenous communities used these playas as logistical activity areas. Projectile points identified along the rim of Punche Lake indicate that this playa was primarily used as a seasonal hunting site between 5500 and 1800 BCE, although there are some tools that indicate such hunting activities continued at the site up until 400 CE. Notably, the Punche Lake points dating to this period are made almost exclusively of dacite, suggesting that Punche Lake may have been part of a localized logistical mobility circuit involving the procurement of dacite from Cerro San Antonio.

Although diagnostic projectile points at Arroyo Punche and Three Basins indicate that they were used during different time periods (Arroyo Punche 1800 BCE–400 CE and Three Basins 4800 BCE–1800 BCE), both chipped stone assemblages contain evidence of intercept hunting and tool refurbishment. These sites are associated with a diverse set of raw materials, including various types of obsidian and Pedernal chert. The presence of non-local materials at Arroyo Punche and Three Basins present an important counterpoint to evidence along the west rim of the Rio Grande Gorge, which is marked by a nearly continuous scatter of largely non-local lithic materials from the Espanola Basin to the San Luis Valley. As a result, the west rim has been perceived as the primary travel corridor for Indigenous Peoples moving north and south through the region between 5500 BCE and 400 CE.[111] In contrast, sites dating to this period within the interior of the Taos Plateau are typically dominated by dacite, suggestive of a more localized exploitation of the area. The Three Basins and Arroyo Punche materials complicate this picture, indicating that Indigenous peoples were not only moving north and south along the Rio Grande during this period but also moving east and west across the Plateau.

In addition to evidence of logistical hunting and mobility, all of the playa landscapes examined here contained stone circles likely constructed by Numic- and/or Athabaskan-speaking peoples. The material record at Punche Lake, Arroyo Punche, and Three Basins reveals two distinct occupational logics: low-intensity logistical mobility sites and high-intensity residential aggregations. The archeological record at Arroyo Punche and Three Basins fits within a "low-intensity" model, characterized by clusters of 2–5 tipi rings and small numbers of associated chipped stone artifacts. The secondary and tertiary debris associated with some tipi rings at these playas suggests that these households were primarily refurbishing rather than producing tools on-site—a strategy consistent with long-distance residential mobility. This interpretation is supported by the presence of non-local obsidian and chert. The absence of external features like hearths as well as the paucity of groundstone and bifacial tools associated with these features strongly suggest that Arroyo Punche and Three Basins were short-term logistical sites revisited multiple times by activity groups moving across the Taos Plateau during seasonal journeys through the northern Rio Grande.

Unlike the stone rings documented at Three Basins and Arroyo Punche, the encampment at Punche Lake is significantly larger both in terms of scale and intensity of occupation. The stone circles identified across Areas 1 and 2 at Punche Lake as well as the thousands of chipped stone debris, formal, and informal tools associated with them are indicative of significant levels of plant and animal processing activities as well as tool manufacture and refurbishment. The large numbers of formal tools made from dacite at this site, particularly when compared to Arroyo Punche and Three Basins, suggests that the Indigenous inhabitants of this playa were primarily using locally available materials—a pattern that is consistent with a medium-term occupation of the area. The small numbers of obsidian flakes and finished tools at Punche Lake indicate that its inhabitants were also traveling or trading across significant distances to acquire raw materials.

Overall, the archaeological record within the Punche Lake basin indicates that this playa was used as a seasonal residential settlement on at least two separate occasions. Diagnostic projectile points associated with these stone rings strongly suggest that an aggregated group of *Ndee* people occupied both areas sometime after the 15th century. Drawing on the Jicarilla concept of *nahkeyaa*, Punche Lake might be better thought of as a "footprint" within a larger interconnected cultural landscape comprised of cultural and natural resources connected together based on functional interdependence and proximity.[112] Ultimately, it is the connections between Punche Lake and its surrounding resources that make this site a persistent place.

In addition to evidence for intercept hunting, tool refurbishment, and various levels of residency, all three playa sites contained rock piles and alignments. These features appear to have been used in a variety of ways, including as part of communal hunting endeavors as exemplified by the blind at Arroyo Punche. The rock piles from Arroyo Punche and Three Basins also may have been used as caches or as landscape markers signaling the location of particular natural resources or trails. For example, George Frison noted that the among the Apsáalooke (Crow), it was common for scouts moving across the landscape to add stones to rock piles, marking their migration route as an act of devotion.[113] Rock alignments and piles are part of a widespread material tradition employed by Indigenous Peoples across the North American West, and offer evidence for a shared set of practices linked to natural resource locations, the need to identify pathways of movement, and the intersection of the spiritual and mundane.

Finally, the archaeological records of Punche Lake, Arroyo Punche, and Three Basins indicate that playa landscapes were also used by 19th- and early-20th-century settlers who constructed boundary markers, fences, and fieldhouses out of locally available basalt rocks. These features represent the imposition of a new cartographic logic onto the Taos Plateau. Rather than the free flow of bodies between topographic nodes guided by seasonal ebbs and flows in resource accessibility and Indigenous initiatives, the colonial mobility circuit is dominated by non-Indigenous settlers who moved sheep and cattle along orthogonal lines within legally parceled plots.

Notes

1 Thomas, 1935: 7.
2 Appadurai, 1996: 198.
3 Church, 2002: 222.
4 Chapin, 2005: 656.
5 Bryan and Butler, 1940: 28–29.
6 Getty, 1972.
7 LaBelle and Spencer, 2013: 51.
8 Vierra, 1990: 64.
9 N.A., 2019.
10 Vierra, 2017: 10.
11 Vierra, 2013; Kuhn, 1989; Irwin-Williams, 1968.
12 Roth, 2000, Shackley, 1990; Vierra, 1994 a, b.
13 Vierra, 2013: 155.
14 McBrinn and Vierra, 2017: 240.
15 Vierra, 2013: 148.
16 Vierra et al., 2018: 244; Hughes, 1998: 371–373; Vierra, 2013: 150.
17 Christenson, 1987: 145; Guernsey and Kidder, 1921: 85; Musil, 1988: 374; Plew and Woods, 1985: 221–222.
18 Huckell, 1996: 334.
19 Kehoe, 1958: 863.
20 Opler, 1971: 314.
21 This summary of the Jicarilla origin story is drawn from Opler, 1938.
22 Reed, 1988.
23 Annand, 1967; Buckles, 1971; Hill and Kane, 1988.
24 Gunnerson, 1969; Kingsbury and Gabel, 1983.
25 Gunnerson, 1969: 27.
26 Kehoe, 1966: 839; Kehoe and McCorquodale, 1961.
27 Chesheir and Kelly (2006) have argued that a thickness-length ratio greater than 0.12 are more durable than smaller ratios.
28 Gunnerson, 1974: 78; Ayer, 1965 [1916]: 41.
29 Eiselt, 2012: 72.
30 Eiselt, 2012; Gunnerson, 1969.
31 Seymour, 2009: 270.
32 Seymour, 2009: 270.
33 Finnigan's (1983) ethno-archaeological study posited the following formula for assessing the number of residents within a given tipi: (FA = NP x 1.86). "FA" represents the floor area of the tipi, "NP" represents the "number of people" who occupy the tipi, and 1.86 m is the estimated constant for the number of square meters of floor space that each person would need.

34 Twitchell, 1914: 150.
35 Kehoe, 1960; Adams, 1983.
36 Adams, 1983.
37 Adams and Chavez, 1956: 252.
38 Brumley and Dau, 1988; Kehoe, 1960.
39 La Flesche, 1932; Laubin, 1977; Oldershaw, 1987; Powers, 1977.
40 Eiselt, 2009: 57; Tiller, 2011: 27.
41 Duncan, 2000: 218 as cited in Montgomery, 2012.
42 Conaty and Tailfeather, 1985; Dempsey, 1956; Kehoe, 1954.
43 Kehoe, 1954: 133; Mirau, 1995: 196.
44 O'Brien, 1990: 71.
45 Gettys, 1972: 36–37, 46.
46 Although both Areas 1 and 2 contain stone tools associated with hide processing and meat consumption, neither Gettys nor the author identified any animal bones at the site. The absence of faunal remains likely reflects the fact that faunal remains were displaced or weathered away as the result of high soil acidity, rodent activity, and seasonal fluctuations in temperature and moisture on the Plateau.
47 Steward, 1997: 127.
48 Gettys, 1972: 53–54.
49 Gettys, 1972: 77–78.
50 Eppler, 1976; Lipman and Mehnert, 1979; Shackley, 2011.
51 Shackley, 2013b; Vierra et al., 2012.
52 Shackley, 2013a.
53 Shackley, 2013c.
54 Shackley, 2013a: Figure 3.
55 Shackley, 2013c: 5.
56 Shackley, 2005.
57 Hurt and Dick, 1946; Snow, 1984; Sunseri, 2018.
58 Sunseri, 2018: 90.
59 For more information on Taoseño identity, see Sanchez, 1967.
60 Church, 2002: 232.
61 Dicks et al., 2016: VI-13.
62 Merlan, 2010: 3.
63 Simmons, 1985: 81–88.
64 Merlan, 2010: 4.
65 Kutsche, Van Ness, and Smith, 1976: 3; Williams, 1986.
66 Eidenbach, 1989.
67 Dicks et al., 2016: VI-41.
68 Vierra, 2013: 150.
69 Benedict, 1996, 2002, 2005; Brink et al., 2003; Cassells, 1995, 2000; LaBelle and Spencer, 2013; McGuire and Hatoff, 1991.
70 Driver, 1937: 61.
71 Matheny et al., 1997: 72; Steward, 1941, 1942.
72 LaBelle and Spencer, 2013: 59.
73 Benedict, 1992: 5.
74 Brunswig, 2005: 147.
75 Shott, 1986: 39; Torrence, 1983: 13.
76 Shott, 1986: 27.
77 LaBelle and Spencer, 2013: 51.
78 Bryan, 1939: 17.
79 Warren, 1974: 87.
80 Smith and Huckell, 2005: 427.
81 Smith and Huckell, 2005: 428.
82 Vierra and Foxx, 2009.

83 Hicks, 1994.
84 Brunswig, 2005: 187..
85 Hicks, 1994: 506.
86 LaBelle and Spencer, 2013: 55.
87 Benedict, 1992: 7.
88 Dicks et al., 2016: I-18.
89 Brunswig, 2003: 20; Hartley and Wolley Vawser, 2005: 7; Haynal, 2000: 172; Sundstrom, 2003: 271.
90 Chartkoff, 1983: 757.
91 Benedict, 1975.
92 Brink et al., 2003: 214.
93 Brink et al., 2003: 216; McKeand, 2000: 20.
94 Montgomery, 2019.
95 The following estimates are based on a formula for estimating the number of inhabitants based on floor area (FA = NP x 1.86) developed by Finnigan, 1983.
96 There is also evidence to suggest that these types of structures served as shelters for women undertaking various domestic activities. See Hartley and Wolley Vawser, 2005: 4.
97 For a discussion of research problems related to tipi rings, see Davis, 1983. For discussions of artifacts at tipi rings also see Malouf, 1960, 1961, and 1966 and Mulloy, 1954, 1960.
98 Church, 2002: 223.
99 Church, 2002: 227.
100 Act of May 20, 1862 (Homestead Act). Public Law 37-64, 05/20/1862. Record Group 11. General Records of the United States Government. National Archives, Washington, DC.
101 Merlan, 2010: 19.
102 Dunbar, 1944; Lawson, 1974.
103 Dicks et al., 2016: VI-16.
104 Merlan, 2010: Vii.
105 United States Bureau of Land Management 2007.
106 Van Ness, 1987.
107 Dicks et al., 2016: VI-20.
108 Jones and Sullivan, 1989.
109 MacDonald, 1989; Rae, 2016.
110 Madis, 1971.
111 Dicks et al., 2016: VI-7.
112 Stoffle et al., 1997: 231.
113 Frison, 1981: 146.

Bibliography

Act of May 20, 1862. (Homestead Act) Public Law 37-64, 05/20/1862. Record Group 11. General Records of the United States Government. National Archives, Washington, DC.

Adams, Elanor B. and Fray Angelico Chavez. 1956. *The Missions of New Mexico, 1776: A Descritpion by Fray Francisco Atanasio Dominguez*. University of New Mexico Press, Albuquerque.

Adams, Gary W. 1983. Tipi Rings at York Factory: An Archaeological-Ethnographic Interface. *Plains Anthropologist* 28(102): 6–15.

Annand, Richard E. 1967. A Description and Analysis of Surface Collected Pottery from the Collbran Region, Colorado. *Southwestern Lore* 33(2): 47–59.

Appadurai, Arjun. 1996. *Modernity at Large: Cultural Dimensions of Globalization.* University of Minessota Press, Mineaopolis.

Ayer, Mrs. Edward E. (translator). 1965 [1916]. *The Memorial of Fray Alonso de Benavides, 1630.* Horn and Wallace, Albuquerque.

Benedict, James B. 1975. The Murray Site: A Late Prehistoric Game Drive System in the Colorado Rocky Mountains. *Plains Anthropologist* 20(69): 161–174.

Benedict, James B. 1992. Footprints in the Snow: High-Altitude Cultural Ecology of the Colorado Front Ranges, U.S.A. *Artic and Alpine Research* 24(1): 1–16.

Benedict, James B. 1996. The Game Drives of Rocky Mountain National Park. Research Report no. 7, Center for Mountain Archaeology, Ward.

Benedict, James B. 2002. A newly discovered game-drive system in Rocky Mountain National Park, North-Central Colorado. *Southwestern Lore* 68(1): 23–37.

Benedict, James B. 2005. Tundra Game Drives: An Artic-Alpine Comparison. *Artic, Antartic, and Alpine Research* 37: 425–434.

Brink, Jack W., Kristine Wrigh-Fedyniak, and Dean Wetzel. 2003. A Review of Certain Stone Alignments and Rock Cairns in Alberta Archaeology. In *Archaeology in Alberta: A View from the New Millennium,* edited by Jack W. Brink and Johan F. Drmaar, pp. 208–241. The Archaeological Society of Alberta, Medicine Hat.

Brumley, John H., and Barry J. Dau. 1988. *Historical Resource Investigations within the Fort Mille Coulee Reservoir.* Archaeological Survey of Alberta,Edmonton.

Brunswig, Robert H. 2003. Archeological, Ethnographic, and Historic Investigations of the 5LR7095 Rock Feature Complex Site, Rocky Mountain National Park, North Central Colorado. Manuscript on file, Department of Anthropology, University of Northern Colorado, Greeley.

Brunswig, Robert H. 2005. Prehistoric, Protohistoric, and Early Historic Native American Archaeology of Rocky Mountain National Park. Final Report of Systemwide Archaeological Inventory Program Investigations by the University of Northern Colorado (1998-2002). University Press of Colorado, Boulder.

Bryan, Kirk. 1939. Stone Cultures Near Cerro Pedernal and their Geological Antiquity. *Bulletin of the Texas Archaeological and Plaeontological Society* 11: 9–42.

Bryan, Kirk, and Arthur P. Butler Jr. 1940. Artifacts Made of the Glassy Andesite of San Antonio Mountain, Rio Arriba County, New Mexico. Anthropology Series, vol. 3., University of New Mexico, Albuquerque.

Buckles, William G. 1971. The Uncompaghre Complex: Historic Ute Archaeology and Prehistoric Archaeology on the Uncompaghre Plateau in West Central Colorado. Unpublished Ph.D. thesis, Department of Anthropology, University of Colorado, Boulder.

Cassells, E. Steve. 1995. Hunting the Open High Country: Prehistoric Game Driving in the Colorado Alpine Tundra. Unpublished Ph.D. thesis, Department of Anthropology, University of Wisconsin, Madison.

Cassells, E. Steve. 2000. Coming into the Colorado High Country: The Archaeology of the Sawtooth Game Drive. In *This Land of Shining Mountains: Archaeological Studies in Colorado's Indian Peaks Wilderness,* edited by E.S. Cassells, pp. 189–215. Center for Mountain Archaeology, Ward.

Chapin, Nicholas Merrill. 2005. Hunter-Gatherer Technological Organization: The Archaic Period in Northern New Mexico. Unpublished PhD thesis, Department of Anthropology, Univeristy of New Mexcio, Albuquerque.

Chartkoff, Joseph L. 1983. A Rock Feature Complex from Northwestern California. *American Antiquity* 48(4): 745–760.

Cheshier, Joseph, and Robert L. Kelly. 2006. Projectile Point Shape and Durability: The Effect of Thickness. *American Antiquity* 71: 353–363.

Christenson, Andrew L. 1987. Projectile Points: Eight Millennia of Projectile Change on the Colorado Plateau. In *Prehistoric Stone Technology on Northern Black Mesa, Arizona*, edited by W. Parry Chistenson and Andrew Christenson, pp. 143–198. Center for Archaeological Investigations, Carbondale.

Church, Minette C. 2002. The Grant and the Grid: Homestead Landscapes in the Late-Nineteenth-Century Borderlands of Southern Colorado. *Journal of Social Archaeology* 2(2): 220–244.

Conaty, Gerald, and Esther Tailfeathers. 1985. The Blood Tribe Historic Site Development Project, 1984. In *Archeology in Alberta 1984*, edited by David Burley, pp. 180–232. Archaeological Survey of Alberta Occasional Paper No. 25, Alberta.

Davis, Leslie B. 1983. Introduction to Tipi Ring Problems and Research. *Plains Anthropologist* 28(102): 1–5.

Dempsey, Hugh A. 1956. Stone "Medicine Wheels," Memorials to Blackfoot War Chiefs. *Journal of the Washington Academy of Sciences* 46(6): 177–182.

Dicks, Merrill, Arron C. Anderson, Jessica Mrstik, Peter Rogers, and Todd Scarbourgh. 2016. Rio Grande Del Norte National Monument Class III Cultural Resources Survey of the Cerro Montoso Project Area, Taos County, New Mexico. Bureau of Land Management, Taos.

Driver, Harold E. 1937. Culture Element Distibutions: VI, Southern Sierra Nevada. *University of California Anthropological Records* 1(2): 53–154.

Dunbar Ortiz, Roxanne. 2014. *An Indigenous People's History of the United States*. Beacon Press, Boston.

Duncan, Clifford. 2000. Consultation on Traditional Ute Sites in Rocky Mountain National Park, August 22-24. Manuscript on file, Department of Anthropology, University of Northern Colorado, Greeley.

Eidenbach, Peter. 1989. *The West That Was Forgotten: Historic Ranches of the Northern San Andres Mountains, White Sands Missile Range, New Mexico*. Human Systems Research Inc., Las Cruces.

Eiselt, B. Sunday. 2009. The Jicarilla Apaches and the Archaeology of the Taos Region. In *Between the Mountains-Beyond the Mountain: Papers in Honor of Paul R Williams*, edited by Emily Brown, Karen Armstrong, David M. Brugge, and Carol Condie, pp. 57–69. Papers of the Archaeological Society of New Mexico vol. 35, Albuquerque.

Eiselt, B. Sunday. 2012. *Becoming White Clay: A History and Archaeology of Jicarilla Apache Enclavement*. University of Utah Press, Salt Lake City.

Eppler, Dean. 1976. The Geology of the San Antonio Mountain Area, Tres Piedras, Taos and Rio Arriba Counties, New Mexico. Unpublished M.S. thesis, University of New Mexico, Albuquerque.

Finnigan, James T. 1983. Tipi to Tipi Ring: A Transformational Model. *Plains Anthropologist* 28(102): 16–28.

Frison, George C. 1981. Linear Arrangments of Cairns in Wyoming and Montana. In *Megaliths to Medicine Wheels: Boulder Structures in Archaeoloy: Proceedings of the Eleventh Annual Chacmool Conference*, edited by Michael Wilson, Kathie L. Road, and Kenneth J. Hardy, pp. 133–147. Archaeological Association of the University of Calgary, Calgary.

Getty, John Marshall. 1972. The Tres Piedras Site of Northern New Mexico. Unpublished M.A. thesis, Department of Anthropology, Eastern New Mexico University, Portales.

Guernsey, Samuel J., and Alfred V. Kidder. 1921. Basket-Maker Caves of Northeastern Arizona: Report on the Explorations, 1916-17. Papers of the Peabody Museum of American Archaeology and Ethnology vol. 7, no. 2. Harvard University, Cambridge.

Gunnerson, Dolores A. 1974. *The Jicarilla Apaches: A Study in Survival.* Northern Illinois University Press, DeKalb.
Gunnerson, James H. 1969. Apache Archeology in Northeastern New Mexico. *American Antiquity* 34(1): 23–39.
Hartley, Ralph J., and Anne M. Wolley Vawser. 2005. A Qualitative Investigation of the Cultural Topography of Hunt and Sheep Mountains, Bighorn National Forest, Wyoming. Report to Midwest Archaeological Center and National Park Service, Lincoln, Nebraska. Manuscript on file, Department of Anthropology, University of Northern Colorado, Greeley.
Haynal, Patrick M. 2000. The Influence of Sacred Rock Cairns and Prayer Seats on Modern Klamath and Modoc Religion and World View. *Journal of California and Great Basin Anthropology* 22(2): 170–185.
Hicks, Patricia. 1994. Dating the Undiagnostic Lithic Scatter Using Patterened Cahnges in Debitage Attributes. In *Archaic Hunter-Gatherer Archaeology in the American Southwest,* edited by Bradley J. Vierra, pp. 478–526. Eastern New Mexico University, Portales.
Hill, David V., and Allen E. Kane. 1988. Characterizations of Ute Occupations and Ceramics from Southwestern Colorado. In *Archaeology of the Eastern Ute: A Symposium,* edited by Paul Nickens, pp. 61–78. Colorado Council of Professional Archaeologists, Denver.
Huckell, Bruce B. 1996. The Archaic Prehistory of the North American Southwest. *Journal of World Prehistory* 10(3): 305–373.
Hughes, Susan H. 1998. Geeting to the Point: Evolutionary Change in Prehistoric Weaponry. *Journal of Archaeological Method and Theory* 5(4): 345–407.
Hurt, Wesley R., and Herbert W. Dick. 1946. Spanish-American Pottery from New Mexico. *El Palacio* 53(10): 280–289, 307–312.
Irwin-Williams, Cynthia. 1968. Archaic Culture History in the Southwestern United States. In *Early Man in Western North America,* edited by Cynthia Irwin-Williams. Eastern New Mexico University, Portales.
Jones, Olive, and Catherine Sullivan. 1985. *The Parks Canada Glass Glossary.* Canadian Government Publication Centre, Ottowa.
Kehoe, Thomas F. 1954. Stone "Medicine Wheels" in Southern Alberta and the Adjacent Portions of Montana: Were They Designed as Grave Markers? *Journal of the Washington Academy of Sciences* 44(5): 133–137.
Kehoe, Thomas F. 1958. Tipi Rings: The "Direct Ethnological" Approach Applied to an Archeological Problem. *American Anthropologist* 60(5): 861–873.
Kehoe, Thomas F. 1960. *Stone Tipi Rings in North Central Montana and the Adjacent Portion of Alberta, Canada: Their Historical Ethnological and Archaeological Aspects.* Bulletin Submitted to Bureau of American Ethnology, Washington, DC.
Kehoe, Thomas F. 1966. The Small Side-Notched Point System of the Northern Plains. *American Antiquity* 31(6): 827–841.
Kehoe, Thomas F., and Bruce A. McCorquodale. 1961. The Avonlea Point-Horizon Marker for the Northwestern Plains. *Plains Anthropologist* 6(13): 179–188.
Kingsbury, Lawrence A., and Lorna H. Gabel. 1983. Eastern Apache Campsites in Southeastern Colorado: A Hypothesis. *Plains Anthropologist* 28(102): 319–325.
Kuhn, Steven I. 1989. Hunter-Gatherer Foraging Organization and Strategies of Aritfact Replacement and Discard. In *Experiments in Lithic Technology,* edited by S. Amick and R. Mauldin, pp. 33–47. BAR International Series, Oxford.
Kutsche, Paul, John R. Van Ness, and Andrew T. Smith. 1976. A Unified Approach to the

Anthropology of Hispano Northern New Mexico: Historical Arhaeology, Ethnohistory, and Ethnography. *Historical Archaeology* 10: 1–16.

LaBelle, Jason M., and Pelton R. Spencer. 2013. Communal Hunting along the Continental Divide of Northern Colorado: Results from the Olson Game Drive (5BL147), USA. *Quaternary International* 297: 45–63.

La Flesche, Francis. 1932. Dictionary of the Osage Language. Smithsonian Institution, Bulletin 109, Bureau of American Ethnology, Washington, DC.

Laubin, Reginald, and Gladys Laubin. 1977. *The Indian Tipi, its History, Construction, and Use*. University of Oklahoma Press, Norman.

Lawson, Merlin P. 1974. *The Climate of the Great America Desert: Reconstruction of the Climate of Western Interior United States, 1800-1850*. University of Nebraska, Lincoln.

Lipman, Peter W., and Mehnert, Harald H. 1979. The Taos Plateau Volcanic Field, Northern Rio Grande Rift, New Mexico. In *Rio Grande Rift: Tectonics and Magnetism*, edited by Robert E. Riecker, pp. 289–311. American Geophysical Union, Washington, DC.

MacDonald, Mary Lee. 1989. Repairing Historic Flat Plaster Walls and Ceilings. Preservation Briefs 21. National Park Service, U.S. Department of the Interior, Washington, DC.

Madis, George. 1971. *The Winchester Book*. Lancaster, Texas.

Malouf, Carling. 1960. Tipi Rings. *Southwestern Lore* 24(4): 3–5.

Malouf, Carling. 1961. The Tipi Rings of the High Plains. *American Antiquity* 26(3): 381–389.

Malouf, Carling. 1966. Tipi Rings. *The Wyoming Archaeologist* 9(4): 4.

Matheny, Ray T., Thomas S. J. Smith, and Deanne Matheny. 1997. Animal Ethology Reflected in the Rock Art of Nine Miles Canyon, Utah. *Journal of California and Great Basin Anthropology* 19(1): 70–103.

McBrinn, Maxine, and Bradley J. Vierra. 2017. The Southwest Archaic. In *The Oxford Handbook of Southwest Archaeology*, edited by Barbara J. Mills and Severin Fowles. Oxford University Press. DOI: 10.1093/oxfordhb/9780199978427.013.12.

McGuire, Kelly R., and Brian W. Htoff. 1991. A Prehistoric Bighorn Sheep Drive Complex, Clan Alpine Mountains, Central Nevada. *Journal of California and Great Basin Anthropology* 13(1): 95–109.

McKeand, Peggy. 2000. Test Excavation of Two Cairns at DkOd-60 in Southwestern Saskatchewan. *Saskatchewan Archaeological Society Newsletter* 21(1):17–20.

Merlan, Thomas. 2010. *Historic Homesteads and Ranches in New Mexico: A Historic Context*. Report Prepared for Historic Homestead Workshop, September 25–26, 2010. Historic Preservation Division, Office of Cultural Affairs, Santa Fe, New Mexico.

Mirau, Neil A. 1995. Medicine Wheels on the Northern Plains. In *Beyond Subsistence: Plains Archeology and the Processual Critique*, edited by Philip Duke, and Michael C. Wilson, pp. 193–210. University of Alabama Press, Tuscaloosa.

Montgomery, Christine M. 2012. Reconstructing a Prehistoric Ute Sacred Landscape in the Southern Rocky Mountains Through Visibility and Orientation Analysis. Unpublished M.A. thesis, Department of Anthropology, University of Wyominig, Laramie.

Montgomery, Lindsay M. 2019. Nomadic Economics: The Logic and Logistics of Comanche Imperialism in New Mexico. *Journal of Social Archaeology* 19(3): 333–355. DOI: 10.1177/1469605319859667.

Mulloy, W.T. 1954. The McKean Site in Northeastern Wyoming. *Southwestern Journal of Anthropology* 10(4): 432–460.

Mulloy, W.T. 1960. Late Prehistoric Stone Circles. *Southwestern Lore* 25(4): 1–3.

Musil, Rober T. 1988. Functional Efficiency and Technological Change: A Hafting Tradition Model for Prehistoric North America. In *Early Human Occupation in Far Western North America: The Clovis-Archaic Interface*, edited by C. Melvin Aikens, Judith A. Willig, and John L. Fagan, pp. 373–387. Nevada State Museum Anthropological Papers, Carson City.

Musil, Rober T. 2019. Climate Assessment for the Southwest. University of Arizona, Tucson. https://www.climas.arizona.edu/sw-climate/southwest-paleoclimate.

O'Brien, Patricia. 1990. Evidence for the Antiquity of Gender Roles in the Central Plains Tradition. *Archaeological Papers of the American Anthropological Association* 2(1): 61–72.

Oldershaw, Barbara. 1987. Blackfeet American Indian Women: Builders of the Tribe. *Places: A Symposium on the Criticism of Place* 4(1): 38–48.

Opler, Morris E. 1938. *Myths and Tales of the Jicarilla Apache Indians*. G.E.: The American Folk-Lore Society.

Plew, Mark G., and James C. Woods. 1985. Observation of Edge Damage and Technological Effects on Pressure-Flaked Stone Tools. In *Stone Tool Analysis: Essays in Honor of Don E. Crabtrees*, edited by Mark Plew, James Woods, and M. Pvesic, pp. 211–228. University of New Mexico Press, Albuquerque.

Powers, William K. 1977. *Oglala Religion*. University of Nebraska Press, Lincoln.

Rae, Haniya. 2016. An Exciting History of Drywall. *The Atlantic*. July 29, 2016. https://www.theatlantic.com/technology/archive/2016/07/an-exciting-history-of-drywall/493502/.

Reed, Alan D. 1988. Ute Cultural Chronology. In *Archaeology of the Eastern Ute: A Symposium*, edited by Paul Nickens, pp. 79–101. Colorado Council of Professional Archaeologists, Denver.

Roth, Barbara J. 2000. Obsidian Source Characterization and Hunter-Gatherer Mobility: An Example from the Tucson Basin. *Journal of Archaeological Science* 27: 305–314.

Sanchez, George I. 1967. *Forgotten People: A Study of New Mexicans*. Calvin Horn Publisher, Albuquerque.

Stechert and Co, Agents. 1971. Jicarilla Apache Territory, Economy, and Society in 1850. *Southwestern Journal of Anthropology* 27(4): 309–329.

Seymour, Deni J. 2009. Distinctive Places, Suitable Spaces: Conceptualizing Mobile Group Occupational Duration and Landscape Use. *International Journal of Historical Archeology* 13(3): 255–281.

Shackley, M. Steven. 1990. Early Hunter-Gatherer Procurement Ranges in the Southwest: Evidence from Obsidian Geochemistry and Lithic Technology. Unpublished Ph.D. thesis, Department of Anthropology, Arizona State University, Tempe.

Shackley, M. Steven. 2005. *Obsidian: Geology and Archaeology in the North American Southwest*. University of Arizona Press, Tucson.

Shackley, M. Steven. 2011. Sources of Archaeological Dacite in northern New Mexico. *Journal of Archaeological Science* 38: 1001–1007.

Shackley, M. Steven. 2013a. Source Provenance of Obsidian and Dacite Artifacts from the Protohistoric Apache Punche Lake Tepee Site (LA 64805) Taos Plateau, Northern New Mexico. Report prepared for Lindsay M. Montgomery. Albuquerque.

Shackley, M. Steven. 2013b. The Secondary Distribution of Archaeological Obsidian in Rio Grande Quaternary Sediments, Jemez Mountains to San Antonito, New Mexico: Inferences for Prehistoric Procurement and the Age of Sediments. Poster presentation at the Paleoamerican Odyssey conference, Santa Fe.

Shackley, M. Steven. 2013c. The Geochemistry and Archaeological Petrology of Volcanic Raw Materials in Northern New Mexico: Obsidian and Dacite Sources in Upland and

Lowland Contexts. In *From Mountain Top to Valley Bottom: Understanding Past Land Use in the Northern Rio Grande Valley, New Mexico*, edited by Bradley Vierra, pp. 17–32. University of Utah Press, Salt Lake City.
Shott, Michael. 1986. Technological Organization and Settlement Mobility: An Ethnographic Examination. *Journal of Anthropological Research* 42(1): 15–51.
Simmons, Virginia McConnell. 2001. *The Ute Indians of Utah, Colorado, and New Mexico*. University of Colorado Press, Boulder.
Smith, Gary A., and Bruce B. Huckell. 2005. The Geological and Geoarchaeological Significance of Cerro Pedernal, Rio Aribba County, New Mexico. In *Geology of the Chama Basin*, edited by Lucas G. Spencer, Kate E. Zeigler, Virgl W. Lueth, and Donald E. Owen, pp. 425–431. New Mexico Geological Society, Albuquerque.
Snow, David H. 1984. Spanish American Pottery Manufacture in New Mexico: A Critical Review. *Ethnohistory* 31(2): 93–113.
Steward, Julian Haynes. 1997. *Basin-Plateau Aborigional Sociopolitical Groups*. University of Utah Press, Salt Lake City.
Steward, Omar C. 1941. Culture Element Distributions: XIV, Northern Paiute. University of California Anthropological Records 4(3): 361–446.
Steward, Omar C. 1942. Culture Element Distributions: XVIII, Ute-Southern Paiute. University of California Anthropological Records 6(4): 231–354.
Stoffel, Richard W., David B. Halmo, and Diane E. Austin. 1997. Cultural Landscape and Traditional Cultural Properties: A Southern Paiute View of the Grand Canyon and Colorado River. *American Indian Quarterly* 21(20): 229–249.
Sundstrom, Linea. 2003. Sacred Islands: An Exploration of Religion and Landscape in the Northern Great Plains. In *Islands on the Plains: Ecological, Social, and Ritual Use of Landscapes*, edited by Marcel Kornfeld and Alan J. Osborn, pp. 258–300. University of Utah Press, Salt Lake City.
Sunseri, Jun. 2018. Situational Identities along the Raiding Frontier of Colonial New Mexico. University of Nebraska Press, Lincoln.
Thomas, Alfred B. 1935. *After Coronado: Spanish Exploration Northeast of New Mexico, 1696-1727*. University of Oklahoma Press, Norman.
Tiller, Veronica E. 2011. *Culture and Customs of the Apche Indians*. Greenwood, Westport.
Torrence, Robin. 1983. Time Budgeting and Hunter-Gatherer Technology. In *Hunter-Gatherer Economy in Prehistory: A European Perspective*, edited by Geoff Bailey, pp. 11–22. Cambridge University Press.
Twitchell, Ralph E. 1914. *The Spanish Archives of New Mexico*. vol. 1. Torch Press, Cedar Rapids.
United States Bureau of Land Management. 2007. The Official Federal Land Records Site. Bureau of Land Management, General Land Office Records. Automated Records Project; Federal Land Patents, State Volumes. Bureau of Land Management, Eastern States, Springfield, VA. http://www.glorecords.blm.gov.
Van Ness, John R. 1987. Hispanic Land Grants: Ecology and Subsistence in the Uplands of Northern New Mexico and Southern Colorado. In *Land, Water, Culture: New Perspectives on Hispanic Land Grants*, edited by Charles L. Briggs and John R. Van Ness, pp. 141–216. University of New Mexico, Albuquerque.
Vierra, Bradley J. 1990. Archaic Hunter-Gatherer Archaeology in Northwestern New Mexico. In *Perspectives on Southwest Prehistory*, edited by Paul Minnis and Charles L. Redman, pp. 57–67. Westview Press, Boulder.
Vierra, Bradley J. 1994a. Archaic Hunter Gatherer Mobility Strategies in the American

Southwest. Excavations and Interpretations of Aceramic and Archaic Sites, vol 14., pp. 385–398. Office of Contrat Archaeology, University of New Mexico, Albuquerque.

Vierra, Bradley J. 1994b. Archaic Hunter-Gatherer Mobility Strategies in Northwestern New Mexico. In *Archaic Hunter-Gatherer Archaeology in the American Southwest*, edited by Bradley J. Vierra, pp. 121–154. Eastern New Mexico University, Poratles.

Vierra, Bradley J. 2013. Archaic Foraging Technology and Land Use in the Northern Rio Grande, New Mexico. In *From Mountaintop to Valley Bottom: Papers in Honor of Paul Williams*, edited by Bradley J. Vierra, pp. 145–160. University of Utah Press, Salt Lake City.

Vierra, Bradley J. 2017. A History of Archaic Research in the Northern Southwest. In *The Archaic Southwest: Foragers in an Arid Land*, edited by Bradley J. Vierra, pp. 3–15. University of Utah Press, Salt Lake City.

Vierra, Bradley J., Margaret A. Jodry, M. Steven Shackley, and Michael J. Dilley. 2012. Late Paleoindian and Early Archaic Foragers in the Northern Southwest. In *From the Pleistocene to the Holocene: Human Organization and Cultural Transformations in Prehistoric North America*, edited by C. Britt Bousman and Bradley J. Vierra, pp. 171–196. Texas A&M University Press, College Station.

Vierra, Bradley J., Richard I. Ford, and Stephen S. Post. 2018. Archaic Foragers of the Northern Rio Grande. In *The Archaic Southweset: Foragers in an Arid Land*, edited by Bradley J. Vierra, pp. 235–253. University of Utah Press, Salt Lake City.

Vierra, Bradley J., and Teralene Foxx. 2009. Archaic Upland Resource Use: The View from the Pajarito Plateau. In *Between the Mountains, Beyond the Mountains: Papers in Honor of Paul R. Williams*, edited by Emily J. Brown, Karen Armstrong, David M. Brugge, and Carol J. Condie, pp. 154–166. The Archaeological Society of New Mexico, Albuquerque.

Warren, A. Helene. 1974. The Ancient Mineral Industries of Cerro Pedernal, Rio Arriba County, New Mexico. In *New Mexico Geological Society 25th Annual Fall Field Conference Guidebook*, edited by Charles T. Siemers, Lee A. Woodward, and Jonathan F. Callender, pp. 87–93. New Mexico Geological Society, Santa Fe.

Williams, Jerry (editor). 1986. *New Mexico in Maps*. Second edition. University of New Mexico, Albuquerque.

IN SEARCH OF VIOLENCE

On March 11, 1849, Lieutenant J.H. Whittlesey left Taos heading north with a force of 67 dragoons, several scouts, and a mountain howitzer.[1] On paper, Whittlesey's mission read as a disciplinary endeavor. He and his men had been ordered by Major Llyod Beall to seek out and "chastise" a groups of *Nuutsiyu* people living along the Rio Colorado who were accused of stealing cattle from Mexican ranchers. In reality, these orders were motivated by revenge. Still reeling over a recent fiasco at Fort Bent during which an allied group of some 2,000 *Kai-i-gwu*, *Inuna-ina*, *Tsitsistas*, *Ndee*, and *Numunu* warriors refused to submit to imprisonment under American control, Beall was looking for an opportunity to restore the respect and authority of his unit.

The next day, Whittlesey received news from two hunters that a party of "Indians" had been seen from Cerro del Yuta, to which the troops hastily proceeded. Peering through the cold, clear air on the morning of March 13th, Whittlesey spied a party of *Nuutisyu* horseman riding onto the Plateau to the west. They were moving towards Cerro de la Olla (Kettle Mountain). Quickly rallying his troops, Whittlesey led his men down the steep cavernous sides of the Rio Grande Gorge, crossing the swift flowing river near modern-day "Sheep's Crossing." Here the group broke into two divisions, a first wave of 23 men struck out across the desolate plains heavy with snow and mud in pursuit of the *Nuutsiyu* travelers. A second wave of men was tasked with carrying the cumbersome howitzer across the river.

About a mile from the base of Cerro de la Olla, five *Nuutsiyu* men on horseback met Whittlesey's group. Speaking in Spanish, one of the men demanded to know why the soldiers were there. In response, Whittlesey declared "*venimos para pelear*" (I have come to fight). The leader of the *Nuutsiyu* entourage reportedly responded to this provocation with an affirmative, "*esta bueno*" (it is good), before retreating to the base of the mountain.

Whittlesey quickly gave the order for his men to charge. Upon drawing close to the mountain, he realized the true size of the enemy's encampment. Concealed among the piñon woodlands covering the mountain's slope were over 100 well-armed *Nuutsiyu* warriors. In vain, the lieutenant called for retreat; his orders swallowed by the wind and clamor of the cavalry's horses.

In an effort to drive the *Nuutsiyu* from the shelter of the trees, Whittlesey led his men in a flank move up the mountainside; however, the deep snow rendered the dragoon's motionless. Capitalizing on this failed maneuver, *Nuutsiyu* soldiers charged forward. The American forces quickly dismounted, continuing the fight on foot. After some 20 minutes of combat, the *Nuutsiyu* withdrew from the battle, fleeing the camp and abandoning all but their horses. Although Whittlesey had his enemy on the run, his horses were in no condition for a rapid pursuit. And so, the lieutenant decided to call for an end to the fighting, just as the howitzer arrived at the abandoned camp.

On March 15, 1849, Whittlesey and his troops returned to Taos, where he wrote his report. According to this account, the American casualties numbered two men killed and three horses lost. The *Nuutsiyu* known losses included five men killed and several wounded. In his closing remarks, Whittlesey hyberbolically bragged

> I killed 10 of the enemy; and from the blood on the snow, I feel confident that many must have been wounded who were carried off…I captured, killed, and wounded about 20 horses. I also captured two women, and the son of one of their chiefs. All this I accomplished with the loss of only two men and three horses, and at no time had more than 23 men in action.[2]

The battle at Cerro de la Olla offers another lens into the layered history of the Taos Plateau. In addition to serving as a camping, hunting, and herding landscape, the Plateau is a place of violence. Small-scale battle stories such as this one are largely absent from traditional histories of Indigenous life under American colonialism. This tendency to forget inconclusive skirmishes in part reflects a historiographic tendency to view such events as irrelevant to the larger arc of US history; they are inconsequential blips on the historical radar. However, when viewed from an archaeological optic, the material residues of such small-scale events are quite literally the stuff of history.

Indeed, I came to Cerro de la Olla in June of 2017 with the aim of identifying the material remains of this 19th-century battle. Over the course of a 4-week field season, we did not identify a single piece of evidence for this conflict. This absence is particularly striking given the significant size of the winter encampment Lieutenant Whittlesey reportedly encountered. The somewhat disappointing results of this field season may in part reflect limitations in survey coverage. It may also point to slippages between the archaeological and archival records. Perhaps the lieutenant exaggerated the size of the Ute encampment to make this battle appear more grandiose in the eyes of his superiors. Such discrepancies in reporting were not uncommon on the colonial frontier and Whittlesey's report likely contained several exaggerations, largely intended to save face in expeditions lacking a definitive outcome.

Alternatively, Whittlesey, a relatively new arrival to New Mexico, may have simply wrote down the wrong mountain; Cerro de la Olla is surrounded by two other imposing peaks—Cerro Montoso and Cerro Chiflo. Future survey of these mountain-scapes would undoubtedly shed light on the accuracy of Whittlesey's account. The 2017 survey results highlight the often messy relationship that exists between documentary evidence and the archaeological record. Rather than searching for material proof of archival (or oral historical) accounts, these lines of evidence are perhaps better seen as parallel and complimentary sources with which to create complex rather than unfussy historical narratives.

6

CERRO DE LA OLLA

Standing at nearly 9,500 feet, Cerro de la Olla looms over the west side of the Rio Grande Gorge. Piñon-juniper woodlands cover the foothills of Cerro de la Olla, gradually giving way to Ponderosa pine, Douglas fir, and scrub oak as one travels upslope. A distinctive basin formed following the collapse of a lava dome on the mountain during the Pliocene covers 20 acres of the summit.[3] This caldera fills with seasonal surface runoff during the spring, offering a reliable water source for both humans and wildlife.

During the summer of 2017, I led a crew of graduate and undergraduate students from the University of Arizona and Barnard College on a non-collection-based survey of the eastern slope of Cerro de la Olla. Over the course of the field season, the team worked systematically in 5 m transects from the base of the mountain, 7,700 feet, upward into the subalpine woodland zone, covering a total of 8.5 km^2. Although we were unable to locate the 1849 battle site, the survey team did document lithic scatters of varying densities as well as isolated tools across the slope. These materials suggest that Cerro de la Olla was used largely by mobile Indigenous groups engaged in piñon harvesting and encounter hunting from roughly 7500 BCE to 400 CE. The survey team also documented material evidence that Euro-American settlers used Cerro de la Olla for logistical activities associated with firewood collecting, hunting wild game, and ranching during the late 19th and early 20th century. The persistent use of Cerro de la Olla reflects its role as an ecological resource niche, its close proximity to raw materials for stone tool production, and its spatial relationship to easy crossing points within the Gorge. These offer new insights into the foraging and procurement patterns of Indigenous people who used this mountain-scape in similar ways over a significant period of time as well as the ways in which settler colonialism transformed the landscape.

The Cerro de la Olla archaeological landscape

Compared to more intensively studied areas in the Rio Grande and Espanola Valleys, archaeological work on the Taos Plateau has largely consisted of extensive landscape surveys rather than excavation-based projects. E.B. Renaud, a professor of anthropology at Denver University, undertook the earliest research in this area, identifying a large number of petroglyphs, pictographs, and lithic scatters through a series of reconnaissance surveys during the 1930s and 1940s along the New Mexico–Colorado boarder.[4] During his 1945 field season, Renaud's team surveyed the northern slope of Cerro de la Olla as well as the prairies to the east. Renaud's report from this season notes the presence of lithic sites comprised of "several medium size biface pieces, some of them well worked, blades, discoids and a fragment of blade. Among the uniface specimens there were medium large worked flakes, side scrapers, blades, some with square end, and a concave scraper, one graver or borer, the fragment of a large blade."[5] Renaud used these findings as evidence for what he called the "Upper Rio Grande Culture" complex. Although a now-defunct archaeological category, as originally conceived, the Upper Rio Grande culture was characterized by high numbers of andesite/dacite tools as well as stemmed projectile points. These tools resemble what Cynthia Irwin-Williams called Jay points, suggesting that Cerro de la Olla was used by residentially mobile Indigenous groups around 5500-4800 BCE.[6]

Renaud's work indicates that substantial ecological changes have occurred across the Plateau over the past 80 years. In his 1946 publication *Reconnaissance Work in the Upper Rio Grande Valley, Colorado and New Mexico*, he notes that "the surface of these sites…is relatively stable" and that "scraping the present, grassy surface of those sites would expose many points and artifacts."[7] The stable surface described in Renaud's field notes has since been deflated to bedrock and regolith and the native grasses replaced by monoculture sagebrush. These changes are largely the result of massive and widespread soil loss caused by overgrazing during the 20th century.[8]

In response to the damaging effects of overgrazing and broad-scale environmental changes on the Plateau, the Bureau of Land Management–Taos office undertook a Class III cultural resource inventory survey of the area surrounding Cerro de la Olla between 2007 and 2012.[9] The *Cerro Montoso Vegetation Treatment Project* covered over 29,000 acres on the west side of the Rio Grande Gorge and documented 266 archaeological sites and thousands of isolated objects. These findings demonstrate an almost continuous human occupation of the area, from roughly 8000 BCE into the mid-20th century.[10] Approximately 70% of these sites are classified as lithic scatters attributed to hunter-gatherer groups moving across the plateau between 7500 BCE and 250 CE.

While the Taos Plateau was an important place within the cultural geography of both Tiwa- and Tewa-speaking people, archaeological evidence of their presence in in the area (e.g black-on-white and incised ceramics, small side-notched points, or pit houses) is relatively sparse (n = 7). This comparatively light material trace offers some preliminary evidence that Indigenous People living in the region used the Plateau less frequently as agriculture became an increasingly central facet of their socioeconomic systems sometime after 950 CE.[11] As discussed in Chapter 5, there is a growing body of evidence that Numic- and Athabaskan-speaking groups established short- and medium-term encampments in the area after the 15th century. The BLM-Taos survey of the Plateau identified ten such encampments comprised of stone rings, distinctive projectile points, and brownware ceramics, as well as hundreds of chipped and groundstone tools. These materials indicate that some Indigenous groups continued to use Cerro de la Olla and its surrounding areas as strategic stopping places within a larger mobility cycle while others chose to aggregate in agricultural villages along the Rio Grande and in the foothills of the Sangre de Cristos on the east side of the Gorge.

Following the arrival of Spanish colonists to the northern Rio Grande, the Plateau continued to be sparsely occupied, largely due to the threat posed to settlers by nomadic raiders. This settlement pattern continued into the 19th century, with traces of temporary shelters and lambing pens offering the primary evidence of settler land use (n = 31).[12] Indeed, it is not until the late 19th century that people settled on the western side of the Taos Plateau in any concerted way—in 1879, Anglo homesteaders established the town of Trés Piedras and established ranching territories across the sweeping prairies of the Taos Plateau.

Fifty-five of the sites recorded by the Cerro Montoso Project are directly located on the slopes of Cerro de la Olla itself. These sites were most frequently (approximately 41%) associated with an early use of the mountain by hunting and gathering Indigenous people. Lithic scatters of hundreds, sometimes thousands, of chipped stone debitage, corner and side-notched projectile points, as well as fire-cracked rock characterize the archaeological record of this period. While approximately half of the sites dating from 7500 BCE to 400 CE also contained chipped stone tools, groundstone was only found at three sites, suggesting that the majority of these occupations were short-term activity camps rather than longer-term base camps.

In addition to these foraging sites, a comparatively large number of lithic scatters from this area are designated as "unknown" or "unknown Aboriginal" (23%), reflecting the general absence of diagnostic projectile points and ceramics at many sites across the Plateau. While most of the sites identified on the slopes of Cerro de la Olla were discrete occupations, there are 11 areas associated with multiple temporal and/or cultural periods—most frequently lithic production and refurbishment locals overlain with late-19th- and early-20th-century objects. This pattern reveals an important gap in the occupational history of the mountain, which appears to have been less intensively used between 950 and 1850 CE.

With the exception of one site that contains several hundred plain and corrugated ceramic sherds, there is a notable absence of material culture made by Tiwa-speaking people at Cerro de la Olla—a finding that is consistent with archaeological evidence documented by the Montoso survey. While Indigenous people appear to have extensively used the mountain slope, this place appears to

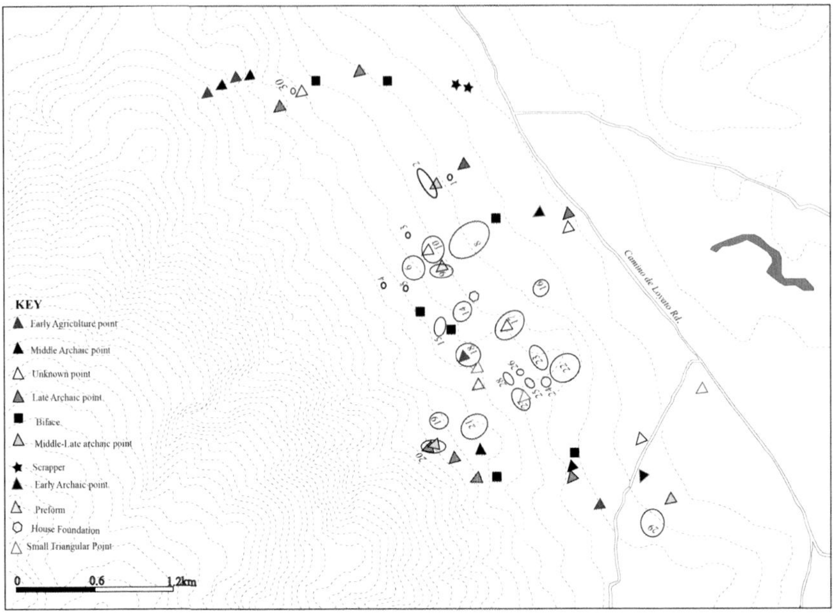

FIGURE 6.1 Map of Cerro de la Olla Scatters and Isolated Finds.

have been largely ignored, at least from an archaeological standpoint, by village-based agricultural communities living in the Taos region.

The logistics of mobile activity areas

The survey team identified 30 lithic scatters and 33 isolated stone tools across the eastern slope of Cerro de la Olla (Figure 6.1). These materials are concentrated along the slope between 8,000 and 8,500 feet in elevation, reflecting the general topographic constraints of the mountain, which becomes steep and densely forested as one moves closer to the peak.

While there are several projectile points dating to roughly 7500 BCE at the site, the majority of diagnostic projectile points within the survey area are less than 6,000 years old (92%).[13] This period coincides with a widespread increase in rainfall across the Southwest, making a larger swath of the landscape inhabitable.[14] In response to changing climatic patterns at the end of the alti-thermal, Indigenous people adopted a more locally oriented foraging subsistence strategy centered on plant collecting and encounter hunting.[15] The localization of foragining rounds in the region is reflected in the predominance of dacite (96%) within the lithic assemblages recorded at Cerro de la Olla.

Thirty-four projectile points were identified within the survey area, roughly 65% of which were isolated finds. Using an Anselin Morans I test, which identifies groupings of high and low values, in ArcGIS, I examined the projectile point data for clusters of tools dating to similar temporal periods.[16] The absence of any statistically significant spatial patterning of similar points suggests that Indigenous peoples were visiting the site in discrete isolated episodes.

These visitations were likely associated with hunting, as suggested by the fact that many of the projectile points documented at Cerro de la Olla had fractured tips, indicative of breakage on impact during hunting. Today, Cerro de la Olla sits within the autumn migration corridor for species like elk, mule deer, and antelope, making this place an ideal location for seasonal hunting. Several of these isolated projectile points also exhibited signs of retouching indicating that they were likely resharpened before use or may have been used as tools before being discarded. Projectile points—over half of which were fragmentary—found in association with scatters comprised predominantly of small dacite flakes offer some additional evidence for tool resharpening at the mountain (scatter 9, 10, 12, 17, 18, 20, 22, 27, and 30 in Figure 6.1). The predominance of broken and refurbished points at Cerro de la Olla suggests that Indigenous people were largely using the eastern slope of the mountain as a resource node for hunting or tool refurbishing activities during logistical mobility rounds.

A multiple regression analysis of the relationship between projectile point type, environmental context (evergreen forest, herbaceous uplands, and shrublands), and find context (i.e., isolated or in a scatter) indicates that there is a weak relationship between the location of points and when they date to. Similarly, there is no statistically significant relationship between other bifacial tools and their location within a particular environmental niche, suggesting that tool production was not influenced by topography. While the lack of statistical significance in part reflects the small sample size, these findings suggest that there was no perceptible shift over time in which areas of the mountain Indigenous people were using to hunt and/or refurbish tools.

Similarly, an spearman rank test assessing the spatial relationship between broken and complete projectile points indicates that there is no statistically significant relationship between whether a point was whole or broken and its topographic location. This analysis indicates that hunting and tool discard were occurring in spatiality unpatterned ways across the mountain over time. These observations are particularly significant, given the wide variety of temporal periods represented at the site.

Almost half of the points identified across the survey area date from roughly 3200 BCE to 250 CE. Research from elsewhere in the northern Rio Grande suggests that after 1800 BCE, foraging groups integrated upland resources like piñon nuts into their seasonal hunting rounds.[17] A corresponding proliferation in projectile point types accompanied the increased use of upland areas as hunters began targeting a greater variety of wild game, particularly during the fall.[18] The preponderance of points dating from 3200 BCE to 400 CE at Cerro de la Olla offers material evidence for the intensive use of upland areas on the Taos Plateau by foraging communities as environmental conditions became moister and piñon-juniper woodlands expanded.[19] As discussed previously, there are no significant differences in the breakage patterns or the location of points dating to different phases within this broad time frame, which suggests that although a more diversified set of hunting strategies were being used by foraging groups in the region overall, the types of hunting activities engaged in on the mountain remained relatively consistent over time. The seasonal use of upland locations like Cerro de la Olla continued to characterize Indigenous mobility patterns in the region until roughly 950 CE.[20]

Projectile points within the survey zone were primarily made from dacite (n = 11)—although obsidian (n = 3) and chert (n = 1) were also represented—pointing to the primary use of locally available raw materials for bifacial tool production during this period. The use of local materials coincides with a general shift in point production strategies during this period towards shorter use-life and higher discard rates.[21] At Cerro de la Olla the majority of discarded dacite projectile points were found in isolated contexts (n = 11). Of these isolated points, approximately half had broken or missing tips (n = 6) while the remaining five points were complete, suggesting a dual discard pattern associated with on-site tool use. While points with missing tips were likely abandoned following hunting activities, whole points made of easily locally available raw materials were more likely discarded following on-site use.

A small sample of projectile points dating to this broad period were associated with scatters (scatters 12, 17, 20, and 22 in Figure 6.1). While some of these points were complete (n = 2), suggesting abandonment following on-site use, others had a combination of fragmentary bases and tips reflecting reflaking (n = 3). Overall, the projectile point dating from 3200 BCE to 400 CE suggests that for roughly 4,000 years foraging groups were engaged primarily in tool refurbishment activities and encounter hunting of medium-sized game on the mountain. The general absence of large bifacial tools like choppers or knives associated with butchering and processing across the survey zone, indicates that these activities took place off-site at base camps located elsewhere on the Plateau.

The other significant cluster (23%) of projectile points identified at Cerro de la Olla date between 400 and 950 CE and are associated with Indigenous groups engaged in a diversified subsistence system, which incorporated some level of cultivation. The eight points dating to this time period were evenly dispersed across isolated and scatter contexts (scatter 10, 12, and 18 in Figure 6.1) and all of these tools were fragmentary, primarily with broken tips (n = 7). The majority (n = 5) of these projectile points are made from dacite, suggesting that Indigenous groups continued to use locally available raw materials for bifacial tool production despite shifting subsistence and settlement patterns. These eight points suggest that Cerro de la Olla continued to be used as a logistical hunting site into the 10th century.

The persistence of Cerro de la Olla as a logistical activity site is likely due to the availability of high-quality protein sources in the area, including deer and piñon nuts. As a result, maize remained a less cost-effective subsistence strategy for Indigenous Peoples living in the northern Rio Grande for a significantly longer period of time than in other areas of the Southwest.[22] Within this evolving subsistence landscape, Cerro de la Olla may have served as a logistical hunting site within a plant-and-go system. Within this hypothetical model, Indigenous people would have continued their yearly rounds across the Plateau, making trips to sites like Cerro de la Olla, while also stopping to plant in the spring and harvest these crops during the late summer or early fall.[23]

Although documentary evidence indicates that Indigenous people continued to use the Taos Plateau from 1000 CE into the present, only three projectile points dating to this latter period were identified within the survey area. The two-notched points in this group were isolated finds with missing tips and date to between 1300 and 1600 CE. These points share many morphological similarities with projectiles from the southern Plains, suggesting that Athabaskan-speaking groups may have visited the mountain on at least two distinct occasions. In contrast, the third stemmed point within this group resembles "Pueblo"-style projectile points and was associated with a medium-sized dacite scatter, which also contained two cores (scatter 27 in Figure 6.1). Although the sample size is too small to draw any large-scale historical trends from, this scatter offers some evidence for on-site tool production and refurbishment by Tiwa or Tewa-speaking people. Although it is difficult to assign a definitive ethnic affiliation to these three points, they do suggest that Indigenous communities engaged in distinct subsistence systems and mobility networks were using the mountain in similar ways.

Despite the general absence of "Pueblo" material culture at Cerro de la Olla, Tiwa-speaking people today recognize the mountain as an important natural and spiritual place on the landscape. In a recent article in the *Daily Post*, Taos Pueblo War Chief Gary J. Lujan stated, "as the primary inhabitants of the Taos Valley, the Red Willow People commonly known as the Taos Pueblo, have always recognized the sacredness of Cerro de la Olla...Our People will continually acknowledge this in perpetuity..."[24] Lujan's comments indicate that Cerro de la Olla occupies an important place within the cosmogeography of the *Ĭăłap°ăĭbâ* and draws attention to the disconnects that often exist between the archaeological record and Indigenous oral histories. Such disjunctures suggest that "sacredness" is not necessarily correlated with overt material evidence of use or occupation, but rather through intangible forms of cultural heritage. In this sense, persistent places are marked by the accumulation of stories (personal and collective) and objects.

▼▽▼

The lithic scatters we recorded across the Cerro de la Olla's eastern slope are comprised predominantly of dacite secondary and tertiary flakes and comparatively small numbers of obsidian and/or chert debitage. These scatters range widely in size, falling broadly within three density concentrations: 14 small-activity areas (1–100 flakes), 12 medium-activity areas (100–200 flakes), and 4 large-activity areas (200–300 flakes). There appears to be no strong relationships between which ecological niche a scatter is located in and its size, suggesting that intensity of stone tool production and use was not influenced by differences in topography or ecology. Similarly, there is no statistically significant relationship between the size of a scatter and the presence and absence of projectile points or other formal bifacial tools. For those scatters with projectile points (roughly 30%) there is also a statistically weak correlation between the size of a scatter and the age of a projectile point, suggesting that there is no significant change over time in the types of lithic production strategies occurring on the mountain. Rather than reflecting changes in the use of Cerro de la Olla, scatter density serves as a better proxy for revisitation. As discussed in Chapter 4, this type of lithic sprawl is a common feature of the archaeological record on the west side of the Taos Plateau and marks this area as part of a continuously used logistical activity area.

More direct evidence of site revisitation over time is found at two of the large scatters we recorded which contain diagnostic points dating to significantly different time periods: a side-notched point (3200–1800 BCE) and a corner-notched point (1800 BCE–400 CE). Notched points such as these were designed to break at the neck, leaving a portion of the blade inside the animal in order to create more tissue damage. These points are part of a replacement prior to failure production and discard pattern that reflect a general shift towards penetration efficiency and localized residential mobility among Indigenous groups in the region that.[25]

Although the relationship between site size, date, and ecological niche is weak, there is some preliminary evidence to suggest that isolated finds and scatters are distributed in patterned ways across the survey area. A Spearman's rank test of the relationship between environmental zone and find-type (isolated or scatter) indicates that there is a positive relationship between these variables ($\rho = .473$; p-value = .05).[26] Specifically, isolated tools, 55% of which are broken projectile points, tend to be located within herbaceous upland areas. This pattern offers preliminary evidence that Indigenous people were targeting game within the herbaceous uplands of the mountain slopes. In contrast to isolated finds, stone tool scatters within the survey area were more likely to be located in evergreen forest and shrubland patches on the mountain. These areas may have been selected for short-term activities, like refurbishment, because of the shade provided by piñon and juniper trees.

Overall, there was a disproportionate number of flakes compared to the number of tools recorded within these scatters, a pattern indicative of tool refurbishment. The high flake to tool flake-to-tool ratio within the survey zone is part of a discard pattern in which tools were abandoned following on-site use; a pattern commonly found in areas where raw materials are abundant. Two isolated dacite bifaces (B12 and B16), which appear to have been projectiles points broken during manufacture and subsequently rejuvenated and used as small scrapping tools before being discarded provide clear evidence of tool reburishment.[27]

To summarize, the scatters at Cerro de la Olla represent the material residues of small logistical activity groups who were using the mountain as a strategic resource node within a larger residential mobility pattern in which base camps served as the primary sites for tool production and intensive food processing activities.

▼▽▼

Evidence of on-site tool production within the survey area is minimal, with only five cores (4 dacite and 1 obsidian) identified across the entire survey area (scatter 18, 20, 27, and 17 in Figure 6.1). The five scatters associated with cores ranged in size from 56 to 211 flakes and were associated with projectile points that spanned a broad temporal range (3200 BCE – 400 CE). These scatters appear to be randomly distributed across the survey area representing discrete, consecutively used tool production areas. The general absence of core reduction at Cerro de la Olla fits a broader pattern of upland resource use by hunting and gathering communities. Higher-elevation areas across the northern Rio Grande typically contain evidence of biface production and maintenance accompanied by lower levels of core reduction.[28] This core-flake pattern in part reflects Cerro de la Olla's proximity to primary sources of dacite at Cerro San Antonio, 18km to the northwest, and suggests that this area was being used are part of a localized mobility network.

As at the playa sites discussed in Chapter 5, Indigenous Peoples occupying Cerro de la Olla were predominantly using locally available raw materials. Nintey-seven percent of flakes and over 70% of formal and informal chipped stone tools within the survey area were made from dacite (Figure 6.2). A comparison of raw material type used for projectile points indicates that dacite remained the primary raw material for tool production over time. The low percentage of obsidian tools and flakes across Cerro de la Olla is consistent with evidence from elsewhere in New Mexico and Arizona indicating that obsidian typically appears in small quantities and as debitage or utilized flakes within pre-agricultural assemblages.[29] This emphasis on locally available raw materials suggests that Indigenous occupants were primarily procuring raw materials during short-distance logistical movements across the Plateau, occasionally undertaking long-distance residential travel or trade to acquire obsidian materials.[30] Within this mobility pattern, residential sites would typically be located around 10 km from a logistical activity area, suggesting that base camps associated with the exploitation of resources at Cerro de la Olla are likely situated within the Rio Grande Gorge, which would have provided protection from the elements and easy access to water.[31]

While dacite is the primary raw material represented at the site, there are several notable exceptions. For example, an Anselin Moran's I test identified a small cluster of chert isolated finds, which includes two scrapers and a biface (p-values = .002, .004, and .034) within the survey area. Chert is not local to the Taos Plateau and is extremely rare at Cerro de la Olla, overall pointing to the curation and transport of tools to the site from elsewhere. These formal tools were either fragmentary and/or retouched suggesting that they were left after being depleted.[32] In contrast, the majority of dacite tools were largely complete (64%) and rarely showed any evidence of retouch (92%), indicating discard prior to exhaustion.[33]

A similar pattern of tool curation for non-local materials is represented at scatter 29. Located within the forested upland zone, this activity area lacks diagnostic tools and obsidian flakes make up over 50% of the assemblage. This scatter

The state of New Mexico formally acquired the remaining unpatented lands surround Cerro de la Olla during the 1960s and 1970s.[53] Today, the majority of the mountain is legally owned by the BLM. However, a small portion in the southern extent of the survey zone does fall within the boundaries of a 640-acre claim issued to another set of brothers, JP, JE, and Ezequiel Rael on December 18, 1961. The Raels received this tract of land in exchange for other holdings in New Mexico as part of the Exchange-Private-Taylor Act (48 Stat. 1269), established in order to prevent overgrazing and soil deterioration and to stabilize the livestock industry across the American West. The passage of what was known as the Taylor Grazing Act in 1916 recognized that arid lands were better suited for ranching, requiring claimants to prove that the land was more valuable for agriculture than as grasslands.[54] This policy was reinforced by the Stock-Raising Homestead Act passed by Congress in the same year, which issued 640 acres of "nonirrigable" land to homesteaders who lived on their parcel for 3 years and used it for pasture.[55] While some settlers established permanent residences on these plots, most of the patented lands surrounding Cerro de la Olla were used for grazing.

In an open, grassy clearing encircled by juniper trees are the remains of a large stone fireplace, likely constructed by 20th century ranchers as part of these federal ranching initiatives (Figure 6.4). Surrounded by rusted can fragments alongside white, green, and brown glass, the fire placeis sealed with cement mortar, which became a widely used construction material during the early 20th century. The use of stone masonry suggests that this structure was built prior to the 1960s when the state of New Mexico began filing legal claims to the remaining acreage on and surrounding Cerro de la Olla. Similar examples of cement-coursed masonry foundations in New Mexico (e.g., LA 73231 and 103482) date to between 1850 and 1945, suggesting that the Cerro de la Olla structure also date to this period.

There is no official land claim registered with the BLM for the area, where this structure is located, suggesting that this structure may reflect a more an illicit settlement strategy. Across northern New Mexico, ranchers and settlers often squatted on remote lands in order to make improvements to the plot before applying for a legal patent.[56] Indeed, the Montoso Survey Project identified a number of similar structures on unpatented lands on the west side of the Taos Plateau (e.g., LA 165974, 165889, 165902, 165889). This preemptive settlement strategy was a creative adaptation to the formal criteria for land ownership laid out in the Homestead Act, which required applicants to build a residence and "improve" an unspecified amount of land for 5 years (this was later reduced to 3 years in 1912) before claiming ownership.[57] It was possible to expedite this process of land acquisition after 14 months of residence by paying the government $1.25 per acre. However, for many poor settlers, this was not a viable option.

If the structural remains at Cerro de la Olla were part of this preemptive settlement pattern, they may have been constructed by Cressie A. Seal, who registered a 640-acre parcel of land under the Homestead Entry-Stocking Raising Act, immediately to the south of the survey area in December of 1916.[58] According to US Census records, Cressie was born in Kentucky around 1890 and was as living

FIGURE 6.4 Stone Fireplace at Cerro de la Olla.

on a homestead near Trés Piedras, New Mexico, with his wife, Mary, in 1930.[59] The Cerro de la Olla structure appears to have been abandoned relatively early on in the homesteading process as it is not associated with large quantities of domestic trash or other structures typically found at homestead sites such as wooden corrals, livestock watering facilities, or outhouses. The material and archival evidence together, suggest that Cressie may have attempted to homestead near his original 640-acre plot, eventually abandoning it for a more secure residence in the predominantly Anglo community of Trées Piedras. Ultimately, who built this fireplace and why it was abandoned remains unclear. A period of drought between 1917 and 1922, along with severe winter storms in 1918, forced many ranchers and homesteaders to abandon such isolated outposts.[60] Once abandoned, these homesteading plots were typically reverted into cattle and sheep ranges.[61]

During the 20th century, the slopes of mountains, like Cerro de la Olla, Cerro Montoso, and Cerro Chiflo, were also used for harvesting juniper posts for fencing or firewood.[62] Harvested juniper posts sold or bartered to households living across the northern Rio Grande provided an important financial supplement to the often-low wages earned by farmers and ranchers in the region.[63] Today, local residents continue to harvest wood from the slopes of Cerro de la Olla, a practice marked by patches of machine and axe cut trees throughout the survey zone. In addition to these cut trees, a contemporary use of the mountain is signaled by material evidence of small temporary camps. For example, interspersed among the chipped stone debris of lithic scatter 2 are the remains of several bullet shells, broken glass, as well as a small rock-lined hearth (Figure 6.1). This transitory camp was likely associated with hunting and/or woodcutting activities in the area during the late 20th century. Archaeological evidence of both permanent and temporary forms of land-use during the 20th century at Cerro de la Olla indicate that the mountain continued to function as a resource node, whether for game, firewood, or pasture, over time.

▼▽▼

The archaeological record at Cerro de la Olla suggests that the Taos Plateau is a "nodal" landscape, characterized by large swaths of sparsely populated unmarked lands punctuated by central sites, marked by accumulative signs of occupation.[64] Diagnostic projectile points found within the survey area indicate that Indigenous groups visited Cerro de la Olla as early as 7500 BCE; however, the site appears to have been most frequently used between 3200 BCE and 400 CE. These findings contrasts with Renaud's earlier fieldwork in the immediately surrounding area, which assigned a large number of lithic scatters on the Plateau to an earlier period of Indigenous use (5500–3200 BCE), characterized by high levels of north-south residential movement, encounter hunting, and tool curation. The archaeological record documented on Cerro de la Olla's eastern slope provide preliminary evidence for an important shift in land-use patterns towards a more intensive exploitation of upland ecological niches sometime around 3200 BCE.

This transition coincides with the expansion of piñon-juniper woodlands across the northern Rio Grande.[65] Archaeological research from eastern New Mexico suggests that upland piñon-juniper landscapes like Cerro de la Olla were part of a broader mobility pattern characterized by movement between riverine campsites in the winter and upland hunting locations in the fall.[66] This upland-lowland pattern was accompanied by an increasing attentiveness to processing plant resources.[67] The piñon trees, which dot the slopes of Cerro de la Olla, would have provided Indigenous people with an alternative source of protein and were likely harvested as part of this localized subsistence system.

The absence of stone features and formal tools associated with intensive plant or animal processing at Cerro de la Olla suggests that the eastern slopes of this mountain were used as a logistical activity site. Not only does the piñon-juniper ecological community, which covers the mountain slope, contain a variety of plant foods for foraging communities, it also offers and reliable source of medium-sized game for hunting.[68] The large number of fragmentary isolated projectile points across the eastern slope also provide evidence for the consistent reuse of the area for encounter hunting over time.[69] These upland resources would have been particularly abundant during the autumn months, suggesting that for much of the past 5,000 years the mountain was primarily visited during the fall as part of a seasonal logistical mobility pattern.

The preponderance of dacite across the survey area indicates that foragers were acquiring locally available materials as part of a more intensive utilization of the Taos Plateau. While the assemblage at Cerro de la Olla largely consists of locally available raw materials, there are examples of obsidian points and debitage across the survey area, indicating that some groups were traveling across significant distances to procure raw materials. The sourcing analysis conducted on a sample of materials from Cerro de la Olla offers preliminary evidence for a nested mobility network characterized by the regularized use of local materials for tool production as well as less-frequent long-distance travel to procure high-quality obsidian.

During the 20th century, Cerro de Olla appears to have continued to function as a strategic resource node. Evidence of bullet casings dating to the mid- to late 1900s indicate that wild game, like antelope, deer, and elk, continued to be hunted at Cerro de Olla over time. Evidence of machine and axe-cut juniper trees across the mountain also mark this place as an important source of building materials and firewood. These 20th-century materials are likely the residues of a clandestine settler land-use pattern that was distinct from the homesteading model found elsewhere in the American West. As marked by the dilapidated house chimney, the ecology and location of Cerro de la Olla defied the establishment of permanent settlements, instead promoting an episodic visitation pattern based on temporary and seasonal use.

The archaeological record at Cerro de la Olla marks this mountain as a persistent place for people practicing a variety of mobility strategies over time. The sheer length of time that the Cerro de la Olla area remained a mobile landscape is striking. The archaeological record of this place is dominated by evidence of hunting and gathering activities by Indigenous foragers as well as by 20th-century settlers. This continuity in land-use practices transcends ethnic identities and subsistence strategies, suggesting that it is something about Cerro de la Olla itself, which both constrained and made possible certain types of activities within this place.

Ecologically, the mountain offers an abundant source of piñon nuts, wild game, and juniper trees for lumber and firewood. In addition to these natural resources, Cerro de la Olla is strategically situated between a variety of raw material sources, including Newman Dome and San Antonio dacite as well as No Agua Peak obsidian, making it a central space within a broader raw material procurement cycle. Finally, Cerro de la Olla is located within 10 km of one of the only crossable areas within the upper Rio Grande Gorge, making it an important landmark for people moving east and west across northern New Mexico.

It is likely for these reasons that Indigenous People like the *Nuutsiyu* encampment identified by Lieutenant Whittlesey chose to camp near Cerro de la Olla well into the 19th century. The archaeological record of the area points to an important shift in land-use practices shortly after the encounter between Whittlesey's dragoons and the *Nuutsiyu* in 1849. Rather than a logistical activity site associated with hunting and piñon collecting, Cerro de la Olla became part of a new mobile landscape linked to pastoralism and wood collecting. As will be discussed in Chapter 7, the transition from a logistical to a pastroal mobility pattern is reflected in the material record of persistent places on both the east and west sides of the Rio Grande Gorge.

Notes

1 This narrative paraphrases a story recounted in Perkins, 1999: 88–90.
2 Perkins, 1999: 89.
3 Dicks, 2016: I-14.
4 Renaud, 1946.
5 Renaud, 1946: 20.
6 Dicks et al., 2016: I-56; Justice, 2002.
7 Renaud, 1946: 41.
8 Dicks et al., 2016: I-57.
9 Dicks et al., 2016: I-58.
10 Dicks et al., 2016: VI-6.
11 Dicks et al., 2016: VI-12.
12 Dicks et al., 2016: VI-6.
13 Chapin, 2005: 583.
14 Montgomery, 2017: 165.
15 Chapin, 2005: 657; Vierra et al., 2018: 240.
16 To run this test, I assigned each projectile point a numerical value based on its relevant age value. Points coded as "1" date to 9000–7500 BCE, whereas points coded as "8" dated to roughly 1600–1900 CE.
17 Vierra et al., 2018.
18 Vierra, 2013: 150.
19 Vierra, 2013: 147.
20 McBrinn and Vierra, 2017.
21 McBrinn and Vierra, 2017.
22 McBrinn and Vierra, 2017.
23 Vierra and McBrinn, 2016: 67.
24 Clark, 2020.
25 Kuhn, 1989.
26 The Spearman's rank-order correlation test is less restrictive than a Pearson product-moment correlation because it does not assume that the relationship between two variables is linear and can be used to determine whether a monotonic or non-monotonic relationship exists across two variables.
27 Shackley, 1990: 277.
28 Vierra and Foxx, 2009: 163.
29 Shackley, 1990: 218.
30 Roth, 2000: 311.
31 Vierra and Foxx, 2009:162.
32 Doleman, 2005: 24.
33 Doleman, 2005: 22.
34 Roth, 2000: 311.
35 McBrinn and Vierra, 2017.
36 Lanner, 1981: 101; Thomas, 1983: 61.
37 Shackley, 1990: 156.
38 Boulanger 2019.
39 The obsidian sample assayed using pXRF represent 100 percent of the obsidian objects within those scatters tested (n = 110, n = 14 , n = 13 respectively). The dacite samples taken from across scatters 14, 15, and 17 (n = 112, 16, and 16 respectively) are less representative of the total number of flakes present (25%, 6%, and 12%).
40 Boulanger 2019: 3.
41 Roth, 2000: 306.
42 Vierra, 2017: 10.
43 Boulanger, 2019: 3.
44 Shackley, 1990: 212.
45 Shackley 1990, 280.

46 Boulanger 2019: 4; Newman 1997; Newman and Nielsen 1980.
47 Vierra 1994a, b; Shackley 1990; Roth 2000.
48 Roth 2000: 312.
49 Roth 2000; Shackley 1990, 1996.
50 Dicks et. al., 2016.
51 Dicks et al. 2016: I-54.
52 Dicks et al. 2016: II-49.
53 United States Bureau of Land Management 2007.
54 Merlan 2010: 17.
55 Merlan, 2010: 20.
56 Dicks et al. 2016: II-108.
57 Merlan 2010:15.
58 United States Bureau of Land Management 2007.
59 United States Census 1930: *3B*.
60 Hinshaw 1976: 154; Cabeza de Baca 1954: 174.
61 Eidenbach and Hart 1994: 51.
62 Dicks et al. 2016: I-54.
63 Dicks et al. 2016: II-71.
64 Dicks et al. 2016: II-8.
65 Vierra et al. 2018: 236.
66 Montgomery 2017: 163.
67 Montgomery 2017: 163.
68 Vierra and Foxx 2009: 158.
69 Vierra 1990: 63.

Bibliography

Boulanger, Matthew T. 2019. *Compositional Analysis by pXRF of Obsidian and Dacite Artifacts from Ute Mountain and Cerro de la Olla, Taos County, New Mexico*. Southern Methodist University, Dallas.

Cabeza de Baca, Fabiola. 1954. *We Fed Them Cactus*. University of New Mexico Press, Albuquerque.

Chapin, Nicholas Merrill. 2005. Hunter-Gatherer Technological Organization: The Archaic Period in Northern New Mexico. Unpublished Ph.D. thesis, Department of Anthropology, Univeristy of New Mexcio, Albuquerque.

Clark, Chris 2020. Heinrich, Udall Introduce Bill to Designate Cerro de la Ollas Wilderness. Daily Post. February 1, 2020. Accessed April 10, 2020. https://ladailypost.com/heinrich-udall-introduce-bill-to-designate-cerro-de-la-olla-wilderness/.

Dicks, Merrill, Arron C. Anderson, Jessica Mrstik, Peter Rogers, and Todd Scarbourgh. 2016. Rio Grande Del Norte National Monument Class III Cultural Resources Survey of the Cerro Montoso Project Area, Taos County, New Mexico. Bureau of Land Management, Taos.

Doleman, Trudy E. 2005. Tool Time: The Influence of Tool Manufacture, Use, and Discard on the Formation and Composition of a Quarry Assemblage. *Lithic Technology* 30(1): 13–28.

Eidenbach, Peter, and Beth Morgan. 1994. *Homes on the Range: Oral Recollections of Family Ranch Life on the U.S. Army White Sands Missile Range, New Mexico*. Human Systems Research, Las Cruces.

Hinshaw, Gil. 1976. Lea, New Mexico's Last Frontier. *Hobbs Daily News-Sun*. Hobbs, New Mexico.

Justice, Noel D. 2002. *Stone Age Spear and Arrow Points of the Southwestern United States.* Indiana University Press, Bloomington.
Kuhn, Steven I. 1989. Hunter-Gatherer Foraging Organization and Strategies of Aritfact Replacement and Discard. In *Experiments in Lithic Technology*, edited by D.S. Amick and R.P. Mauldin, pp. 33–47. BAR International Series, Oxford.
Lanner, Ronald M. 1981. *The Piñon: A Natural and Cultural History.* University of Nevada Press, Reno.
McBrinn, Maxine, and Bradley J. Vierra. 2017. The Southwest Archaic. In *The Oxford Handbook of Southwest Archaeology*, edited by B.J. Mills and S. Fowles. Oxford University Press. DOI: 10.1093/oxfordhb/9780199978427.013.12.
Merlan, Thomas. 2010. *Historic Homesteads and Ranches in New Mexico: A Historic Context.* Report Prepared for Historic Homestead Workshop, September 25-26, 2010. State of New Mexico, Historic Preservation Division, Office of Cultural Affairs, Santa Fe.
Montgomery, John L. 2017. The Archaic of Eastern New Mexico. In *The Archaic Southwest: Foragers in an Arid Land*, edited by B.J. Vierra, pp. 156–166. University of Utah Press, Salt Lake City.
Newman, Jay R. 1997. Patterns of Lithic Procurement and Utility in the Rio Grande del Rancho Valley of the Northern Rio Grande Region, New Mexico. Unpublished Ph.D. dissertation, Department of Anthropology, Southern Methodist University, Dallas.
Newman, Jay R., and R.L. Nielsen. 1980. Initial Notes on the X-ray Fluorescence Sourcing of Northern New Mexico Obsidians. *Journal of Field Archaeology* 12: 377–383.
Perkins, James E. 1999. *Tom Tobin: Frontiermans.* Pueblo Herodotus Press, West.
Renaud, E.B. 1946. *Archaeology of the Upper Rio Grande Basin in Southern Colorado and Northern New Mexico.* Anthropological Paper No. 6.University of Denver, Department of Anthropology, Denver.
Roth, Barbara J. 2000. Obsidian Source Characterization and Hunter-Gatherer Mobility: An Example from the Tucson Basin. *Journal of Archaeological Science* 27: 305–314.
Shackley, M. Steven. 1990. Early Hunter-Gatherer Procurement Ranges in the Southwest: Evidence from Obsidian Geochemistry and Lithic Technology. Unpublished Ph.D. thesis, Department of Anthropology, Arizona State University, Tempe.
Shackley, M. Steven. 1996. Range and Mobility in the Early Hunter-Gatherer Southwest. In *Early Formative Adaptations in the Southern Southwest*, edited by B.J. Roth, pp. 1–16. Monographs in World Archaeology No. 25. Prehistory Press, Madison.
Thomas, David Hurst. 1983. The Archaeology of Monitor Valley: Epistemology. *Anthropological Papers of the American Museum of Natural History* 58(1).
United States Bureau of Land Management. 2007. Bureau of Land Management, General Land Office Records. Automated Records Project; Federal Land Patents, State Volumes. Bureau of Land Management, Eastern States, Springfield.
United States Census. 1930. Tres Piedras, Taos, New Mexico. Enumeration District: 0015; FHL microfilm: 2341135; Roll 23. National Archives, Washington, DC.
Vierra, Bradley J. 1990. Archaic Hunter-Gatherer Archaeology in Northwestern New Mexico. In *Perspectives on Southwest Prehistory*, edited by P. Minnis and C.L. Redman, pp. 57–67. Westview Press, Boulder.
Vierra, Bradley J. 1994a. Archaic Hunter Gatherer Mobility Strategies in the American Southwest. Excavations and Interpretations of Aceramic and Archaic Sites, vol. 14, pp. 385–398. Office of Contrat Archaeology, University of New Mexico, Albuquerque.
Vierra, Bradley J. 1994b. Archaic Hunter-Gatherer Mobility Strategies in Northwestern New Mexico. In *Archaic Hunter-Gatherer Archaeology in the American Southwest*, edited by B.J. Vierra, pp. 121–154. Eastern New Mexico University, Portales.

Vierra, Bradley J. 2013. Archaic Foraging Technology and Land Use in the Northern Rio Grande, New Mexico. In *From Mountaintop to Valley Bottom: Papers in Honor of Paul Williams*, edited by B.J. Vierra, p. 145–160. University of Utah Press, Salt Lake City.

Vierra, Bradley J. 2017. A History of Archaic Research in the Northern Southwest. In *The Archaic Southwest: Foragers in an Arid Land*, edited by B.J. Vierra, pp. 3–15. University of Utah Press, Salt Lake City.

Vierra, Bradley J., Richard I. Ford, and Stephen S. Post. 2018. Archaic Foragers of the Northern Rio Grande. In *The Archaic Southweset: Foragers in an Arid Land*, edited by B.J. Vierra, pp. 235–253. Univeristy of Utah Press, Salt Lake City.

Vierra, Bradley J., and Teralene Foxx. 2009. Archaic Upland Resource Use: The View from the Pajarito Plateau. In *Between the Mountains, Beyond the Mountains: Papers in Honor of Paul R. Williams*, edited by E.J. Brown, K. Armstrong, D.M. Brugge, and C.J. Condie, pp. 154–166. Archaeological Society of New Mexico, Albuquerque.

Vierra, Bradley J., and Maxine McBrinn. 2016. Resistant Foragers: Foraging and Maize Cultivation in the Northern Rio Grande Valley. In Late Holocene Research on Foragers and Farmers in the Desert West, edited by B.J. Roth and M.E. McBrinn, pp. 58–77. University of Utah Press, Salt Lake City.

IN SEARCH OF MULTIVOCALITY

The volcanic peaks that emerge skyscraper-like from the rolling prairies of the Taos Plateau, have intimately shaped and been shaped by the worldviews of Indigenous people in the region. For Tiwa- and Tewa-speaking People, mountains are spiritual beings who play an important role in ceremonies within the village space.[1] As first laid out in the work of Tewa anthropologist Alfonso Ortiz, *Ohkay Owingeh* as well as *Kah'p'oo Owinge* (Santa Clara) and *Po-woh-ge-oweenge* (San Illdefonso) Pueblos, conceptualize the Rio Grande landscape as a series of four nested circles defined by natural and cultural features, including mountains, flat-topped hills, shrines, and the village plaza itself.[2] The outermost ring within this cosmogeography is bound by four sacred peaks: *Keh pin* (San Antonio Mountain) in the north, *Tsikamu* (Chicoma Peak) to the west, *Oku Pin* (Sandia Crest) to the south, and *Ku Sehn Pin* (Truchas Peak) in the east.[3] Spirits referred to as *Towa é*, live on the peaks of these mountains, looking down upon and protecting the Tewa world. Earth navel shrines at the top of each peak, called *Nan sipu,* connect to rain roads that direct water and prayers toward each Tewa village.

The mountain-scapes of the northern Rio Grande also play an important role in Jicarilla origin stories and worldviews. Anthropologist James Mooney recorded one such story in November 1897 during an interview with tribal member Ed Ladd. According to Ladd, the body of White Shell Woman was transformed into four sacred peaks by her son Killer-of-the Enemies. Through bodily acts of walking the landscape and performative retellings of this origin story, the Jicarilla have passed on this place-based understanding of history from one generation to the next.

For the Spanish colonizers who entered the Plateau landscape in the 16th century, mountains did not embody spiritual figures or culture heroes. Rather, they were conceptualized through the lens of Catholicism and given names plucked from a pantheon of Christian saints and icons: San Antonio, San

Francisco, and San Luis. While Spanish-naming practices and ways of relating to the land were markedly different from the cosmogeographies of Indigenous People, nonetheless they marked these places in similar ways, constructing shrines on mountaintops and hills and etching images—primarily crosses—into the basalt boulders of the Rio Grande Gorge.

By the mid-1800s, a new wave of settlers had entered the region. Much like their colonial predecessors, early American explorers sought to map previously uncharted territories and establish overland routes to the Pacific Ocean. One such notable expedition was John William Gunnison's 1853 trek across the Sangre de Cristo Mountains in search of a railroad route through the Rocky Mountains. Although Gunnison's excursion failed, the path he laid out would later become part of the Denver-Rio Grande Rail Line that passed through the towns of Antonito, No Agua, and Trés Piedras on the Taos Plateau. The waves of Euro-American homesteaders enticed westward by the railway brought with them yet another way of relating to mountains, this time through the intensive mineral mining and logging. Under American control, mining camps sprang up across New Mexico. By 1900, over $110 million in minerals had been extracted, permanently disfiguring the landscape while leaking toxic chemicals into its water sources. These distinct occupational histories have create a unique material tapestry on the Taos Plateau, a landscape which continues to evolve to this day.

7

CERRO DEL YUTA

I led a small team of graduate students from Columbia University on a landscape-based survey of Cerro del Yuta during the summers of 2011 and 2012. Although the original aim of the 2011 field season was reconnaissance, survey in the area identified a discrete multilayered site, which we recorded and maped. Perched along a ridge overlooking the Rio Grande Gorge, were some two dozen circular rock alignments, historic debris, chipped stone tools, and flakes, as well as a small number of ceramic sherds. This multifaceted material assemblage provides evidence for the long-term use of the Cerro del Yuta area from the 10th century into the 20th century by various communities, employing a variety of subsistence strategies.

The following summer we returned to the mountain, undertaking a non-collection-based survey on the western slope of Cerro del Yuta. Walking in 5 m transect lines up and down the mountain slope, the team surveyed a roughly 10 km^2 area, ranging in elevation from 7,500 to 8,000 feet (Figure 7.1). This area contained a chipped stone scatter comprised almost exclusively of undiagnostic dacite tools and flakes.

The large dispersed lithic carpet documented on the slopes of Cerro del Yuta obscures archaeological attempts to reconstruct visitation patterns and procurement strategies. In many ways, the archaeological record at Cerro del Yuta reveals the ineffectiveness of applying interpretive models developed for agricultural communities to groups engaged in seasonal task-based activities that produce similar types of material signatures over time. The lithic carpet that covers this mountain-scape encourages archaeologists to move away from research questions focused on elucidating cultural differences across Indigenous communities, instead drawing our attention towards why certain places are consistently used in similar ways over extensive periods of time.

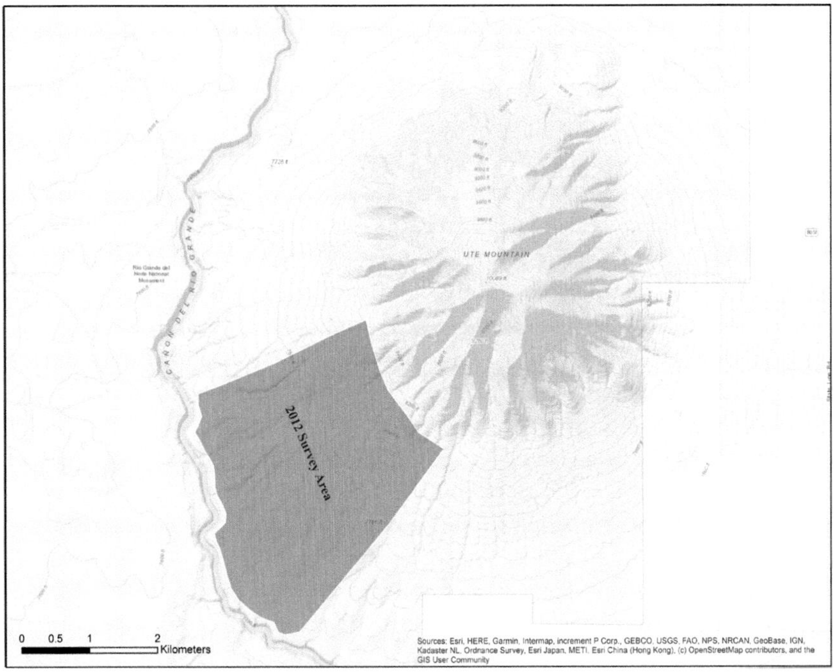

FIGURE 7.1 Cerro del Yuta 2012 Survey Area.

Previous research ear Cerro del Yuta

During the 1930s and 1940s, E.B. Renaud undertook a series of field survey projects in the area directly surrounding Cerro del Yuta. These efforts were part of the larger reconnaissance project discussed in Chapter 6, which encompassed the upper Rio Grande drainage in southern Colorado and northern New Mexico. In 1942, Renaud and a small field crew set out to document archaeological sites on both sides of the modern state border, eventually recording some 47 sites. His survey style primarily involved travel by car to areas previously identified by other archaeologists and local residents including A.L. Pearsall, Eugene Sutherland, and C.C. Wortman.

During the 1942 survey, Renaud's team documented a variety of archaeological materials including pecked petroglyphs depicting abstract and anthropomorphic designs, rock shelters, stone circles, and large dispersed lithic scatters which he referred to as "workshops." Traveling along the east side of Cerro del Yuta and turning west along its southern slope, Renaud's team recorded two sites, NM 271 and NM265, that are of particular interest to my findings at Cerro del Yuta. NM 271 is a dispersed scatter of "poorly worked" chipped stone tools made from dacite. Similarly, the overwhelming majority of chipped stone tools and flakes documented on the slopes of Cerro del Yuta are made from dacite. As Renaud notes, dacite or what he calls black rhyolite, is the "material most common in all that country."[4]

At NM 265, located on the southeast side of the mountain, Renaud recorded a rock shelter associated with some chipped stone flakes and enclosed by a dry-laid stone fence. Renaud identified many similar rock features across the eastern rim of the Gorge and excavated a subset of them. These excavations unearthed various ceramic types, including plainwares and black-on-white painted shards dating to the 11th century as well as one-handed manos. Unlike the material record on the west side of the Gorge, these findings indicate that the east side of the Taos Plateau was used by Indigenous Peoples engaged in early forms of agriculture. These occupations were placed on top of much earlier Indigenous inhabitations signaled by the presence of large projectile points. Renaud's reports, along with excavated faunal remains from rock shelters in the Gorge, reveal an important shift in subsistence patterns in this area from bison consumption to antelope, deer, and smaller game some time during the 10th century.[5]

During the 1942 field season, Renaud also recorded a series of stone enclosures along the edge of the cliff overlooking the Rio Grande, which he attributed to mobile hunting and gathering groups moving into the area during the 15th century.[6] While the precise location of Renaud's findings are somewhat ambiguous based on his maps, these stone features resemble those we recorded at the base of Cerro del Yuta in 2011. Overall, Renaud's research indicates that Indigenous people engaged in a variety of mobility and subsistence practices occupied the area on and surrounding Cerro del Yuta from roughly the 4th-century BCE into the 15th century.

The majority of subsequent archaeological work in the area surrounding Cerro del Yuta has been done by Cultural Resource Management firms and the Bureau of Land Management. These recording efforts have primarily documented sites along the eastern rim of the Rio Grande Gorge or along highway 522, which runs north from Taos along the base of the Sangre de Cristo mountains. Several sites have also been documented within the scrubland plains immediately to the east and south of Cerro del Yuta as part of housing development projects in Sunshine Valley.

Approximately 40% of sites currently identified in the Cerro del Yuta area are designated as "Unknown Aboriginal" or "Unknown Prehistoric" within the Archaeological Records Management System database. Like many of the sites documented on the east side of the Gorge, these sites are typically large lithic scatters ranging in size from small, discrete concentrations of 1 m^2 to large, dispersed scatters of artifacts over several hundred meters—the largest of which is a staggering 2,800 × 500 m. While many of these scatters (about 40%) contained chipped stone tools or other evidence of tool manufacturing, most lack diagnostic projectile points. Lithic scatters at which diagnostic projectile points were identified tend to cluster around the rim of the Gorge and are associated with an early Indigenous use of the area dating from roughly 5500 BCE to 250 BCE.[7]

Approximately 20% of sites in the area surrounding Cerro del Yuta were also associated with rock features, including rock cairns, stone circles, as well as U-shaped and linear alignments. As discussed in Chapters 4, these rock alignments may have been used for a variety of purposes, including as blinds to conceal hunters, as drive lines, temporary shelters, or as part of the emergent pastoral landscape constructed by Euro-American settlers during the 19th and early 20th centuries.

The logic of lithic carpets

Much like Renaud's findings, the western slope of Cerro del Yuta consists of a large, dispersed, culturally undiagnostic lithic scatter dominated by dacite. These archaeological materials suggest that the higher and lower elevations of the mountain were being used in distinct way. The survey area above 7,700 feet appears to have been part of a lithic workshop associated with repeated episodes of tool production and refurbishment. Sixty-eight percent of all the cores identified within the survey area were found within the higher elevation zone, indicating that primary tool production was typically occurring within this "workshop" area. The four projectile points identified within this portion of the survey zone had fragmentary bases, suggestive of breakage during repair. An Anselin Local Morans I test is a spatial statistic that identifies significant correlations between tool types at a 95% confidence level. The results of this test indicate that retouched and utilized dacite flakes are often found together and that these clusters are primarily located at higher elevations. This trend suggests that retouched and utilized flakes were likely used on-site as part of an expedient tool kit before being discarded.

In contrast, the archaeological record below 7,700 feet in elevation consists exclusively of discrete single-use activity areas, specifically, four small chipped stone concentrations (Area 4, 10, 11, and 12 in Figure 7.1). Three of these scatters are associated with rock piles situated at the end of a series of adjacent ridges (Figure 7.2). The location of these stacked piles at the base of the mountain suggest that they may have been used as trail or site markers. Alternatively, *Nuutsiyu* elders have suggested that small rock cairns, such as these, were constructed in order to mark places of offering—perhaps represented by chipped stone tools found in association with these features—given to spirit people.[8]

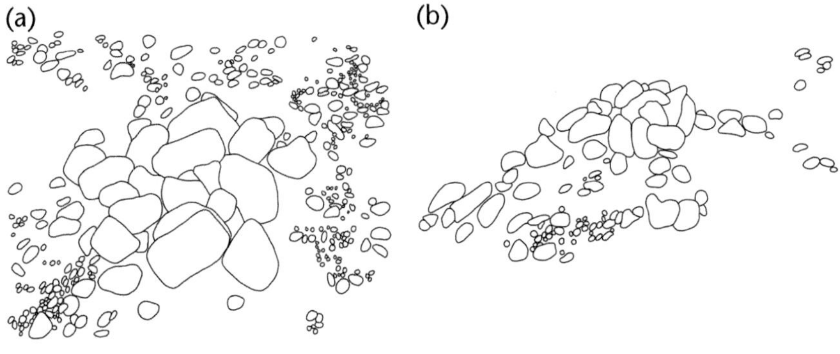

FIGURE 7.2 Line drawings of two rock piles at Cerro del Yuta.

The chipped stone surrounding these scatters is densest immediately next to each feature and gradually diminishes as it extends outward along the ridge. Overall, these scatters are quite large—up to 100 dacite flakes in some cases—and include dacite retouched and utilized flakes, scrapers, bifaces, and projectile points. Although these points were too fragmentary to classify definitively, their general morphology suggests that they date sometime between 1800 BCE and 700 CE. Compared to the higher elevation areas, these artifact clusters have larger ratios of formal bifacial tools suggestive of onsite tool use followed by discard.

The fourth discrete low-lying scatter was not directly associated with any features (Area 12 in Figure 7.1) and consists of an andesite chopper, a single large flake, and four projectile points: two obsidian side-notched points (3200 BCE–400 CE), 1 dacite corner-notched point (3200–1800 BCE) and a obsidian point tip. All four of the points were fragmentary, three of which had fractured tips and bases, indicating that they were broken during use and subsequently repaired. The general absence of other types of tools or flakes suggest that Area 12 is an isolated cache of tools rather than a tool production or use area.

▼▽▼

While there are clear differences between lower and higher elevation assemblages, there are also striking consistencies across the survey zone. Sixty-seven percent of the lithic materials recorded along the western slope of Cerro del Yuta were flakes. Twenty-one percent of this total assemblage was made up of informal dacite tools (retouched and utilized flakes), while formal tools (bifaces, scrapers, and blades) made up 10%. The low ratio of flakes to chipped stone tools within the survey area along with the large numbers of informal tools, suggests that Indigenous visitors to the area were primarily producing tools for on-site use. The large quantities of informal tools at Cerro del Yuta is consistent with observations of intra-site tool use from elsewhere in the western United States, which suggest that local materials, like dacite, are often used to produce expedient tools.[9] The 25 cores in various stages of exhaustion, identified across the survey area, provide additional evidence that Indigenous People were undertaking primary forms of tool production at the site.[10]

Ninety-nine percent of the artifacts, including 62% of projectile points, identified at Cerro del Yuta were dacite, indicating that Indigenous groups visiting the mountain were primarily engaged in a local raw material procurement pattern. A geochemical analysis of a non-culturally modified piece of dacite along with 16 dacite artifacts, including two cores, five bifaces, and eight flakes of different sizes was undertaken in the field by Mathew Boulanger using a pXRF device. The unmodified specimen taken from the survey area as well as nearly all of the sampled artifacts sourced to the *San Antonio Mountain A* complex. This sourcing data offers preliminary evidence for a unique manifestation of San Antonio Mountain A dacite at Cerro del Yuta and suggests that Indigenous People may have used the mountain for raw material procurement as well as primary tool manufacture.[11]

The absence of obsidian cores along with the presence of 5 fractured obsidian projectile points within the survey zone indicates that some Indigenous groups were refurbishing tools made from non-local materials rather than producing them on-site. Boulanger geochemically sourced a small number of the late-stage reduction obsidian flakes (n = 4) at the site. Although the sample size was small, these flakes all sourced to locations in the Jemez Mountains, specifically El Rechuelos and Cerro del Medio (see Figure 5.7 for location of sources).[12] This trend is consistent with the sourcing work conducted at sites on the west side of the Gorge as well as regional evidence that the Jemez Mountains are the largest and most frequently used source of obsidian in the American Southwest. The presence of obsidian materials from sources located more than 100 km to the southwest of Cerro del Yuta suggests that the Indigenous activity groups using the area were participating in large-scale travel or trade networks.

Nearly 75% of the tools identified at Cerro del Yuta had edge angles greater than 58 degrees, suggesting that they were likely used in scraping tasks.[13] The preponderance of possible scraping tools across the survey zone, along with the large numbers of utilized flakes typically used as disposable tools often found in sagebrush grasslands throughout the region, suggests that most of these artifacts were produced by small logistical activity groups engaged in on-site hunting and gathering tasks.

The large numbers of expediently made retouched and utilized flakes at the site may signal a change in Indigenous tool production strategies towards flake tool technologies. Indigenous assemblages after the 10th century in the region are characterized by an increase in of marginally retouched flakes, small numbers of formal tools, low levels of non-local materials, and a high flake-to-tool ratio.[14] The core-flake pattern and larger numbers of informal tools at Cerro del Yuta suggests that the use of this area likely coincides with decreasing levels of residential mobility between roughly 400 and 950 CE.[15]

The chipped stone assemblage at Cerro del Yuta may be indicative of what Lewis Binford called a "collector" strategy, in which people lived for at least part of the year on stored foods acquired by logistically organized procurement groups operating in a higher population context.[16] This subsistence pattern reflects the targeted exploitation of specific resource patches, like piñon nuts, seeds, deer, antelope, elk, and bighorn sheep.[17] Cerro del Yuta's location within the southern Rocky Mountain piñon-juniper woodlands suggests that this mountain was likely used as a reliable seasonal food source over time.

What types of food resources Indigenous task groups may have been acquiring from Cerro del Yuta is less clear. Direct archaeological evidence of piñon procurement and consumption is often difficult to detect because storage pits are typically located outside of residential bases and the same types of grinding tools are used for other plant resources.[18] Despite these limitations, it is clear from ethno-archaeological studies that upland piñon-juniper woodlands were part of most Indigenous procurement rounds in the arid West.[19] The vast lithic carpet which covers the slopes of Cerro del Yuta indicates that residentially mobile and village-based communities integrated the mountain into their procurement practices, of which autumn piñon harvesting was a consistent feature.[20] As anthropologist Julian Steward remarked, the piñon nut is "the most important single food species where it occurs."[21]

Given the intensity of stone tool reduction within the survey zone, the small number of projectile points identified in this area is notable (Figure 7.3). Specifically, 13 projectile points were documented, which fall into two general size ranges: eight points that are 4–8 cm in length and 2.5–4.5 cm in width and a group of six smaller points 2–3.75 cm in length and 1.5–3 cm in width. All of these points were fragmentary, either having missing tips (n = 3), fractured bases (n = 5), or a combination of both (n = 5). The large number of points with broken bases and shafts suggests that these tools were being refurbished on-site.

The fragmentary nature of the majority of points within the survey zone made stylistically typing these tools difficult. Of the five points that were complete enough to confidentially affiliate, three resemble side- and corner-notched types dating to roughly 3200–1800 BCE and the other two were stemmed- and side-notched points dating to 1800 BCE–400 CE. These two points morphologically resemble the "Rio Grande Points" collected by Renaud, which he described as having "a stem marked off from the body of the point by a small notched, cut or shoulder, usually oblique, more rarely horizontal or roundish; with a concave or notched base."[22] While Renaud never assigned a formal date range to his Rio Grande point style, his drawings and description suggest that these tools were

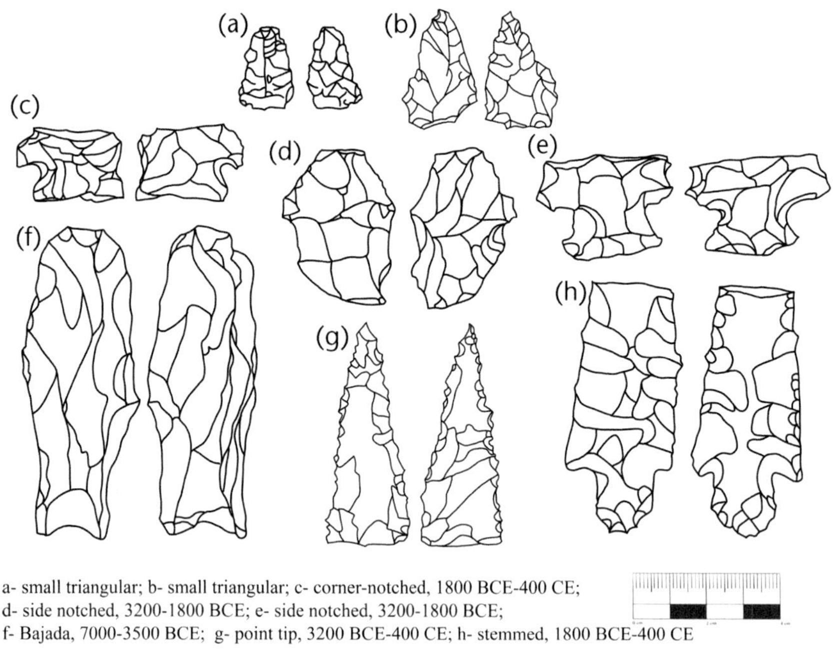

FIGURE 7.3 Sample of Projectile Points Identified at Cerro del Yuta.

similar to the San Jose (3250–1850 BCE) and Armijo (1850–850 BCE) points documented by Cynthia Irwin-Williams. Although the sample size of typable points is small, they offer some evidence that residentially mobile Indigenous groups were using Cerro del Yuta between 3200 BCE and 400 CE; a similar period of occupation to that of Cerro de la Olla. Similarities in the assemblages associated with Cerro del Yuta and Cerro de la Olla, suggest that free-standing mountains likely functioned as resource nodes for logistical activity groups moving between the east and west side of the Rio Grande Gorge.

As the projectile point data demonstrates, much of the archaeological record across the western slope of Cerro del Yuta is culturally and temporally undiagnostic, highlighting the challenges of interpreting Indigenous assemblages on the Taos Plateau. However, those points which could be stylistically typed, suggest that Indigenous People were using this mountain landscape from roughly 3200 BCE to 400 CE. Furthermore, the preponderance of expedient technologies made from locally available dacite within the survey zone also suggests that Indigenous groups engaged in lower levels of residential mobility were likely using the area as a logistical site for tool production and on-site activities sometime after 400 CE.

The sustained use of Cerro del Yuta by Indigenous People in the Taos area resonates with recent scholarship on "Pueblo" Peoples. Contributors to *The Continuous Path* volume, edited by Samuel Duwe and Robert Preucel, have argued that movement is not simply a response to subsistence needs or social conflict.[23] In documenting the continued small- and large-scale mobility of Indigenous People after the adoption of agriculture their research demonstrates that mobility is a key ontological principle shared across communities.[24] These authors draw our attention away from radical change and towards the persistent ways in which Indigenous groups used particular places, like Cerro del Yuta, over time for similar types of activities, including as a raw material source, tool production and refurbishment location, and hunting and gathering area.

Multivocal landscapes

A ridge overlooking the Rio Grande, approximately 2 km south of the 2012 survey area offers additional evidence for the sustained use of the Cerro del Yuta landscape by people engaged in varying levels of mobility. Along this ridge are over 30 stacked rock features surrounded by chipped stone flakes, ceramic fragments, and 20th-century debris (Figure 7.4).

These circular and semicircular features fall within two size groupings, linked to distinct purposes. There are nine small circular and semicircular structures, between 1.4 and 3 m in diameter, distributed throughout the ridge. The small size of these structures, along with the absence of clearly defined entranceways or associated artifacts suggest that they may have functioned as storage pits.

Accompanying these smaller structures are seven large circular structures that range in size from 3 to 7 m in diameter. These features are composed of piled medium- and large-sized rocks built into natural basalt outcrops near the terminus

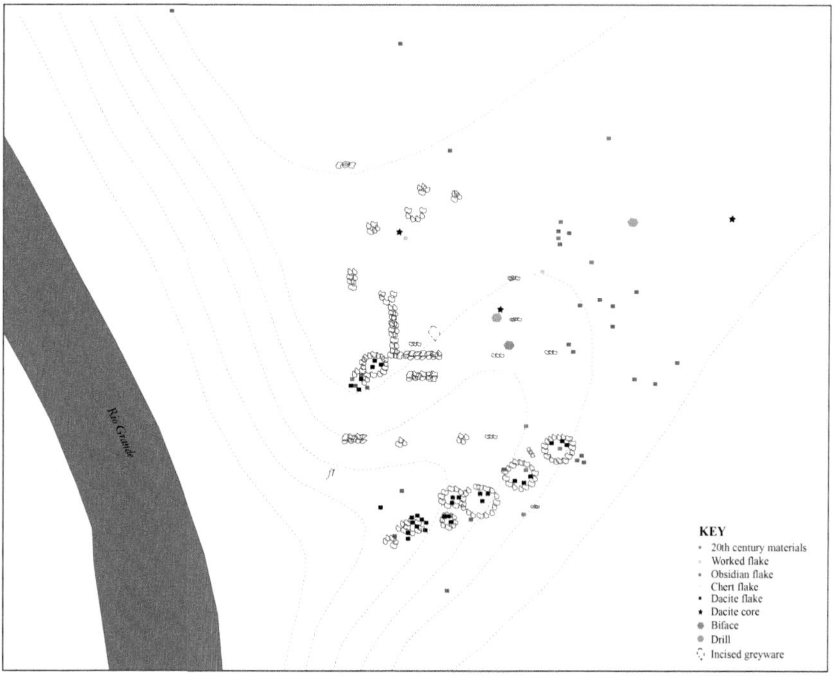

FIGURE 7.4 Map of the Cerro del Yuta Ridge Site.

of the ridge, where a drainage provides an easy pathway down to the Rio Grande (Figure 7.5). The interior of these features is generally clear of grasses or sagebrush and scattered throughout with small amounts of dacite and obsidian flakes.

Renaud describes a variety of similar round and oval shaped dry-laid circular structures, ranging from 2 to 6 m in diameter and reaching up to half a meter in height in his 1932 field report.[25] He posits that these structures were built by non-"Pueblo" people using a combination of horizontal and vertical slabs placed against exposed outcrops of natural basalt boulders.[26] The features Renaud identified were found in isolation as well as in small clusters of between two and ten structures.[27] Circular and linear dry-laid structures like those identified along the ridge are widespread across the region and were produced by various different communities as early as 1800 BCE and continued to be produced into the 20th century. Such features served a variety of purposes including as defensive outposts, tipi rings, hunting blinds, ceremonial structures, habitations, and animal pens.[28]

In addition to these circular features, six linear alignments were documented along the ridge. Like the alignments identified at Punche Lake, these features have widely variable lengths and possible functions. For example, there is a 2-m long single-layer stone alignment stretching across a drainage leading down to the Rio Grande that likely acted as a water management device. There are also larger linear and curvilinear features of piled rocks between 5 and 20 m long and approximately 1 m in height located on the ridgetop which likely served as shelters of some kind.

FIGURE 7.5 Large Circular Stone Features at Cerro del Yuta Ridge Site.

Interspersed throughout these features are seven loosely clustered rock piles, which range in size from 0.5 to 2 m in diameter. These piles were not directly associated with any artifacts and likely represent discard piles produced by the construction and modification of the circular, C-shaped, and linear structures.

The artifacts surrounding these rock features are associated with three temporally distinct uses of the Cerro del Yuta area, making it challenging to determine how and who used these structures. Future excavations, if permitted by Tribal Nations in the area, have the potential to clarify these temporal and functional questions. In the absence of such subsurface research, the following sections use architectural style and assessments of surface artifacts to present a series of possible functions for these features.

Defensive structures?

The location of the Cerro del Yuta features within an open ridge visible from either side of the Rio Grande Gorge would have made it a poor ambush site. Nor would this location have been particularly defensible, especially given the availability of other natural fortifications in the region, such as the mesa tops used at *Po-woh-ge-oweenge* and *Hemes* (Jemez Pueblo) to construct defensive villages during the 1680 Pueblo Revolt.[29] Indeed, many of the Cerro del Yuta features are under 1 m in height, providing little protection against incoming attacks. Finally, the surrounding surface record offers no clear evidence for the intensive production or firing of weapons that one might expect to be associated with a defensive site.

Tipi Rings or Hunting Blinds?

Unlike the rock alignments at Punche Lake, Three Basins, and Arroyo Punche, the Cerro del Yuta stone circles are stacked into several dry-laid levels—an architectural feature unnecessary for holding down hide tents. While C-shaped hunting blinds are a common feature found throughout northern New Mexico and southern Colorado, the walls of the circular and C-shaped structures at Cerro del Yuta are too low to provide effective cover from prey emerging from the drainage.

Ceremonial Structures?

Circular rock rings similar to those recorded at Cerro del Yuta (an average of 2 × 2 m) have been documented in the hills surrounding Tiwa-speaking villages in the Toas area dating from 1150 to 1600 CE. These features are typically located on hills where small and large game congregated and were constructed by men undertaking or returning from hunting expeditions.[30] In addition to these smaller shrines, Severin Fowles has documented a distinctive network of elongated upright rocks and bermed circles to the south of Cerro del Yuta in the Rio del Rancho basin. Fowles argues that these structures were made by ancestral Tiwa-speaking peoples living at *T-aitöna* sometime after the 13th century.[31] This shrine system was part of a ritual "villagescape" created in order to delineate social and ceremonial boundaries and to materialize a shared cosmology in response to aggregation.[32]

Within Tiwa cosmogeography, rivers, like the Rio Grande, and mountains, like Cerro del Yuta, are considered points of power, where one might expect to find similar types of shrines. According to Fowles, Tiwa shrines in the region often appear in pairs; a reference to the dual division of *Ĭăłap°ăĭbâ* into Feather/Summer People who treat the Rio Grande Valley as their former home and the Day/Winter People who are believed to have migrated from the north.[33] While most of the circular structures on the Cerro del Yuta ridge are free standing, there are several that share an adjoining wall (Figure 7.4). Like the features identified by Fowles in the Rio del Rancho basin, the Cerro del Yuta paired structures are comprised of unworked cobbles loosely mounded to 1 m in height in a circular arrangement 3–6 m in diameter with a small depression in the center.[34]

Although it is certainly possible that some of the paired circular structures at Cerro del Yuta may have functioned as shrines, there are several lines of evidence that shed doubt on the use of these features in Indigenous doings. While sharing some morphological similarities with ceremonial structures in the region, the Cerro del Yuta features are not deliberately stacked in the way that most shrines appear to be. Furthermore, rock features made by northern Tiwa-speaking people are typically located within a 500m radius of the main village or on important high places, such as the rock shrine complex documented on Mount Tsikamu. In contrast, the rock complex identified at Cerro del Yuta is situated in a low-lying area some 90 km away from any currently occupied or historically documented Tiwa-speaking village. These structural and spatial characteristics suggest that the rock features documented along the ridge are more likely associated with either a Numic-speaking People or with a Hispano or Euro-American transhumance pattern.

While it is unlikely that any of the circular features at Cerro del Yuta were used as shrines, a small pot drop of unpainted incised greyware pieces offers some evidence for the presence of Tiwa-speaking people on the ridge. Incised greywares were the dominant ceramic type produced in the region between the late 10th through early 13th century, suggesting that the Cerro del Yuta landscape was at least visited by Tiwa-speaking peoples during this period.[35] Ethnographic evidence from *Ĭăłap°ăĭbâ* supports a northern-Tiwa use of the Cerro del Yuta area, which lies within the roughly 2,500 km^2 area throughout which community members regularly traveled.

Habitation structures?

In addition to a northern Tiwa use of the ridge, several lines of evidence suggest that the large stone circles at Cerro del Yuta may have been used as domestic structures sometime during or after the 11th century. Similar circular features have been documented throughout southern Colorado, northern New Mexico, and the Texas and Oklahoma panhandles. Often accompanying these circular features are long rock wall alignments as well as C- and D-shaped features. Scholars have assigned these features to an archaeological culture called the "Apishapa Focus"

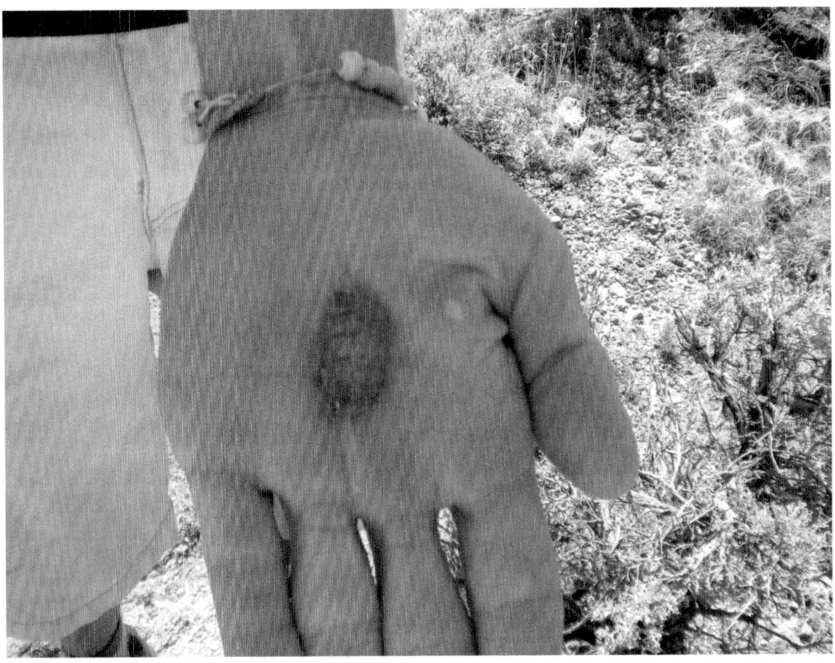

FIGURE 7.6 Incised Greyware Sherd from Cerro del Yuta Ridge.

(1000–1300 CE).[36] Indigenous People associated with this archaeological culture practiced a multifaceted subsistence strategy centered on hunting and some small-scale horticulture.[37]

To date, the largest number of "Apishapa Focus" sites in New Mexico have been identified along the Dry Cimarron and middle Canadian Rivers as well as near the towns of Mora, Logan, and Las Vegas.[38] The Cerro del Yuta features share many striking morphological similarities with "Apishapa Focus" stone features identified by Christopher Lintz in the Oklahoma panhandle to the east of New Mexico. According to Lintz's typology, "Type 8" features are rounded, circular or d-shaped structures made from vertical or horizontally laid slabs. Type 8 features range in size from 1.6 to 12 m^2 in floor space and are typically found along canyon rims and benches overlooking rivers.[39] The large rings at Cerro del Yuta are similarly sized and positioned, providing Indigenous inhabitants with an expansive view of the surrounding area. The ability to see game like elk, deer, and pronghorns from great distances would have made the Cerro del Yuta ridge a particularly attractive inhabitation area.[40]

Using Lintz's classificatory scheme, the Cerro del Yuta ridge complex may represent a "complex sub-homestead" comprised of three or more subordinate rooms without evidence of dominant households or clearly defined hearths and internal storage facilities.[41] In Lintz's study, sub-homestead sites were associated with a variety of domestic artifacts, including chipped stone debitage, projectile points, knives, awls, and brownware ceramics as well as archaeological evidence of butchering, hide preparation, horticultural digging sticks, and grinding implements.[42] However, parallel work conducted by Lynne Drake in southeastern Colorado indicates that artifacts as well as definite hearths and prepared floors are not always present at "Apishapa" phase habitations.[43] While some of the associated artifacts at the site have likely been displaced due to erosion, the artifact assemblage at the Cerro del Yuta more closely resembles Drake's findings in Colorado, rather than the intensive domestic occupations documented by Lintz on the plains.

▼▽▼

The lithic assemblages associated with the circular features follows a distinct compositional logic from the pattern described for the slope of Cerro del Yuta. While the 2012 survey area likely represents a lithic workshop associated with tool production and the on-site use of expedient tools, the assemblage along the ridge primarily points to tool refurbishment and curation. Specifically, chipped stone flakes (n = 56) in various stages of reduction were the primary artifacts documented in the survey area.

Unlike the dacite-dominated scatters identified across the western slope of Cerro del Yuta, the chipped stone assemblage along the ridge contained a more diverse set of raw materials, including dacite (n = 31), obsidian (n = 14 pieces), and chert (n = 11) materials. The comparatively large quantities of obsidian present along the ridge is consistent with archaeological evidence from elsewhere in the northern Rio Grande, which shows that obsidian was increasingly incorporated into stone toolkits over time, offering proxy evidence for a post-10th-century occupation of these stone features.

The obsidian assemblage documented along the ridge was comprised entirely of secondary or tertiary flakes, suggesting that Indigenous People were resharpening formal tools made elsewhere. Similarly, chert was found at the site primarily in the form of small flakes, some of which were worked into expedient tools. The general absence of obsidian or chert bifaces across the ridge is indicative of a tool curation strategy linked to relatively high levels of residential mobility. Overall, the lack of artifacts, particularly ceramics, formal trough metates, and large manos all suggest that the ridge was occupied for a relatively short period of time.[44] While the larger circular structures along the ridge were likely used as temporary shelters, the C-shaped features may have provided windbreaks.

Archaeological evidence of domestic structures dating from 700 to 1190 CE in the Taos region further supports the conclusion that the Cerro del Yuta structures were likely constructed and used by a non-"Pueblo" group. During this period, Tiwa-speaking people used "pit houses" characterized by clearly defined central hearths, four corner postholes, and ventilators. While circular free-standing surface structures were also built during this period, those structures typically have rock foundations with adobe superstructures and many of them contain interior hearths, storage areas, and postholes.[45] Unlike the structures built by Tiwa-speaking communities, the Cerro del Yuta stone circles lack any obvious interior features like hearths, roof support, prepared floors, or evidence of adobe.[46]

Instead, similarities between the Cerro del Yuta features and comparable "Apishapa" sites in the region, suggests that these structures were constructed by Numic-speaking People primarily engaged in a hunting and gathering subsistence system sometime between the 11th and 14th centuries. Numic-speaking groups, along with Caddoan-speaking communities, are typically considered to be the descendants of the "Apishapa" cultural phase.[47] The potential association of the ridge structures with early Numic-speaking people is supported by archaeological migration models which suggest that ancestral *Nuutsiyu* groups moved into the northern Rio Grande sometime between 1100 and 1400 CE in response to changing environmental conditions.[48] Ethnographic and archival evidence shows that some *Nuutsiyu* groups followed a seasonal migration pattern within the New Mexico–Colorado borderlands, suggesting that the Cerro del Yuta features may be early evidence of a Numic-speaking residential mobility circuit in the region.

Herding features and sheepscapes?

There is some preliminary evidence to suggest that sheepherders reused the large circular structures at Cerro del Yuta during the 20th century. The material remnants of sheepherding take many forms, including stock drives, dendroglyphs, wooden and stone corrals, lambing pens, cairns, dry-laid stone blinds, campsites, trenches, hearths, ponderosa pine peels, and sweat lodges. Andrew Gulliford has referred to these archaeological features as *sheepscapes*. These sheepscapes have been identified in wooded highlands, mesa tops, and near streams across New Mexico, particularly near Trés Piedras, Tierra Amarilla, and in the Trés Ritos hills.[49]

Herding sites are characterized by scatters of steel food and tobacco cans accompanied by small clearings marked by circular rock or wood structures, which served as pens. These pens range in size significantly, depending on location, function, and herd size. For instance, lambing pens are typically small, circular enclosures, roughly 1 × 1.5 m in size, while pens holding hundreds of animals may be up to 20 m in diameter.[50] The large, circular stone features at Cerro del Yuta are between 4 and 7 m in diameter, falling within the lower end of the reported size range for sheepherding pens. Herders have also been known to repurpose stone-building materials, from previously occupied sites to create dry-laid masonry corrals. For example, Diné people are known to have constructed a corral and hogan within the Una Vida great house at Chaco Canyon sometime during the late 1800s. The re-use and re-occupation of archaeological sites was a common across New Mexico and may also be present at the Cerro del Yuta ridge site.

Sarah Schlanger and Linda Goodman documented one such sheepscape near the village of Ocate, which contained four semicircular dry-laid masonry features about 4–5 m in diameter along with can fragments, wire nails, and barbed-wire suggestive of fencing.[51] Curtis Schaafsma recorded a similar set of stone features that he attributes to *Diné* people living within the Abiquiù reservoir sometime during the 18th century. This particular site contained a large stonewall made of roughly piled sandstone boulders standing about 1 m high. Surrounding this structure was a retaining wall and seven rectangular, square, D-shaped dry-laid structures representing domestic dwellings.[52] Schlanger, Goodman, and Schaafsma's findings suggest that herders used a relatively consistent type of architecture for corralling their herds over time and across ethnic groups.

In addition to circular corrals, Gulliford has documented semicircular structures and linear dry-laid walls coursed up to 1.5 m in height in association with herding campsites.[53] Several dry-laid walls, ranging from 5 to 12 m in size, at the Cerro del Yuta fit Gulliford's description and may have been used to control and protect animals overnighting on the ridge (see Figure 7.4). These features may also have been repurposed by herders as windbreaks in case of storms.[54]

A variety of artifacts along the ridge, including nails; can fragments; gun cartridges; shells; rubber fragments; a small white porcelain handle; and broken blue, brown, and purple glass, offers additional evidence for a 20th century use of the area, likely by herders. Notably, the presence of blue and purple glass accompanied by the presence of non-ribbed metal cans typical of pre–World War I domestic goods, suggest that the site was likely used prior to the 1930s.[55] While the artifacts associated with sheepherding camps are often similar to those found at homestead sites, the Cerro del Yuta assemblage can be distinguished from domestic trash dumps based on its small density and as well as by the absence of large numbers of building materials and household goods like Whitewares sherds[56].

An early 20th century use of the Cerro del Yuta ridge for sheepherding is consistent with historic evidence of sheepherding in the region from the mi-1700s onwards. Hispano herding activities were governed by the *partidio* system in which an owner or *rico* supplied a breeding herd to his *pastores* (tenant) who agreed to return two lambs for every 100 ewes at the end of a year. In exchange, the tenant was entitled to all the wool produced by the herd and the right to graze his own sheep on the *ricos* land.[57] Over the course of the 18th century, herding evolved from a subsistence industry into a central facet of New Mexico's exchange economy. By 1827, Governor Antonio Narvona reported that there were 62,000 head of sheep and goats in the city of Santa Fe alone and an estimated 240,000 in the territory of New Mexico.[58]

Twenty years later, Lieutenant James Albert remarked on the growing importance of sheep herding in the Taos area in particularly noting that, "the hills are covered with very good grass, which furnishes subsistence to herds of cattle and horses, as well as to fine flocks of sheep and goats. In them lie the principal wealth of the inhabitants."[59] With the arrival of the railroad, pastoralism became a truly profitmaking operation. In addition to expanding in scale, sheep ownership was gradually consolidated into the hands of an increasingly small number of powerful herding families still operating under the *partido* system. In 1880, 20 families owned nearly three quarters of all the sheep in New Mexico.[60]

On the Taos Plateau in particular, sheepherding expanded on the heels of the Denver and Rio Grande railroad, known as the Chili Line, which ran from Alamosa Colorado, through Antonito down to Santa Fe.[61] The presence of the railroad fueled the growth of towns like Trés Piedras, Servilleta, Calienta, Palmilla, Volcano, No Agua, and Barranca, whose inhabitants used the Plateau for commercial pastoralism. In 1895, New Mexico was producing some 14 million pounds of wool for export from over 3 million heads of sheep.[62] The herding boom of the late 19th century had largely cooled by the mid-20th century as a result of the economic downturn brought on by the Great Depression and increasing competition from cattle ranchers.

Contextualized within this broader history of pastoralism, the Cerro del Yuta ridge was likely reused as a sheep-penning site sometime between 1850 and 1930. On average, a herder would travel anywhere between 9 and 20 km a day, moving their herd from protected often-wooded areas in elevated locations downslope in order to graze and water their flock. The location of the Cerro del Yuta features in the open grasslands of the Plateau some 18 km from the nearest town of Costilla, suggests that it was likely used as an overnight camp rather than as part of a daily herding cycle.

This site would have served as convenient stopping place within a broader system of seasonal transhumance that alternated between warm season camps in the mountains, often marked by carved aspen trees bordering large meadows, and lower altitude cold season pastures. According to Jeffrey Boyer, while sheep would have been allowed to roam in longer-term high- or low-altitude locations, circular pens like those at Cerro del Yuta would have been used to control sheep overnight or during seasonal moves.[63] Ethnographic and historical evidence suggests that seasonal transhumance routes could cover over 600 km. One such mobility circuit involved wintering in the desert sagebrush region near Chaco, moving northwest to Los Ojos in the spring, and then traveling northeast to summer into the high elevations of the San Juan Mountains in Colorado.[64] As part of a similar herding network, the Cerro del Yuta ridge site may have served as a short-term penning area for herders moving north into Colorado or east into the Sangre de Cristo Mountains during the summer months.

While there is some preliminary evidence to suggest that the stone features at Cerro del Yuta were used as herding pens, further testing will be required to confirm this. Research by Schaafsma in the Chama Valley, along with more recent work by Wade Campbell on *Diné* corral sites located on Navajo Nation lands, suggests that chemically analyzing soil samples for spherulites—microscopic crystals of calcium salt in manure—offers one concrete avenue for identifying herding sites without excavation or faunal remains.[65]

The archaeological record at the Cerro del Yuta ridge site offers insights into the evolving land-use patterns of the Taos Plateau over the course of 2,000 years. The dry-laid stone structures along the ridge provide material evidence for the use of this area as a short-term habitation site by Indigenous people practicing a multifaceted hunting-gathering mobility pattern. The presence of incised ceramics along the ridge offers compelling evidence that this particular area was also likely incorporated into an Tiwa-speaking cultural landscape. Finally, the scatter of early 20th-century materials along the ridge suggests that these stone structures were reconstructed to create sheep corrals.

▼▽▼

The archaeological record at Cerro del Yuta constitutes what Chip Colwell and T.J. Ferguson have referred to as a *multivocal cultural landscape*.[66] This term refers to the fact that landscapes are constantly being inscribed with new cultural meanings and practices by a variety of different communities. Cerro del Yuta is multivocal in that multiple distinct social systems, material traditions, and levels of mobility, ranging from large-scale residential movement to localized logistical mobility to seasonal transhumance, are evident at the mountain. Specifically, projectile points identified throughout the survey area offer clear evidence that Indigenous hunting and gathering groups were visiting Cerro del Yuta sometime between 3200 BCE and 400 CE. These tools suggest that Cerro del Yuta was part of a seasonal logistical activity pattern associated with an increasingly localized mobility circuit centered on the northern Rio Grande.

There is also compelling evidence that Cerro del Yuta continued to be used by Indigenous People for logistical activities as village-based agriculture became an essential facet of their subsistence system. The core-flake production pattern and large numbers of informal tools documented across Cerro del Yuta are consistent with procurement patterns among Tiwa-speaking people. While it is certainly possible that non-"Pueblo" groups were also using a core-flake production strategy, the small pot drop of incised greyware on the ridge site offers clear evidence for a Tiwa presence in the area.

While it appears that tool construction using locally available materials continued over time at Cerro del Yuta, there were some notable differences in how particular areas of the mountain-scape were used. Within the 2012 survey zone, the types of activities occurring as well as the frequency of use differ between higher and lower elevations. The higher-elevation areas contain an extensive dispersed lithic workshop comprised primarily of flakes and informal tools made from local materials. This area constitutes a lithic carpet produced through multiple visits to the area by small activity groups engaged in tool production and on-site processing tasks. The absence of diagnostic materials associated with this lithic workshop makes it difficult to track when or who was re-visiting the area. Such interpretive challenges draw our attention away from questions of identity and towards "how" the landscape was being used consistently over time. In contrast to this higher elevation area, the area below 7,600 feet is comprised of discrete scatters of formal tools, particularly projectile points, as well as secondary and tertiary flake. The size of these low-lying assemblages suggest that they are likely the result of singular visitations to the mountain in association with hunting and/or tool refurbishment activities.

In addition to a potential Tiwa-speaking use of the mountain, the stacked dry-laid masonry structures along the ridge near Cerro del Yuta resemble "Apishapa Focus" features suggesting that this area was used as a short-term habitation area by Numic-speaking people sometime between 1000 and 1300 CE. A possible Numic-speaking occupation of the mountain is supported by the pronounced absence of grinding tools and ceramics typically associated with early agricultural occupations in the region.

Finally, early-20th-century debris across the ridge along with ethnohistoric evidence of pastoralism in northern New Mexico suggests that sheepherders may have repurposed some of the stone structures along the Cerro del Yuta ridge, using these features as pens for overnighting sheep during seasonal movements across the northern Rio Grande.

The culturally and temporally layered nature of this ridge reflects several unique aspects of its location and geology. The drainage which borders the ridge site provides an easily accessible pathway down into the Gorge, whose sheer cliffs make it difficult to cross the river. As an access point to one of the few traversable areas within the northern portion of the Gorge, this ridge would have provided an important throughway for both Indigenous and non-Indigenous peoples moving east to west across the Taos Plateau. Preliminary evidence for a variant of San Antonio A dacite at Cerro del Yuta also suggests that the mountain may have served as a primary source of raw materials on the east side of the Rio Grande Gorge. Finally, this ridge offers sweeping views of the surrounding landscape allowing visitors and short-term occupants to easily spot game or human movement across the Plateau. These factors help to explain why Cerro del Yuta has become a persistent place and point to the important role of the George in shaping land-use patterns over time.

Notes

1 Parsons 1939.
2 Duwe 2011: 106; Ortiz 1969.
3 There are currently two different interpretations of the northern peak within the Tewa cosmology. According to Harrington (1916: 44), San Antonio Peak is the northern boundary, while Alfonso Ortiz (1969: 19) states that it is *Tse Shu* (Canjilon Peak). This discrepancy is likely because Ortiz spoke exclusively o People from Ohkay Owingeh while Harrington conducted interviews with People from Santa Clara and San Ildefonso as well as Ohkay Owingeh.
4 Renaud 1942: 10
5 Renaud 1942: 34.
6 Renaud 1942: 11.
7 Specifically, these sites were associated with Armijo, San Pedro, Datil, and side notched projectile points.
8 Brunswig 2003: 55.
9 Odell 2000: 279; MacDonald 1995; Andrefsky 1994.
10 Vierra 2005: 202.
11 Boulanger 2019: 4.
12 Boulanger 2019.
13 Getty 1972; Gould 1971.
14 Bullock 1997:63.
15 Vierra 2005: 187.
16 Binford 1980: 10.
17 Akins and Bullock 1992: 33; Irwin-Williams 1984: 9-10.
18 Shackley 1990: 158.
19 Thomas 1973.
20 Shackley 1990: 154.
21 Steward 1997: 27; Clemmer 1985: 135.
22 Renaud 1942: 29.
23 Preucel and Duwe 2019.
24 Lyons 2003; Nelson and Strawhacker 2011; Ortman 2012.
25 Renaud 1932.
26 Lintz 1984: 50.
27 Evans 2012:1; Lintz 1984: 50.
28 Drake 1992: 18.
29 Aguilar 2019; Liebmann 2014; Preucel 2002; Wilcox 2009.
30 Duwe 2011: 346; Parsons 1939: 241.
31 Duwe 2011: 322.
32 Fowles 2009: 455.
33 Fowles 2004: 519.
34 Fowles 2004: 157.
35 Fowles 2004: 157.
36 Campbell 1969: 422; Krieger 1946.
37 Renaud 1932, Campbell 1969; Lintz 1986; Gunnerson 1989, Zier and Kalasz 1999.
38 Holden 1931; Moorehead 1931; Stuart and Gauthier 1981; Winter 1988; Zamora and Oaks 2004: 12.
39 Evans 2012: 26.
40 LaBelle 2012: 148.
41 Lintz, 1984: 245.
42 Lintz, 1984: 264.
43 Drake, 1992: 18.
44 Fowles 2004: 144.
45 Fowles 2004: 210.
46 Fowles 2004: 145.

47 Echo-Hawk 2000: 280-281.
48 Brunswig 2005: 88; Bettinger 1994.
49 Boyer 1995: 8; Boyer 1983, 1984, 1988, 1994.
50 Wade Campbell, 2020, personal communication.
51 Schlanger and Goodman, 1993.
52 Schaafsma 1979: 42-52.
53 Gulliford, 2018: 19.
54 Gulliford, 2018:18.
55 Boyer 1995: 16; Gulliford 2018: 18.
56 Boyer, 1995: 16.
57 Gonzaléz, 1967: 47.
58 Dunmire, 2013: 62.
59 Dunmire, 2013: 64.
60 Gulliford, 2018: 29.
61 Boyer, 1990: 9.
62 Gulliford, 2018: 32.
63 Boyer 1995: 38.
64 Gulliford 2018: 41.
65 Brochier et al. 1992; Schaafsma 1979: 220-222, Schaafsma 2002; 186; Wade Campbell, 2002, personal communication.
66 Colwell-Chanthaphonh and Ferguson 2006.

Bibliography

Akins, Nancy J., and Peter Y. Bullock. 1992. Test Excavations at Two Sites on the Bernalillo Grant in Sandoval County. Archaeology Notes 70. Office of Archaeological Studies, Museum of New Mexico, Santa Fe.

Aguilar, Joseph R. 2019. Asserting Sovereignty: An Indigenous Archaeology of the Pueblo Revolt at Tunyo, San Illdefonso Pueblo, New Mexico. Unpublished Ph.D. dissertation, Department of Anthropology, University of Pennsylvania, Philadelphia.

Andrefsky, William, Jr. 1998. *Lithics: Macroscopic Approaches to Anlaysis*. Cambridge University Press, Cambridge.

Bettinger, Robert L. 1994. How, When, and Why Numic Spread. In *Across the West, Human Population Movement and the Expansion of the Numa*, edited by D.B. Madsen and D. Rhode, pp. 44–55. University of Utah Press, Salt Lake City.

Binford, Lewis R. 1980. Willow Smoke and Dogs' Tails: Hunter-Gatherer Settlement Systems and Archaeological Site Formation. *American Antiquity* 45(1): 4–20.

Boulanger, Matthew T. 2019. *Compositional Analysis by pXRF of Obsidian and Dacite Artifacts from Ute Mountain and Cerro de la Olla, Taos County, New Mexico*. Southern Methodist University, Dallas.

Boyer, Jeffrey L. 1983. *The Taos Municipal Airport Expansion: A Cultural Resources Survey of the Proposed Runway Extension*. Contract Archaeology Report No. 2. Taos: Kit Carson Memorial Foundation.

Boyer, Jeffrey L. 1984. *Archaeological Investigations at the San Antonio Mountain Scoria Mine, rio Arriba County, New Mexico*. Contract Archaeology Report No. 5. Kit Carson Memorial Foundation, Taos.

Boyer, Jeffrey L. 1988. *Colorado Aggregate Company's Planned Red Hill Scoria Mine: Archaeological Inventory Survey*. Report No. 88-03. Taos.

Boyer, Jeffrey L. 1990. The Tres Piedras Project: Archaeological Testing at LA 71740, Taos County, New Mexico. Archaeology Notes No. 19. Museum of New Mexico, Office of Archaeological Studies, Santa Fe.

Boyer, Jeffrey L. 1994. Valle Vista Subdivision: Archaeological Survey in Taos County, New Mexico. Report 94-02. Taos.

Boyer, Jeffrey L. 1995. NM 150-NM 522 Intersection: Archaeological Testing and a Data Recovery Plan for LA 53678, Taos County, New Mexico. Archaeology Notes 174. Museum of New Mexico, Office of Archaeological Studies, Santa Fe.

Brochier, Jaques E., Paola Villa, Mario Giacomarra, and Antonio Taliacozzo. 1992. Shepherds and Sediments: Geo-ethnoarchaeology of Pastoral Sites. *Journal of Anthropological Archaeology* 11(1): 47–102.

Brunswig, Robert H. 2003. Archeological, Ethnographic, and Historic Investigations of the 5LR7095 Rock Feature Complex Site, Rocky Mountain National Park, North Central Colorado. Manuscript on file, Department of Anthropology, University of Northern Colorado, Greeley.

Brunswig, Robert H. 2005. Prehistoric, Protohistoric, and Early Historic Native American Archaeology of Rocky Mountain National Park: Final Report of Systemwide Archaeological Inventory Program Investigations by the University of Northern Colorado (1998-2002). University Press of Colorado, Boulder.

Bullock, Peter Y. 1997. U.S. 84-Sunshine Breaks: The Testing of Ten Sites Southeast of Santa Rosa, New Mexico. Archaeology Notest 165. Santa Fe.

Campbell, Robert Gordon. 1969. Prehistoric Panhandle Culture on the Chaquaqua Plateau, Southeast Colorado. Unpublished Ph.D. dissertation, Department of Anthropology, University of Colorado, Boulder.

Clemmer, Richard O. 1985. The Pinon-Pine: Old Ally or New Pest? Western Shoshone Indians vs. the Bureau of Land Management in Nevada. *Environmental Review* 9(2): 131–149.

Colwell-Chanthaphonh, Chip, and T.J. Ferguson. 2006. Memory Pieces and Footprints: Multivocality and the Meanings of Ancient Times and Ancestral Places among the Zuni and Hop. *American Anthropologist* 108(1): 148–162.

DeKorne, James B. 1970. *Aspen Art in the New Mexico Highlands*. Museum of New Mexico Press, Santa Fe.

Drake, Lynne. 1992. Archaeological Testing of an Apishapa Phase Structure in Union County. Archaeology Notes No. 73. New Mexico. Museum of New Mexico, Office of Archaeological Studies, Santa Fe.

Dunmire, William W. 2013. *New Mexico's Spanish Livestock Heritage Four Centuries of Animals, Land, and People*. University of New Mexico, Albuquerque.

Duwe, Samuel. 2011. The Prehispanic Tewa World: Space, Time, and Becoming in the Pueblo Southwest. Unpublished Ph.D. dissertation, School of Anthropology, University of Arizona, Tucson.

Echo-Hawk, Roger C. 2000. Ancient History in the New World: Integrating Oral Traditions and the Archaeological Record in Deep Time. *American Antiquity* 65(2): 267–290.

Evans, Charles Edward. 2012. The Sain Charles River Project: An Exploraiton of Prehistoric Trade, Exchange, and Apishapa Architectural Patterning in Southeastern Colorado. Unpublished Ph.D. thesis, Department of Anthropology, Colorado State University, Fort Collins.

Ferguson, T.J., and Chip Colwell-Chanthaphonh. 2006 *History Is in the Land: Multivocal Tribal Traditions in Arizona's San Pedro Valley*. University of Arizona Press, Tucson.

Fowles, Severin. 2004. The Making of Made People: The Prehistoric Evolution of Hierocracy Among the Northern Tiwa of New Mexico. Unpublished Ph.D. dissertation, Anthropology Department, University of Michigan, Ann Arbor.

Fowles, Severin 2009. The Enshrined Pueblo: Villagescape and Cosmos in the Northern Rio Grande. *American Antiquity* 74(3): 448–466.

Getty, John Marshall. 1972. The Tres Piedras Site of Northern New Mexico. Unpublished MA thesis, Department of Anthropology, Eastern New Mexico University, Portales.

Gonzaléz, Nancie L. 1967. *The Spanish-Americans of New Mexico: A Heritage of Pride.* University of New Mexico Press, Albuquerque.

Gould, Richard A. 1971. The Archaeologist as Ethnographer: A Case from the Western Desert of Australia. *World Archaeology* 3(2): 143–177.

Gulliford, Andrew 2018. *The Wolly West: Colorado's Hidden History Sheepscapes.* Texas A&M University Press, College Station.

Gunnerson, James H. 1989. Apishapa Canyon Archaeology: Excavations at the Cramer, Snake Blakeslee and Nearby Sites. Reprints in Anthropology, vol. 41. J&L Reprint Company, Lincoln, Nebraska.

Harrington, John Peabody. 1916. *The Ethnography of the Tewa Indians.* Government Printing Office, Washington, DC.

Holden, W.C. 1931. Texas Tech Archaeological Expedition Summer 1930. *Bulletin of Texas Archaeological and Paleontological Society* 3: 43–52.

Julyan, Robert Hixson. 2006. *The Mountains of New Mexico.* University of New Mexico Press, Albuquerque.

LaBelle, Jason M. 2012. Hunter-Gatherer Adaptations of the Central Plains and Rocky Mountains of Western North America. In *Hunter-Gatherer Behavior: Human Response during The Younger Dryas*, edited by M.I. Eren, pp. 139–164. Left Coast Press, Walnut Creek.

Liebmann, Mathew. 2014. *Revolt: An Archaeological History of Pueblo Resistane and Revitalization in 17th-Century New Mexico.* Tucson: University of Arizona Press.

Lintz, Christopher Ray. 1984. Architecture and Community Variability within the Antelope Creek Phase of the Texas Panhandle. Unpublished Ph.D. dissertation, Department of Anthropology, University of Oklahoma, Norman.

Lyons, Patrick D. 2003. *Ancestral Hopi Migrations.* Anthropological Papers of the University of Arizona No. 68. University of Arizona Press, Tucson.

MacDonald, Douglas H. 1995. Mobility and Raw Material Use at the Huntgin Camp Spring Site (35WA96) Blue Mountains, Oregon. *North American Archaeologist* 16: 343–361.

Moorehead, Warren K. 1931. *Archaeology of the Arkansas River Valley.* Phillips Academy, Andover.

Nelson, Margaret C., and Colleen Strawhacker (editors). 2011. *Movement, Connectivity and Landscape Change in the Ancient Southwest.* University Press of Colorado, Boulder.

Odell, Georg H. 2000. Stone Tool Research at the End of the Millennium: Procurement and Technology. *Journal of Archaeological Research* 8(4): 269–331.

Opler, Morris E. 1938. *Myths and Tales of the Jicarilla Apache Indians.* The American Folk-Lore Society. G.E. Stechert and Co., Agents.

Ortiz, Alfonso. 1969. *The Tewa World: Space, Time Being, and Becoming in a Pueblo Scoeity.* University of Chicago Press, Chicago.

Ortman, Scott. 2012. *Winds from the North: Tewa Origins and Historical Anthropology.* University of Utah Press, Salt Lake City.

Parsons, Elsie Clews. 1939. *Pueblo Indian Religion.* University of Chicago Press, Chicago.

Preucel, Robert W. (editor). 2002. *Archaeologies of the Pueblo Revolt: Identity, Meaning, and Renewal in the Pueblo World.* University of New Mexico, Albuquerque.

Preucel, Robert W., and Samuel Duwe. 2019. Introduction: Engaging with Pueblo

Movement. In *The Continuous Path: Pueblo Movement and the Archaeology of Becoming*, edited by S. Duwe and R.W. Preucel, pp. 1–33. University of Arizona Press, Tucson.

Schaafsma, Curtis. 1979. *The Cerriot Site (AR-4) A Piedra Lumbre Phase Settlment at Abiquiu Reservoir*. School of American Research, Santa Fe.

Schaafsma, Curtis. 2002. *Apaches de Navajo: Seventeenth-Century Navajos in the Chama Valley of New Mexico*. University of Utah Press, Salt Lake City.

Shackley, M. Steven. 1990. Early Hunter-Gatherer Procurement Ranges in the Southwest: Evidence from Obsidian Geochemistry and Lithic Technology. Unpublished Ph.D. dissertation, Department of Anthropology, Arizona State University, Tempe.

Schlanger, Sarah H., and Linda J. Goodman. 1993. *Archaeological Tests and Ethnohistoric Research at LA 74220, An Early Twentieth-Century Sheep Camp Near Ocate, Mora County, New Mexico*. Archaeology Notes 95. Museum of New Mexico, Office of Archaeological Studies, Santa Fe.

Steward, Julian Haynes. 1997. *Basin-Plateau Aborigional Sociopolitical Groups*. University of Utah Press, Salt Lake City.

Stuart, David A., and Rory P. Gautheir. 1981. *Prehistoric New Mexico: Background for Survey*. Historic Preservation Division, Santa Fe.

Nelson, Margaret C., and Colleen Strawhacker (editors). 2011. *Movement, Connectivity and Landscape Change in the Ancient Southwest*. University Press of Colorado, Boulder.

Teofilo. 2019. Gambler's House: Chaco Canyon, Its World, and Ours. Accessed on March 4, 2020. https://gamblershouse.wordpress.com/2009/07/21/a-virtual-tour-of-una-vida/.

Thomas, David Hurst. 1973. An Empirical Test for Steward's Model of Great Basin Settlement Patterns. *American Antiquity* 38(2): 155–176.

Renaud, E.B. 1932. Archaeological Survey of Eastern Colorado, First Report. University of Denver, Denver.

Renaud, E.B. 1942. Reconnaissance Work in the Upper Rio Grande Valley, Colorado and New Mexico. *Archaeological Series* 3: 1–35.

Vierra, Bradley J. 2005. Ancient Foragers of the High Desret Country. In *The Peopeling of Bandelier: New Insights from the Archaeology of the Pajarito Plateau*, edited by R. Powers, pp. 19–26. School of American Research, Santa Fe.

Wescott, Konnie L., Jennifer M. Abplanalp, Jeff Brown, Brian Cantwell, Merrill Dicks, Brian Fredericks, Angie Krall, Katherine E. Rollins, Robert Sullivan, Arnie Valdez, Bruce Verhaaren, Joseph Vieira, Lee Walston, and Emily A. Zvolanek. 2016. San Luis Valley-Taos Plateau Landscape-Level Cultural Heritage Values and Risk Assessment Final Report. Report Prepared for the Bureau of Land Management by Argonne National laboratory, Argonne, Illinois.

Wilcox, Michael V. 2009. *The Pueblo Revolt and the Mythology of Conquest: An Indigenous Archaeology of Contact*. University of California-Berkeley, Berkeley.

Winter, Joseph C. 1988. *Stone Circles, Ancient Forts, and Other Antiquities of the Dry Cimarron Valley: A Study of the Cimarron Seco Indians*. Office of Contract Archaeology, Univeristy of New Mexico, Albuquerque.

Yoshida, Twyla. Supporting Background: An Autoethnographic Look at Three Jicarilla Creation Myths. Unpublished Ph.D. dissertation, Department of Mythological Studies, Pacifica Graduate Institute, Carpenteria, CA.

Zamora, Dorothy A., and Yvonne R. Oakes. 2004. Entrepreneurship and the Settlement of Des Moines, Union County, New Mexico. Archaeology Notes 349. Museum of New Mexico, Office of Archaeological Studies, Santa Fe.

Zier, Chrstian J., and Stephen M. Kalasz. 1999. Colorado Prehistory: A Context for the Arkansas River Basin. Colorado Council of Professional Archaeologists, Denver.

A CLOSING VERSE

The story that was told throughout this book was whispered to me on the wind, as I crossed the dried, cracked floor of a playa. Each rock an adjective, describing the people who had been there before.

The story that was told here was an echo reverberated back to me while walking through the piñon pines that dot the slopes of a mountain. Each tool along the slope a verb denoting actions taken in the past.

The story that has been told here was a song that tickled my throat as I stood on a ridge and stared across the gaping expanse of the Rio Grande Gorge. Each flake along this craggy outcrop a note connecting together actions and people.

At their essence, archaeological narratives are simply stories we tell ourselves about our—or quite often somebody else's—ancestors. These histories are not just entertaining or informative reading, they are vital to our very survival, as humans, as communities, as nations. As Leslie Marmon Silko so eloquently wrote in *Ceremony*, stories "are all we have, you see, all we have to fight off illness and death. You don't have anything if you don't have the stories."[1] What I take Silko to say here is that stories are our lifeline. They ground our identity in a richer, deeper past while proffering guidance for how to act in the present. Perhaps most critically, stories give us ideas about what we might do, say, or become in the future.

8

PERSISTENT PLACES

A great deal of research on Indigenous history in the northern Rio Grande has focused on the timing, context, and logistics of maize agriculture.[2] The decrease in residential mobility that accompanied an investment in maize cultivation and the increased reliance on food storage is seen as a definitive moment for Indigenous people in the region. As Bruce Huckell has argued, this historical moment marks the "termination of the purely hunting-gathering, Archaic lifeway."[3] While maize cultivation in the Rio Grande occurs around the same time as other regions in the American Southwest, roughly 1000 BCE, "Late Archaic" foraging practices continue for a much longer period of time—up until 800 or 900 CE—in the north.[4] The eventual emergence of farming as the dominant subsistence strategy in the Rio Grande region occurred during the 12th century as effective moisture rates increased, making lowland farming more efficient. Scholars have often framed this transition from a hunting and gathering subsistence system to a mixed farming-foraging economy in terms of competition for territory and resources. The story goes that a growing sedentary population challenged foraging communities for access to desirable land, eventually compelling residentially mobile groups to either intermarry with agriculturalists or to move north and east where hunting and gathering remained advantageous.[5] Understanding precisely why Indigenous people did not change their cultural patterns for so long despite the availability of maize has, and continues to be, a central question of archaeological research in the region.[6]

Maxine McBrinn and Bradley Vierra have referred to the continuation of hunting and gathering in the northern Southwest as "resistant foraging."[7] Although it is clear that shifting climatic conditions and inter-community dynamics played an important role in shaping the life-ways of Indigenous People living in the Rio Grande region, the term "resistant foragers" assumes that the adoption of agriculture was inevitable—what Indigenous people were resisting was the pull to adopt sedentism and cultivation. By placing Indigenous people into bounded socio-economic categories, forager versus agriculturalist, current models describing the emergence of large-scale agriculture gloss over the ways in which Indigenous communities undertook subsistent practices that often blurred such categories. "Pueblo" people continued to engage in various forms of logistical and residential mobility throughout the region and "Nomadic" hunter-gatherers occupied and settled the northern Rio Grande landscape for varying lengths of time.

The archaeological record of the Taos Plateau offers material evidence for long-term human use of the northern Rio Grande from roughly 5500 BCE into the present. Material evidence for continuous land use in the region presents an opportunity to develop an alternative model for writing about the relationship between place, subsistence, and mobility. The model promoted in this book attempts to step away from long-standing archaeological interests in the "Neolithic revolution" and instead focuses on how particular features of the local landscape structured and were structured by Indigenous and non-Indigenous mobility practices over time.

Attending to persistence, upends traditional archaeological modes of inquiry that have often explained why people, practices, and places change. The argument for moving away from "transitions" and towards "persistence" is in part a pragmatic one. The archaeological record across the Taos Plateau is largely made up of low-intensity and/or undiagnostic "sites" that obfuscate efforts to document shifts in social, economic, and political patterns. When diagnostic materials are present at these occupations, they often map on to lengthy time periods that stretch over hundreds, sometimes thousands, of years and which encompass a broad range of descendent communities and lifestyles. In the end, the overall impression that one gets from the material record of the Taos Plateau is not of radical change but rather one of continuity both over time and across Indigenous People.

The arguement for abandoning change for continuity is also an explicitly political; I do so in order to challenge current modes of writing Indigenous history. As outlined in Chapter 2, archaeologists and anthropologists have often facilitated the erasure and alienation of Indigenous Peoples by focusing on culture change—European colonization being the most radical of these transitions. As outline in Chapter 3, they have also done so through various acts of categorization, like the creation of archaeological cultures (e.g., "Apishapa Focus") and temporal groupings (e.g., "Middle Archaic"). These practices have more often than not produced stories of abandonment, collapse, and acculturation that disconnect contemporary Tribal Nations from their material pasts. A focus on place rather than chronology takes seriously how Indigenous People say they think about history and its connection to the land. Incorporating Indigenous perspectives more fully into our scholarly engagements with the material record offers one small means of Indigenizing the discipline.

What has emerged from this approach is a series of place-based histories documenting the life-ways of human societies engaged in various levels of residential and logistical mobility. How human communities used playas and mountain-scapes changed over time in response to the needs and ideologies of the people who inhabited them. While there are obvious as well as subtle shifts in land-use practices on the Taos Plateau over time, the archaeological record from these playas and free-standing volcanic domes also provides evidence for remarkable continuities. Over thousands of years, these places have remained important resource nodes and activity centers for Indigenous and non-Indigenous communities. As will be discussed, this persistence reflects a variety of factors including the unique ecology and topography of each location as well as the geospatial position of these places in relationship to crossing points and natural resources.

Mobility corridors and the East-West pattern

Roughly 72% of sites currently documented on the Taos Plateau date from 3500 BCE to 400 CE, a period of increased population density and decreasing residential mobility.[8] On the Pajarito Plateau, Bradley Vierra has documented the emergence of an upland-lowland mobility system during this period in which Indigenous people moved between riverine valleys in low-lying areas and higher-elevation forested zones.[9] This mobility pattern represents a strategic adaptation to the unique topography of the region which, unlike southern New Mexico, has higher levels of rainfall and a more varied ecology.[10] The archaeological records at (Punche Lake, Arroyo Punche, Three Basins, and Cerro de la Olla on the west side of the Gorge and Cerro del Yuta on the east side, contain complimentary evidence for the emergence of a more localized residential mobility pattern after 3200 BCE. The extant archaeological evidence at these locales suggests that in addition to an upland-lowland pattern, Indigenous Peoples during this period were moving east and west across the Rio Grande Gorge. This east-west system structured the movement cycles of logistical activity groups traveling across the open grasslands of the Taos Plateau between intercept hunting sites and upland forest zones.

The movement of Indigenous people across the Taos Plateau in an east-west pattern was likely driven by the presence of large high quality source of dacite on the west side of the Gorge (Cerro San Antonio). The influence of dacite on the mobility logics of the area is demonstrated by the fact that dacite tools and chipped stone debitage make up 90% of every assemblage I documented (Figure 8.1). As depicted in Figure 8.1, obsidian and particularly chert made up a small proportion of the assemblages at Punche Lake, Arroyo Punche, and especially at Cerro del Yuta.

This pattern is consistent with previous research on the Taos Plateau and distinguishes the Indigenous occupation of this area from other locations within the northern Rio Grande, in which archaeologists have documented a general decrease in the use of dacite over time in favor of obsidian. This emergent preference for obsidian has been attributed to its particular affordances as a raw material; obsidian can be use of produce weapons with higher levels of penetration—an increasingly important factor as Indigenous communities

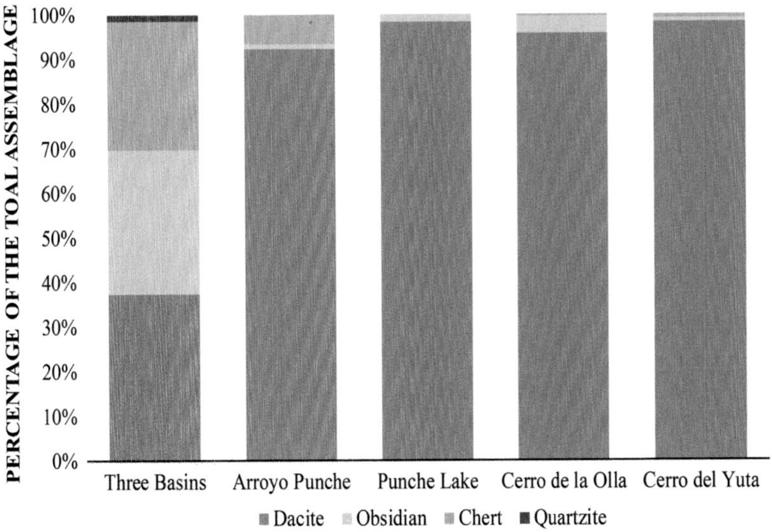

FIGURE 8.1 Stone Tool Material Types Across Sites.

moved from an intercept to an encounter hunting strategy in upland settings.[11] The continued reliance on dacite by Indigenous People moving across the Plateau over a roughly 7,000-year period is particularly striking given the pronounced changes that occurred over time in residential mobility patterns and subsistence strategies during this time. The preponderance of dacite at habitation areas across the Taos Plateau suggests that proximity to this raw material source was a primary reason why playas and mountains on the Plateau became persistent places.

While the large quantities of dacite chipped stone at sites on the Plateau demonstrate the intensive use of local resources, there is also some evidence for continued long-distance travel and/or trade. Obsidian objects sampled from Cerro de la Olla, Cerro del Yuta, and Punche Lake were geochemically sourced to locations along the Chama River and in the Jemez Mountain. The absence of obsidian cores or large numbers of flakes at sites on both the east and west side of the Gorge indicates that non-local material were primarily entering the Taos Plateau in the form of finished bifacial tools refurbished on-site. Noteably, obsidian and chert flakes made up a much more substantial portion of the chipped stone assemblage documented at Three Basins, suggesting that Indigenous occupants of this playa were engaged in a more varied raw material procurement strategy requiring higher levels of residential mobility and tool curation. These findings indicate that Indigenous people moving through the Plateau were also engaged in large-scale mobility networks in which the Rio Grande Gorge functioned as a north-south corridor.

Compositional differences in the quantities of dacite, obsidian, and chert materials documented within each of these areas draws attention to the heterogeneity of Indigneous mobility rounds. Despite similarities in subsistence practices, the archaeological record of the Plateau obscure attempts to impose one-dimensional procurement models onto Indigenous communities organized into autonomous small groups for much of the year.

In addition to nuances in raw material use, the archaeological record of persistent places on the Taos Plateau suggests that Indigenous people were engaging in different types of activities at playas and volcanic mountains on the west and east sides of the Gorge. For example, broken and isolated projectile points dating from roughly 5500 BCE to 400 CE and clustered around the rims of playas suggests that these places were used primarily for logistical activities, likely associated with intercept hunting, rather than as base camps. Specifically, over 75% of the points identified at Punche Lake, Arroyo Punche, and Three Basins date to between 5500 and 1800 BCE, suggesting that these landscape features were more frequently used by Indigenous groups engaged in a large-scale north-south residential mobility round during a climatic period characterized by heighted aridity.[12] In addition to providing a seasonal source of water, these play as were used in similar ways over time in part because of their strategic location within the natural migration corridors of medium-sized game.

While playas appear to have been consistently used as intercept hunting sites by residentially mobile Indigenous People, mountainscapes on both sides of the Gorge appear to be more frequently associated with etool refurbishment activities as well as hunting. Diagnostic tools identified in association with both lithic scatters and as isolated tools at Cerro de la Olla predominantly date from 3200 BCE to 400 CE, suggesting that as residential mobility networks became more concentrated, mountain slopes were increasingly used for logistical activities associated with upland resource procurement. That Cerro de la Olla served primarily as a short-term activity area is supported by the pronounced absence of constructed stone features or stone tools indicative of on-site processing activities typically associated with more intensive occupations.

The archaeological record at Cerro del Yuta suggests that mountain slopes on the east side of the Taos Plateau were also used largely for logistical activities rather than as base camps. The majority of points identified at Cerro del Yuta were too fragmentary to stylistically type, indicating that these tools were being refurbished extensively on-site and then discarded upon exhaustion. Those points that were complete enough to assign to a temporal category, dated to a similar period of use to those found at Cerro de la Oll (3200 BCE and 400 CE). These diagnostic points had broken tips caused likely fractured during logistical hunting activities. This pattern suggests that Cerro del Yuta was a logistical activity node within an upland-lowland mobility circuit similar to the one proposed by Vierra. The chipped stone assemblages documented at Cerro de la Olla and Cerro del Yuta suggest that mountainous areas became particularly important logistical activity areas for Indigenous people as residential mobility circuits contracted.

As the most imposing geological feature on the Rio Grande landscape, the Gorge itself likely played a role in shaping land-use practices on the east and west sides of the Plateau. Although the sample size is small, the sourcing analysis conducted at Punche Lake, Cerro de la Olla, and Cerro del Yuta offer evidence for the development of a nested procurement pattern. Within this pattern, the Gorge served as a geological boundary, which incentivized the use of extra-local raw materials. The sourcing data from Punche Lake and Cerro de la Olla indicates that at least some Indigenous activity groups were using dacite collected from Newman Dome and Cerro San Antonio on the west side of the Plateau. These sources are located within a 10-km radius of both sites. Similarly, preliminary evidence for a possible source of San Antonio A dacite at Cerro del Yuta supports the idea that Indigenous groups were using locally available raw materials to produce new tools when needed. While more geochemical sampling will be needed to fully demonstrate this pattern, the initial sourcing data would seem to represent a distinctive localized procurement pattern which made tool curation unnecessary.

The material record from sites directly located within the Gorge and along the rim offer additional insights into the particular role this landscape feature played in shaping Indigenous mobility patterns. A reviews of sites files in the ARMS database, indicates that there are 103 sites currently documented between the Rio Grande Gorge Bridge and the New Mexico–Colorado border.[13] Sites within and surrounding the Gorge rim consist primarily of undiagnostic chipped stone scatters, suggesting that this area was also used for logistical activities rather than as base camps. Approximately 30% of these sites, however, did contain dateable projectile points associated with Indigenous foragers living in the region between 5500 BCE and 900 CE (Figure 8.2). Roughly half of those sites with diagnostic projectile points contained tools directly dating to the 2nd-century BCE or later, a period that coincides with an increase in regional population and the more intensive use of the local landscape.[14] Despite wide-scale shifts in mobility patterns during this period, there are no notable differences in terms of site size, composition, or location across sites assigned to this period in the ARMS database.

Lithic scatters dating from 5500 BCE to 900 CE fall into two general groupings which offer evidence for a dual logistical mobility system associated with different levels of intensity. The majority of scatters in this subsample (n = 21) were discrete activity areas comprised of several dozen pieces of chipped stone debitage. These discrete scatters were likely produced by small groups or individuals undertaking short-term logistical trips that made little archaeological impact on the landscape.

In contrast, large dispersed scatters were likely produced by task groups engaged in significant levels of on-site tool use and production. Although Indigenous people rarely reoccupy the same locations, they do often camp near old sites. Over time these locations increase in size as well as in the diversity of associated artifacts.[15] Such revisitation practices have produced large lithic workshops comprised of hundreds of pieces of debitage, chipped stone tools, and projectile points along

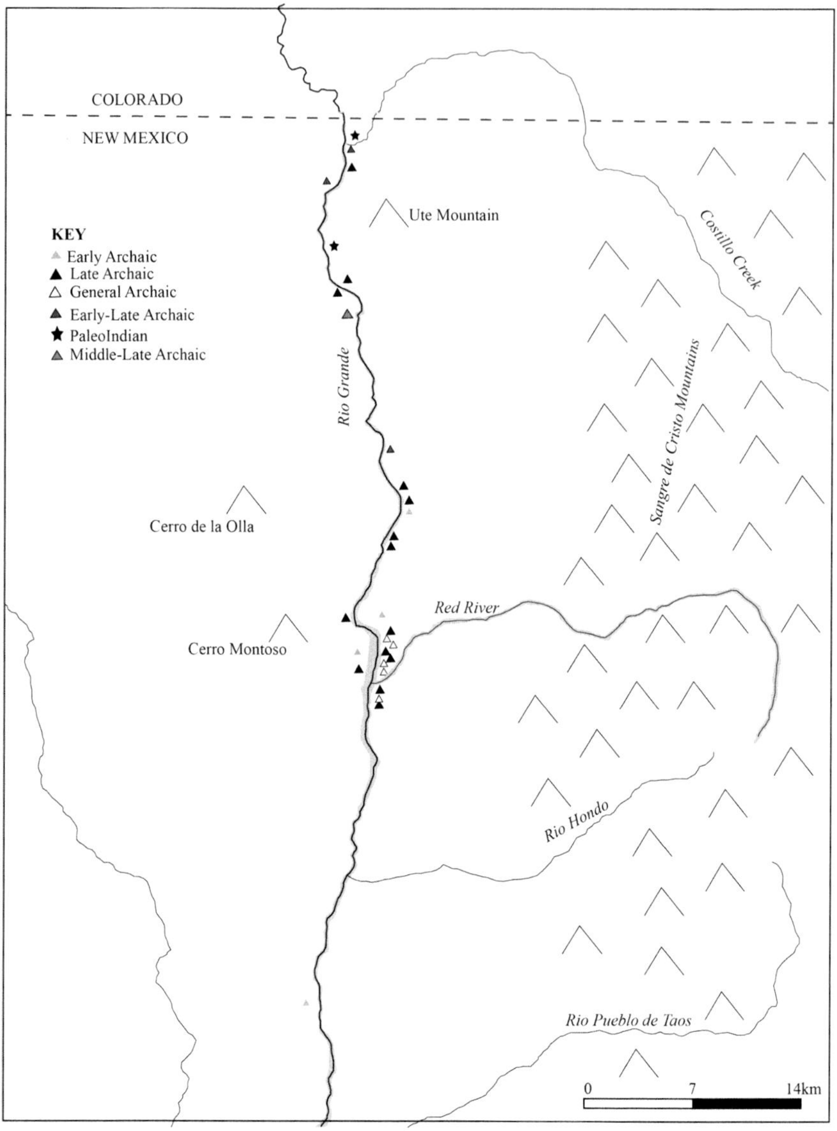

FIGURE 8.2 Sites Associated with Indigenous People Living in the Rio Grande Gorge between 5000 BCE and 400 CE.

the rim of the Gorge (n = 10). Many of these large scatters are also associated with on-site tool use (n = 6), primary tool manufacturing (n = 4), and plant processing activities (n = 3).

The densest concentration of "Archaic" sites within the Gorge is located at the confluence of the Red River and the Rio Grande. The two largest scatters, LA 167551 (10,000+ lithics) and LA 70753 (1,000+ lithics) within this area, are situated on the west and east sides of the Gorge respectively. Eleven smaller lithic scatters have been recorded directly below these sites within the Gorge itself. The density of these artifact scatters likely reflects several features of the local topography and ecology. Specifically, this confluence provides an easy crossing point between the east and west sides of the Plateau, likely serving as a key thoroughfare for people and wild game moving across the Taos Plateau. The Red River-Rio Grande confluence is also associated with several natural springs, commonly referred to as Big and Little Arsenic springs. Big Arsenic springs is a complex of several large northern springs along with a single southern spring, whereas Little Arsenic consists of a single small spring.[16] Natural springs are considered to be particularly powerful places by Indigenous people, a belief that likely informed the accumulation of material culture in this area.[17]

The importance of springs within Indigenous cosmogeographies is recorded within oral narratives. According to stories told by the *Ĭălap°ăĭbâ*, at the end of the world, a deity known as *Pâköałanna* would make the hot springs boil over and flood the earth.[18] The origin stories of northern Tiwa-speaking peoples also indicate that hot springs like Ponce de Leone as well as a small spring referred to as *Tsipapu* near Taos were where their ancestors first emerged into the region.[19] Tewa-speaking communities also consider springs to be places of emergence and the dwellings of important culture heroes. For example, according to *Kah'p'oo Owinge* tribal members, the culture hero *Posejemsu* lived and sometimes still lives at the springs near Ojo Caliente.[20]

Hot springs held similar types of meanings passed down through oral histories for Indigenous groups engaged in higher levels of residential mobility than these Tiwa- and Tewa-speaking communities. According to one *Ndee* narrative, a monster named He-Kicks-them-in-the-Water lived in a hot spring and would terrorize travelers by kicking them into the water and feeding them to his four daughters. It was not until the culture hero Killer-of-Enemies killed this monster, that this terrorizing stopped.[21] Hot springs were also an important part of *Nuutsiyu* seasonal rounds throughout New Mexico and Colorado and are believed to have healing properties.[22] These oral histories indicate that Indigenous groups, practicing varying levels of residential mobility, consider springs to be particularly important spaces. While we can only speculate as to why Indigenous groups moving through the Gorge may have frequently stopped at the Red River-Rio Grande confluence, what is clear is that the large scatters in this area represent persistent places reused multiple times by Indigenous people moving both through and across the Rio Grande Gorge.

Unlike the Pajarito Plateau, there is a notable lack of evidence for storage features, intensive domestic processing materials, or on-site tool use in this riverine setting, suggesting that the northern extent of the Gorge may not have been used for seasonal residential base camps.[23] Although there are currently four sites within the northern portion of the Gorge that contain groundstone artifacts indicative of plant processing activities, in general, sites within this area are ephemeral single-use areas. This pattern contrasts with the large scatters documented along the east (n = 7) and west sides (n = 3) of the rim and suggests that the Gorge largely served as a natural travel corridor for Indigenous People moving through and across the Taos Plateau.[24]

Rock art documented within the Rio Grande indicates that Indigenous people were using this area to record hunting and gathering activities between 5500 BCE and 900 CE. There are currently 25 rock art sites between the Rio Grande Gorge Bridge and Cerro del Yuta, which contain deeply pecked petroglyphs.[25] These glyphs depict abstract and geometric images, including concentric circles, dots, wavy and zigzag lines, as well as footprints, animal tracks, and quadrupeds, particularly deer (Figure 8.3).

The clustering of many of these abstract images, particularly wavy and zigzag lines, near hot springs and confluences within the Gorge (n = 15 sites) suggests that these images may have been used to mark or "tap into" the power located within these particular places. The tracks and dots—which may represent scat lines—etched into the basalt boulder of the Gorge may have served as a kind of representational map of the tracking logics employed by Indigenous hunters in and outside of the Gorge. The presence of naturalistic images associated with hunting and gatherings activities along with the general absence of substantive domestic camps indicate that the northern extent of the Rio Grande Gorge was part of a sophisticated logistical mobility pattern associated with the targeting of wild game on the east and west sides of the Taos Plateau.

Roughly 88% of petroglyph sites dating to this period also contain images created by Tiwa-speaking people. The iconography used by these "Pueblo" Peoples, include figurative depictions of humans, animals, and ceremonial entities, which present a striking contrast to the abstract style of earlier residentially mobile groups. The move away from abstract images and toward representational depictions of animals as well as disarticulated hands and feet, is part of a broader series of transitions in image selection among Indigenous groups in the region.[26] As suggested by Severin Fowles, the turn towards representing bodies is directly associated with the adoption of village-based agricultural practices and marks an important shift in both representational style and the logic of image depiction among Indigenous people in the region.[27] Much like the lithic scatters discussed on the Taos Plateau, the layering of images over top of one another points to the creation of persistent places within the Gorge itslef by Indigenous people engaged in varying levels of residential mobility.

Natural boundary markers and Indigenous mobility

As the possibilities of agriculture drew *some* Indigenous People towards village life in the Rio Grande Valley, the Gorge appears to have become a natural eastern boundary marker within this emergent cultural landscape. As E.B. Renaud notes, "the Pueblos seemed to have favored the route east of the river, either because more direct or more accessible."[28] The consolidation of particular Indigenous groups on the east side of the Gorge opened up other space on the west side of the

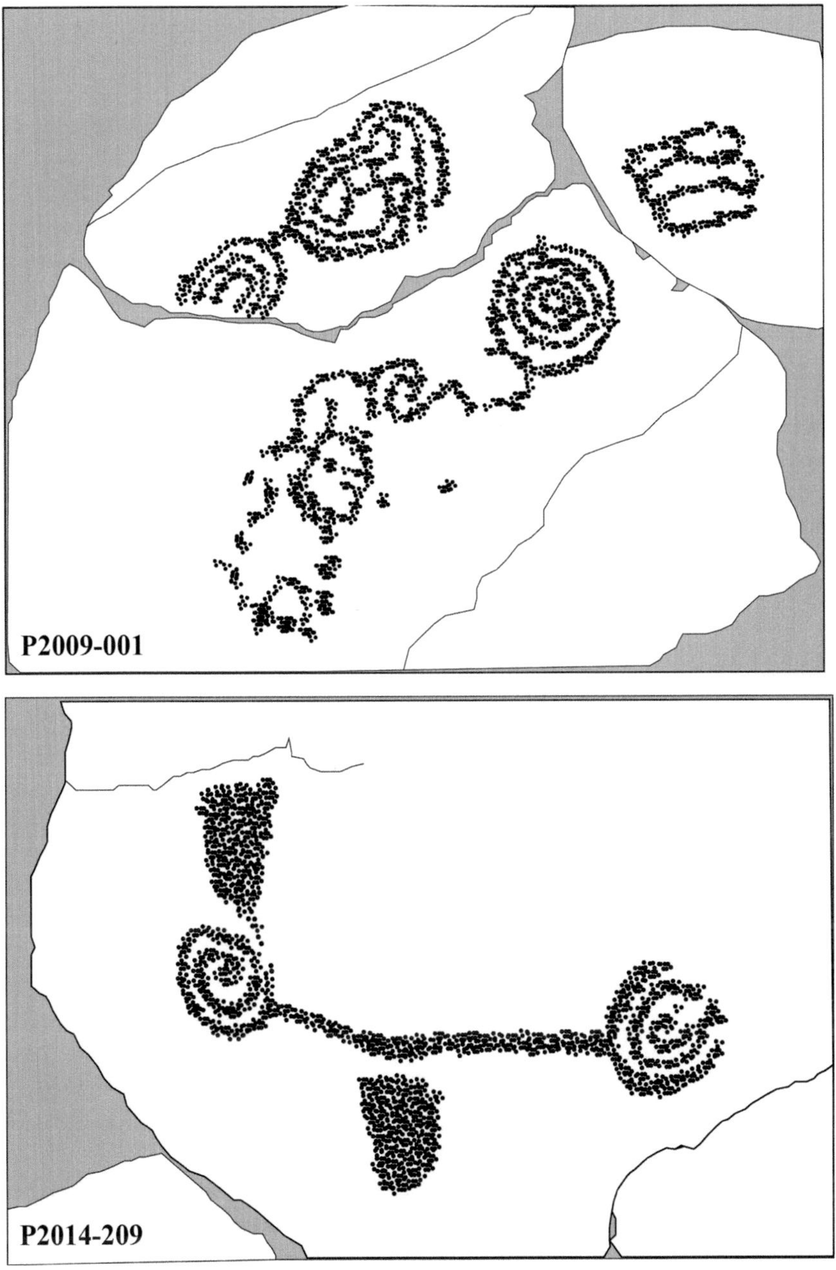

FIGURE 8.3 Drawing of Petroglyphs 2014-208 and 2009-001 Recorded by the Rio Grande Gorge Project.

Taos Plateau for alternative types of subsistence and residency patterns centered on hunting, gathering, raiding, and trade.

The surface assemblages documented on the east and west sides of the Gorge offer evidence for two distinct land-use patterns: one associated with a village-based mobility logic and the other associated with continued residential mobility. The coursed dry-laid masonry as well as Tiwa ceramics, rock shelters, and petroglyphs identified along the eastern rim of the Gorge all point to a more substantial investment in constructing place and to the incorporation of this area into a subsistence pattern increasingly centered on agriculture. In contrast, the archaeological record on the west side of the Gorge is characterized by discrete tool refurbishment areas, as found at Cerro de la Olla, Three Basins, and Arroyo Punche, and evidence of large seasonal encampmements as found at Punche Lake suggesting that this area was largely used by different residentially mobile communities over time.

As the Hispano name *La Otra Banda* suggests, this portion of the Taos Plateau remained a "unsettled" territory from 5500 BCE well into the 19th century. However, the lack of substantive settlement on the west side of the Plateau should not be read as absence of occupation. The archaeological record of this region requires a different understanding of land-use from the dominant Western model of "occupation" based on sustained investment in the land through agriculture and evidence of permanent residency in the form of architecture. In this context, occupation must be disassociated from notions of private property, cultivated acreage, and material forms of boundary maintenance and instead measured by consistent, albeit episodic, use. This understanding of occupation is materially marked in subtle ways, in the small lithic scatters, rock piles, or stone circles that dot the landscape and immaterially in the form of personal narratives and oral histories rooted in place.

▼▽▼

The archaeological evidence from Cerro Del Yuta on the east side of the Gorge suggests that this portion of the plateau was persistently if not consistently visited by Indigenous groups from approximately 3200 BCE into the 14th century. This evidence indicates that the Plateau was not "abandoned" as Indigenous groups began to experiment with cultivation and village-based modes of living in the Rio Grande Valley.

Archaeological evidence from Cerro del Yuta points the use of the Plateau by various Indigenous groups, practicing different levels of residential mobility over time. The slope of Cerro del Yuta is covered by a dispersed chipped stone scatter comprised largely of informal dacite tools and flakes. The preponderance of lower-quality materials and expedient flake technologies reflect a shift in tool production strategies linked to the incorporation of cultivation into Indigenous subsistence rounds.[29] These materials indicate that Indigenous people occupying the region after 400 CE, continued to use the eastern Plateau for logistical hunting and gathering activities as well as stone tool production and maintenance. The coursed dry-laid structures documented along the ridge at Cerro del Yuta resemble domestic features associated with "Apishapa Focus" sites found elsewhere in the region, suggesting that this area may also have been used as a short-term settlement by ancestral Numic-speaking groups sometime after the 10th century. Finally, the presence of incised greyware ceramics, associated with northern Tiwa-speaking people at the Cerro del Yuta ridge site indicates that this area was used by Indigenous agriculturalists as early as the 1050 CE.

While Indigenous groups engaged in early forms of cultivation may have focused their activities on the east side of the Plateau, there is also evidence to suggest that Tiwa-speaking people crossed the Gorge to undertake logistical trips on the west side of the Plateau. Chipped stone materials collected from T'aitöna and Sagebrush Pueblo indicate that dacite from Newman Dome located on the west side of the Gorge was the preferred raw material for stone tool production, suggesting that Tiwa-speaking communities continued to procure raw materials from the west side of the Gorge over time.[30] As discussed in Chapter 6, the *Ĭăłap°ăĭbâ* recognize western mountain-scapes like Cerro de la Olla as "sacred," indicating that the west side of the Gorge was not "abandoned" by Indigenous groups classically considered "sedentary".

Indeed, the oral tradition documents the continued importance of logistical mobility practices and foraging activities for the *Ĭăłap°ăĭbâ*. Their origin stories describe the existence of a dual economy in which Athabaskan-speaking Winter People from the north specialized in hunting while Tiwa-speaking Summer People from the south focused on farming.[31] This narrative presents an intriguing road map to the community's ethnogenesis, positing a merger of residentially mobile big-game-hunting groups with agriculturally oriented ones—a merger which may have entailed a symbolic and physical bridging of the Rio Grande Gorge. Ultimately, the persistence of foraging as a central subsistence practice for Indigenous people living throughout the northern Rio Grande region reveals the ways in which archaeological research interests and assumptions obscure important continuities in search of disruption.

Although there is evidence that Tiwa-speaking people continuously used both sides of the Plateau, albeit at different intensities, there is a notable lack of direct material evidence for Numic- or Athabaskan-speaking equestrian groups on the east side of the Taos Plateau. Unlike the tipi encampements documented on the west side of the Taos Plateau, the stacked stone circles documented at Cerro del Yuta represent a distinct type of domestic feature. This absence of material evidence of equestrian nomadism conflicts with Spanish archival accounts that suggest Cerro del Yuta was positioned at the nexus of three territorial zones, occupied by Numic-, Athabaskan-, Tiwa-speaking peoples.

During an expedition in 1694 into Colorado, Don Diego de Vargas recorded the following ethno-geography for the region while camped some ten leagues, about 56 km, north of Arroyo Hondo:

> They informed me that the mountains that run along the edge of the Rio Colorado are inhabited by the Apache del Acho, and that the Yuta nation, which we are looking for, does not countenance them in their land, for which reason I should flee from this place which is also the farthest point to which the rebel Taos Indians … come out on the trail of the buffalo, the dung of which has been found in different parts, as along the descents from the mountain to the river.[32]

De Vargas's account documents spatial division between mobile bison hunting groups, with *Ndee* people residing to the east of the Rio Grande River, along the Sangre de Cristo Mountains and *Nuutsiyu* peoples occupying the area to north. In light of De Vargas's account, the current absence of Numic- or Athabaskan-speaking sites near Cerro del Yuta notable, a trend that becomes more puzzling when one reflects on the fact that the mountain is named after the *Nuutsiyu*.

Archaeological survey work conducted in the areas directly south and east of Cerro del Yuta reveal a similar dearth of definitively *Ndee* or *Nuutsiyu* material culture. A single isolated metal projectile point similar to those identified in the Rio del Oso Valley in association with Jicarilla encampments, was documented in the open valley surrounding Cerro del Yuta and offers the only clear evidence of a early 19th-century use of the area.[33] Metal points are made from barrel hoops, using a combination of chisels, hammers, and sandstone sharpening tablets. The use of metal as an alternative material to stone for projectile points was relatively short lived, beginning sometime during the early 1800s and subsiding by the 1870s when rifles became widely distributed.[34] Although metal points are temporally diagnostic, Indigenous people were not the only producers of these objects. Evidence of metal debitage and finished points at Vecino settlements such as San Lorenzo, indicate that Hispano settlers were also making or trading for metal arrow points at this time.[35] In the absence of other material signatures like tipi rings or micaceous ceramics, the metal point documented near Cerro del Yuta may just as readily be interpreted as evidence for a Hispano presence on the eastern side of the Taos Plateau.

While Numic- and Athabaskan-speaking groups in the area would have most certainly known about del Yuta, the absence of stone rings as well as diagnostic projectile points or ceramics associated with these groups creates an interesting slippage between the archival and archaeological records. There are several potential reasons for this disconnect. For instance, it is possible that stone rings and culturally associated artifacts do exist on Cerro del Yuta but were simply missed by surveyors or are located outside the confines of our survey area. These features may be in areas that have yet to be systematically surveyed, including the east or north face of the mountain and the vast tracks of open prairie surrounding it. Preservation is also certainly an issue in highly erosional contexts like mountain slopes, where surface collections as well as ephemeral features like stone circles are easily displaced. Similarly, brush structures, often found in mountain environments used by the

Nuutsiyu, do not often preserve in the archaeological record over time. As a result of these preservation issues, material evidence for Numic- or Athabaskan-speaking groups may have simply been erased over time.

In addition to sampling limitations and preservation biases, the slopes of Cerro del Yuta itself are in many ways unfit for residential encampments. While the mountain provides sweeping views of the surrounding landscape, it has little tree cover, leaving potential inhabitants exposed to inclement weather or detection by hostile groups. This latter concern would have been a particularly salient factor in deciding where to camp after the 16th century, as tensions escalated among Indigenous groups as well as between Indigenous people and European settlers. During a council of war held in Santa Fe, General Don Antonio Valverde Cosío describes these growing hostilities:

> However, I find, according to my experiences, the number of men, twenty-five, too small. The reason is that, although these [Jicarilla] Apaches acknowledge their submission, since they have offered themselves for catechizing, they have for enemies, the Ute and Comanche tribes in the northeast, and to the east the Faraones, which, although an Apache tribe, is ordinarily hostile. This being the situation, it is necessary for arms to defend and protect them from their enemies.[36]

In June of 1720, when this report was penned, *Nuutsiyu* and *Numunu* people were joined together with the Faraones in hostilities against colonial authorities in New Mexico. In contrast, the Jicarilla had submitted (at least in the eyes of colonial officials) to the Spanish Crown and were now considered allies of the colonial state. Cosío's account documents the fact that Indigenous groups took different approaches to interethnic interactions and that these strategies changed over time, variously influencing where they chose to establish domestic encampments or undertake trading and raiding activities.

Much like Cerro del Yuta, there is a notable absence of archaeological evidence that Numic- or Athabaskan-speaking groups were using the eastern slope of Cerro de la Olla. Again, the material record contrasts with archival documents from the mid-19th century, which note the presence of *Nuutsiyu* encampments on the mountain. As discussed in Chapter 6, this lapse between the archaeological and documentary records may be a matter of unfamiliarity with the local topography on the part of American officials, gaps in survey coverage, or preservation issues related to ephemeral surface collections and erosion. Regardless, the current pattern suggests that such free-standing mountains may not be the best place to locate tipi encampments, which are more often found on the open expanses of the west side of Taos Plateau. The stone rings identified at playa sites indicate that Numic- and Athabaskan-speaking groups occupied these spaces for varying lengths of time and at different times of the year. The domestic use of playas is distinct from previous uses of these areas for logistical activities by residentially mobile groups. This shift reflects a variety of factors, including new modes of

periods of time. During the 1890s and 1950s, the already stark environmental conditions on the Plateau were made worse by two intervals of severe drought, leading many would-be settlers to abandon their homesteads.[43] As many Euro-American settlers came to learn, the Taos Plateau was best suited for transitory activities like herding and ranching rather than permanent settlement.

In addition to this new mode of dividing up and using to the land, American colonization introduced a more intensive set of land use practices. The exhaustive mining of natural resources on the Plateau following New Mexico's statehood has resulted in severe deforestation and the degradation of many watersheds.[44] As discussed in Chapter 1, cattle ranching has also had a profound effect on the landscape, leading to diminished ground cover, the extinction of many wild grass species, the invasion of mesquite shrubs, sheet erosion, and the formation of coppice dunes.[45]

In many ways, the ecology and topography of the Taos Plateau seems to have effectively limited more permanent types of settlement, instead facilitating the continuation of a mobile lifestyle in various forms into the 20th century. Rather than housing dense population centers, the open expanses of the Plateau provid an optimal space for traveling between resource nodes. Over time, how human groups traveled across this particular landscape evolved from pedestrianism to equestrianism to what might be considered a hypermobility pattern made possible by the construction of the Santa Fe Branch of the Denver and Rio Grande Western Railroad in the 1880s. The railroad brought New Mexico's economy into the capitalist age for the first time, collapsing the time-space continuum at new speeds and ushering in a new era of mobility materially marked by rail lines and eventually asphalt highways.

▼▽▼

By focusing on continuity rather than change, I have tried to draw attention to how specific places remain central features of cultural landscapes at the same time that mobility and subsistence patterns evolve. This alternative historical focus untethers socioeconomic change from harmful notions of abandonment and disappearance. My goal in adopting such an approach is to challenge archaeological models that frame Indigenous history in the American Southwest as a unidirectional progression towards immobility. This linear timeline is punctuated by various moments of "radical" change, such as evidence for plant and animal domestication in the 6th century, the imposition of Spanish missions in the 16th century, and the creation of reservations by the US government in the 19th century. While it is important to recognize the dynamic and evolving nature of Indigenous societies, this linear historical approach has obscured the centrality of mobility to human life-ways across time and space. The unacknowledged consequence of such models is a separation of contemporary Tribal Nations from their cultural heritage in the deep past.[46] Rather than viewing mobility as a subsistence choice which becomes increasingly untenable as societies "advance," it may be better conceptualized as a philosophy enacted at different levels (individual, group, and community), to different degrees, and at different times. As a way of thinking and being, mobility is not something that ends but rather continues in modified forms, connecting the past, present, and futures of Indigenous People in the Southwest.

Notes

1 Silko, 1977: 2.
2 Boyer, 1986; Dello-Russo, 2003; McNutt, 1969; Post, 2002; Schmader, 2001; Vierra, 2008; Vierra and Ford, 2005 in Vierra and Ford.
3 Huckell, 1996: 343.
4 Vierra and Ford, 2007: 123.
5 Vierra and Ford, 2007: 125.
6 McBrinn and Vierra, 2017.
7 Vierra and McBrinn, 2016: 63.
8 Vierra, 2003; Dicks et al., 2016: VI-6.
9 McBrinn and Vierra, 2017.
10 McBrinn and Vierra, 2017.
11 Vierra, 1990: 153.
12 Huckell, 1996: 317.
13 This sample is based on the data available in the Archaeological Records Management System of New Mexico as of May 2020 and includes any sites within the data based that were located within 500 m of the Gorge itself.
14 Vierra, 2013.
15 Vierra, 1990: 64.
16 Bauer et al., 2007: 11.
17 Ellis, 1974: 124–126; Fowles, 2004: 507.
18 Parsons, 1936: 113; Fowles, 2004: 295.
19 Ellis, 1974: 113; Parsons, 1936: 109; Fowles, 2004: 506.
20 Harrington, 1916: 164.
21 Opler, 2012 [1938]: 66.
22 Simmons, 2001; Stoffel et al., 2008: 114.
23 Montgomery, 2017: 163; Vierra, 2003.
24 Vierra and Foxx, 2009: 162.
25 This site sample reflects site reports registered with the ARMS database as of May 2020 as well as sites recorded by the Rio Grande Gorge Project directed by Severin Fowles.
26 Severin Fowles, personal communication, 2020.
27 Vierra et al., 2018: 250–251.
28 Renaud, 1942: 20.
29 Vierra, 2017: 12.
30 Boulanger, 2019: 5; Newman, 1997.
31 Fowles and Eiselt, 2019: 184; Vierra et al., 2018: 252.
32 Espinosa, 1939: 85.
33 Eiselt, 2006: 288–290; Montgomery, 2015: 155–156.
34 Betzinez and Nye, 1958: 5, 85; Boyer, 2014: 32.
35 Moore, 1992, 2004.
36 Thomas, 1935: 159.
37 Benedict, 1992.
38 Kornfeld, 2010: 402.
39 Thomas, 1940: 68.
40 de Mendinueta, 1773.
41 Patton, 2000: 123; Scholes, 1942: 50.
42 Dicks et al., 2016: VI-15.

43 Towner and Salzer, 2013.
44 Julyan, 2006: 33.
45 Hall, 2017: 28.
46 Preucel and Duwe, 2019: 25.

Bibliography

Bauer, Paul W., Peggy S. Johnson, and Stacy Timmons. 2007. *Springs of the Rio Grande Gorge, Taos County, New Mexico: Inventory, Data Report, Preliminary Geochemistry*. New Mexico Bureau of Geology and Minearl Resources, Socorro.

Benedict, James B. 1992. Footprints in the Snow: High-Altitude Cultural Ecology of the Colorado Front Ranges, U.S.A. *Artic and Alpine Research* 24(1): 1–16.

Betzinez, Jason, and Wilbur Sturtevant Nye. 1959. *I Fought with Geronimo*. University of Nebraska Press, Lincoln.

Boulanger, Matthew T. 2019. *Compositional Analysis by pXRF of Obsidian and Dacite Artifacts from Ute Mountain and Cerro de la Olla, Taos County, New Mexico*. Southern Methodist University, Dallas.

Boyer, Jefferey L. 1986. Non-Sedentary Sites on the Taos Plateau and in the Rio Ojo Caliente Drainage: The Hernandez-Taos Archaeology Project. Contract Archaeology Report No. 19, Kit Carson Memorial Foundation, Taos.

Boyer, Jefferey L. 2014. Is There a Point to This? Contexts for Metal Projectile Points in Northern New Mexico. *Papers of the Archaeological Society of New Mexico* 38: 27–36.

Dello-Russo, Robert D. 2003. The Responses of Basketmaker II Foragers to Climatic Stress in the Middle Rio Grande Valley of New Mexico. In Anasazi Archaeology at the Millennium: Proceedings of the Sixth Occasional Anasazi Symposium, edited by P. Reed, pp. 23–28. Center for Desert Archaeology, Tucson.

Dicks, Merrill, Arron C. Anderson, Jessica Mrstik, Peter Rogers, and Todd Scarbourgh 2016. Rio Grande Del Norte National Monument Class III Cultural Resources Survey of the Cerro Montoso Project Area, Taos County, New Mexico. Bureau of Land Management, Taos.

Eiselt, B. Sunday. 2006. The Emergence of Jicarilla Apache Enclave Economy during the 19th Century in Northern New Mexico. Unpublished Ph.D. dissertation, Department of Anthropology, University of Michigan, Ann Arbor.

Ellis, Florence Hawley. 1974 [1962]. Anthropological Data Pertaining to the Taos Land Claim. In *Pueblo Indians I*, 29–150. Garland Publishing Inc., New York

Espinsoa, J. Manuel. 1939. Journal of the Vargas Expedition into Colorado, 1694. *The Colorado Magazine* XVI(3): 81–90.

Fowles, Severin. 2004. The Making of Made People: The Prehistoric Evolution of Hierocracy Among the Northern Tiwa of New Mexico. Unpublished Ph.D. dissertation, Anthropology Department, University of Michigan, Ann Arbor.

Fowles, Severin, and Sunday B. Eiselt. 2019. Apache, Tiwa, and Back Again: Ethnic Shifting in the American Southwest. In *The Continuous Path: Pueblo Movement and the Archaeology of Becoming*, edited by S. Duwe and R.W. Preucel, pp. 166–194. University of Arizona Press, Tucson.

Hall, Stephen A. 2017. Paleoenvironments of the American Southwest. In *The Archaic Southwest: Foragers in an Arid Land*, edited by B.J. Viera, pp. 16–30. The University of Utah Press, Salt Lake City.

Harrington, John Peabody. 1916. *The Ethnography of the Tewa Indians*. Government Printing Office, Washington, DC.

Huckell, Bruce B. 1996. The Archaic Prehistory of the North American Southwest. *Journal of World Prehistory* 10(3): 305–373.

Julyan, Robert Hixson. 2006. *The Mountains of New Mexico.* University of New Mexico Press, Albuquerque.

Kornfeld, Marcel, Georg C. Frison, and Mary Lou Larson. 2010. *Prehistoric Hunter-Gatherers of the High Plains and Rockies.* Left Coast Press, Walnut Creek.

McBrinn, Maxine, and Bradley J. Vierra. 2017. The Southwest Archaic. In *The Oxford Handbook of Southwest Archaeology*, edited by B.J. Mills and S. Fowles. Oxford University Press. DOI: 10.1093/oxfordhb/9780199978427.013.12.

McNutt, Charles H. 1969. Early Puebloan Occupations at Tesuque By-Pass and in the Upper Rio Grande Valley. Anthropology Papers No. 40, Museum of Anthropology, University of Michigan, Ann Arbor.

de Mendinueta, Pedro Fermin. 1773. Letter Concerning Comanche Activities. John L. Kessell Papers, MSS 767, Box 2, Folder 66, plate 103 and 65. Southwest Research Center, University of New Mexico, Albuquerque.

Montgomery, John L. 2017. The Archaic of Eastern New Mexico. In *The Archaic Southwest: Foragers in an Arid Land*, edited by B.J. Vierra, pp. 156–166. University of Utah Press, Salt Lake City.

Montgomery, Lindsay M. 2015. Yndios Bárbaros: Nomadic Archaeologies of Spanish New Mexico. Unpublished Ph.D. dissertation, Department of Anthropology, Stanford University, Stanford.

Moore, James L. 1992. Spanish Colonial Stone Tool Use. In *Current Research on the Late Prehistory and Early History of New Mexico*, edited by B.J. Vierra, pp. 239–244. Special Publication No. 1. New Mexico Archaeological Council, Albuquerque.

Moore, James L. 2004. Spanish Chipped Stone Artifacts. In *Adaptations on the Anasazi and Spanish Frontiers: Excavations at Five Sites near Abiquiu, Rio Arriba County, New Mexico*, by J.L. Moore, J.L. Boyer, and D.F. Levine, pp. 179–200. Archeology Notes 187. Office of Archaeological Studies, Museum of New Mexico, Santa Fe.

Newman, Jay R. 1997. Patterns of Lithic Procurement and Utility in the Rio Grande del Rancho Valley of the Northern Rio Grande Region, New Mexico. Unpublished Ph.D. dissertation, Department of Anthropology, Southern Methodist University, Dallas.

Opler, Morris E. 2012 [1938]. *Myths and Tales of the Jicarilla Apache Indians.* American Folk Lore Society, New York.

Parsons, Elsie Clews. 1936. *Taos Pueblo.* General Series in Anthropology No. 2. George Banta Publishing Company Agent, Menasha.

Patton, Paul R. 2000. *Deleuze and the Political.* Routledge, London.

Post, Stephen S. 2002. Emerging from the Shadows: The Archaic Period in the Northern Rio Grande. In *Traditions, Transitions and Technologies: Themes in Southwestern Archaeology*, edited by S. Schlanger, pp. 33–48. University of Colorado Press, Boulder.

Preucel, Robert W., and Samuel Duwe. 2019. Introduction: Engaging with Pueblo Movement. In *The Continuous Path: Pueblo Movement and the Archaeology of Becoming*, edited by S. Duwe and R.W. Preucel, pp. 1–33. University of Arizona Press, Tucson.

Renaud, E.B. 1942. Reconnaissance Work in the Upper Rio Grande Valley, Colorado and New Mexico. Archaeological Series No. 3. University of Denver, Department of Anthropology, Denver. 3.

Schmader, Matthew. 2001. Gimme Shelter: Uncovering Archaic Structures in Rio Rancho and Santa Fe, New Mexico. Rio Grande Consultants, Albuquerque.

Scholes, Frances V. 1942. *Troublous Times in New Mexico, 1659–1670.* Historical Society of New Meixco Publications in History, Albuquerque.

Silko, Leslie Marmon. 1977. *Ceremony*. Viking Press, New York.

Simmons, Virginia McConnell. 2001. *The Ute Indians of Utah, Colorado, and New Mexico*. University of Colorado Press, Boulder.

Stoffel, Richard W. Kathleen A. Van Vlack, Rebecca S. Toupal, Sean M. O'Meara, Jessica L. Medwied-Savage, Henry F. Dobyns, and Richard W. Arnold. 2008. *American Indians and the Old Spanish Trail*. Bureau of Applied Research in Anthropology, University of Arizona, Tucson.

Thomas, Alfred B. 1935. *After Coronado: Spanish Exploration Northeast of New Mexico, 1696–1727*. University of Oklahoma Press, Norman.

Thomas, Alfred B. 1940. *The Plains Indians and New Mexico, 1751–1778: A Collection of Documents Illustrative of the History of the Eastern Frontier of New Mexico*. University of Oklahoma Press, Norman.

Towner, Ron H. 2016. Early Navajo Land Use in Northwestern New Mexico: Big Bead Mesa in Regional Perspective. *Journal of Field Archaeology* 41(1): 118–129.

Vierra, Bradley J. 1990. Archaic Hunter-Gatherer Archaeology in Northwestern New Mexico. In *Perspectives on Southwest Prehistory*, edited by P. Minnis and C.L. Redman, pp. 57–67. Westview Press, Boulder.

Vierra, Bradley J. 2003. Late Archaic Settlement Systems in the Northern Rio Grande. Paper Presented at the Annual Meetings of the Society for American Arachaeology. Seattle, WA.

Vierra, Bradley J. 2008. Early Agriculture on the Southeastern Periphery of the Colorado Plateau: A Case of Diversity in Tactics. In *Archaeology without Borders: Contact, Commerce and Change in the US Southwest and Northwestern Mexico*, edited by M. McBrinn and L. Webster. University of Colorado Press, Boulder.

Vierra, Bradley J. 2013. Archaic Foraging Technology and Land Use in the Northern Rio Grande, New Mexico. In *From Mountaintop to Valley Bottom: Papers in Honor of Paul Williams*, edited by B.J. Vierra, p. 145–160. University of Utah Press, Salt Lake City.

Vierra, Bradley J. 2017. A History of Archaic Research in the Northern Southwest. In *The Archaic Southwest: Foragers in an Arid Land*, edited by B.J. Vierra, pp. 3–15. University of Utah Press, Salt Lake City.

Vierra, Bradley J., and Maxine McBrinn. 2016. Resistant Foragers: Foraging and Maize Cultivation in the Northern Rio Grande Valley. In Late Holocene Research on Foragers and Farmers in the Desert West, edited by B.J. Roth and M.E. McBrinn, pp. 58–77. University of Utah Press, Salt Lake City.

Vierra, Bradley J., and Richard I. Ford. 2005. Early Maize Agriculture in the Northern Rio Grande Valley, New Mexico. In *Histories of Maize: Multidisciplinary Approaches to the Prehistory, Biogeography, Domestication and Evolution of Maize*, edited by J. Staller, R. Tykot, and B. Benz, pp. 497–510. Elsevier, Boston.

Vierra, Bradley J., and Richard I. Ford. 2007. Foragers and Farmers in the Northern Rio Grande Valley, New Mexico. *Kiva* 73(2): 117–130.

Vierra, Bradley J., Richard I. Ford, and Stephen S. Post. 2018. Archaic Foragers of the Northern Rio Grande. In *The Archaic Southweset: Foragers in an Arid Land*, edited by B.J. Vierra, pp. 235–253. University of Utah Press, Salt Lake City.

Vierra, Bradley J., and Teralene Foxx. 2009. Archaic Upland Resource Use: The View from the Pajarito Plateau. In *Between the Mountains, Beyond the Mountains: Papers in Honor of Paul R. Williams*, edited by E.J. Brown, K. Armstrong, D.M. Brugge, and C.J. Condie, pp. 154–166. Archaeological Society of New Mexico, Albuquerque.

INDEX

Note: *Italicized* page numbers refer to figures

For Product Safety Concerns and Information please contact our EU representative GPSR@taylorandfrancis.com Taylor & Francis Verlag GmbH, Kaufingerstraße 24, 80331 München, Germany

Batch number: 10722136

Printed by Printforce, the Netherlands